The Art of

Successful Failure

Stephan Poulter, Ph.D.

BALBOA.
PRESS
A DIVISION OF HAY HOUSE

Balboa Press books may be ordered through booksellers or by contacting:

Balboa Press
A Division of Hay House
1663 Liberty Drive
Bloomington, IN 47403
www.balboapress.com
1 (877) 407-4847

Because of the dynamic nature of the Internet, any web addresses or links contained in this book may have changed since publication and may no longer be valid. The views expressed in this work are solely those of the author and do not necessarily reflect the views of the publisher, and the publisher hereby disclaims any responsibility for them.

The author of this book does not dispense medical advice or prescribe the use of any technique as a form of treatment for physical, emotional, or medical problems without the advice of a physician, either directly or indirectly. The intent of the author is only to offer information of a general nature to help you in your quest for emotional and spiritual well-being. In the event you use any of the information in this book for yourself, which is your constitutional right, the author and the publisher assume no responsibility for your actions.

Any people depicted in stock imagery provided by Thinkstock are models, and such images are being used for illustrative purposes only. Certain stock imagery © Thinkstock.

Print information available on the last page.

ISBN: 978-1-5043-5415-8 (sc)
ISBN: 978-1-5043-5417-2 (hc)
ISBN: 978-1-5043-5416-5 (e)

Library of Congress Control Number: 2016905440

Balboa Press rev. date: 06/30/2016

Other Books by the Author

Your Ex-Factor:
Overcome Heartbreak and Build a Better Life

The Mother Factor:
How Your Mother's Emotional Legacy Impacts Your Life

The Father Factor:
How Your Father's Legacy Impacts Your Career

Father Your Son:
How to Become the Father You've Always Wanted to Be

Mending the Broken Bough:
Restoring the Promise of the Mother-Daughter Relationship

Audio Tapes by the Author

Relaxation Factor:
Self-Empowerment Series I-Light Your Emotional Load

Relaxation Factor:
Self-Empowerment Series II-Mindfulness in a Mindless Moment

Relaxation Factor:
Self-Empowerment Series III-Fear of Flying

Dedication Page

To the close loving souls who have helped me to become the person I chose prior to coming to this life: Miriam, Jonathan Brett, Madison Wendy, Pete and Charlotte, Ricardo, Samantha and Stella.

In addition, I dedicate this book to all the people who are trying so hard to make sense of their life and sufferings, and wish to discover their intuitive, soulful nature/spirit.

Table of Contents

Acknowledgments

I want to personally acknowledge the incredible souls who have helped me to create and have the courage to describe our collective process of spiritual transformation: Miriam C, Pete, Charlotte, Debbie D, Barry W, Julia W, Eddie C, Paramahansa Y, Dr. Jay G, Kye H, Bill M, Bill K, Darlene K, Marlene C, Lisa J, Jane S, David O, Winston G, Jim M, Carla M, Carter F, Pam S and Beat, and lastly my guarding angels.

In addition, from the bottom of my heart and soul, I want to thank all the different people whom are too numerous to mention in the creation of this book and journey. All the people at Balboa Press, Hay House Publishers, Jan W, Debbie B, Melissa G and all my spiritual teachers (many of whom had no idea that they were part and parcel of my spiritual transformation-realization).

Author's Note

All of the non-personal stories by the author, third-party references, names, clinical vignettes and examples are a vast composite of many different individuals designed to protect privacy and anonymity. Therefore, any similarity between the names and the stories of individuals that the reader might recognize is inadvertent and purely coincidental in nature. All the names used in this book are for illustration purposes only. The people are fictional and have no relationship to any person known by the author.

Foreword

"All great truths begin as blasphemies."
—George Bernard Shaw

Let's begin our introduction with Shaw's classic quote and my personal sentiment about the following pages of this book that are in your hands. This is going to be quite a ride, a journey with a profound end result—maybe there is a plan, a purpose and a divine reason for your life: blasphemies, hyper-positive psychology, or possibly something different. This book isn't about the philosophical debate regarding the existence of God/Spirit but rather your personal and ever-expanding experience of the divine within you. You want a present day personal "divine intuitive" experience—not something from the first century. That's a fair and appropriate desire. Your life is all about experiences that have shaped, formed and directed you. The following chapters are hopefully going to shed some new insights into your experiences of "successes" and seemingly painful "failures" that are highly purposeful. It's of no concern where you currently are on the path of your life—it's merely a starting point, not an ending point. You can be 21 years old and wondering about your career or purpose, or 33 years old hoping to have children and a family, or 62 years old, divorced for the third time and feeling like you have missed the deeper meaning of your life or "Life" in general. Wherever you are, it's a beginning point to take a look at the six common areas of your personal life journey. Rather than explore the ideas of this book ahead of time, let's agree that your spiritual awakening is personal and necessary.

There is no wrong path or way to awaken to your life's purpose, mission and passion. Yes, you have a purpose, passion, mission and reason for living at this time. The only problem is when you stop on your life path and cease trying to find out why. No one quits, it's just a "time out" based on your fear of life. Your life will always be more than your acquisitions, wealth, fears, family issues, health concerns and success, but rather how you have fulfilled your life purpose and improved the world around you. We aren't discussing politics, or same sex-marriages or government policies, but rather your intuitive soul awakening and where that path takes you. This may all sound like rainbows and unicorns, but it is really much more and worth your time and exploration. Let's say Buddha, Allah, Lord Krishna, Jesus, Gandhi, your guardian angels and Moses are all meeting for lunch tomorrow to catch-up on the state of affairs of your life. I don't think you want to ignore this priceless dialogue because it is happening within your heart. It's the East spirituality meets the West materialism—each needing to understand the other. Both parts are within you.

I promise to be honest (about myself), to share new insights and be brave in sharing this unfolding life path that is secretly disguised as your own spiritual path. You don't need to join any group, become religious, attend any meetings or donate money. In fact, it is preferable that you take time for your inner exploration about the topics and ideas in the following pages. Just open your heart and soul to the possibilities that your inner feelings are telling you something very important and valuable. Yes, it could be nonsense, but then again it could be the seemingly random start to a brand new chapter in your story of hope, self-acceptance and love. Let's find out, and it will be at least be an interesting read. Before we move on to this book, I want to leave you with this incredible story about three dogs (beagles) facing their own mortality.

Prologue: Three adult beagles are living together in a small metal cage at a Los Angeles dog shelter, hoping to be rescued by a loving person/ family—or they will never see daylight again. Soon the dogs will be delivered (euthanized) into their new world, but they are not sure what that "other side" will be like. The following parable is a composite of many themes, ideas, beliefs and concerns about the life journey that we all have, but never quite articulate.

First beagle: (to the second beagle): "Do you believe that there is life after we leave here (i.e., die)?

Second beagle: "Yes, of course. There is the next life after this one. We all have done great things here and then pass forward to the other side. I know we are alone without our humans and their love, but our life still matters."

First beagle: "That's magical thinking or some kind of fairy tale idea. There is no after life after this life or any past lives for that matter. We have only one life to live and then we die."

Second beagle: "I know that this life isn't our only existence. Maybe on the other side there are different things like new bodies, different things to see, different feelings, insights, love and acceptance. Maybe we will have new experiences and see our lives differently. We could also become much more aware of the universe and how the different aspects of life might all work together."

Third beagle: "I am going back to sleep—I'm not worried about any of these after-life or heaven issues. I am resting and don't really care or believe in anything other than this life. I was physically abused and abandoned by my owner and life is confusing. Stop hoping for a miracle. We are doomed, and that's how a dog's life is!"

First beagle: "We will enter into complete nothingness after we leave here. There is no higher power or God; we just live good dog lives and die. There is no heaven or wonderful next life. Look at all the beagles that are killed for research and killed for food every day! If there was a loving God, why would he allow us or our friends to be abused? This life is a one-time event with no next-life following. I am mad at my owner for abandoning me. I loved him, and look what has happened to me."

Second beagle: "I don't know about how and why certain things happen or don't happen in life, but I do know that our life has purpose, lessons to learn, love to give and to receive. We must learn how to forgive and help other lost or abused dogs. We can't lose hope or forget that we all belong to a higher power."

First beagle: "If God exists, then where is she now? Seriously, life is unfair. All my brothers and sisters were killed when we were puppies. I hate the man who did that, and I hope he dies a thousand deaths."

Second beagle: "He (God/Spirit) is all around us, inside our hearts and souls. Can't you feel him when you breathe, think and feel? Who do you think created us? We once had a good life, and even though things are bleak right now, that doesn't mean we should give up on life—right?"

First beagle: "Well, if I can't see her or him then they don't exist. I don't believe in religion anyway. I am a realist, and God isn't real to me. We are going to die this week!

Third beagle (suddenly awaking): "Maybe there is something to all of us being together here in this cold place. Maybe there is order or purpose."

Second beagle: "You can hear things from the other side if you are still; there are feelings, impressions and silent words. Trust me, we are all here together and something really good is happening now and in our future. No matter how our story ends at this shelter, this isn't the end of our story."

So, one question before we start . . . what kind of beagle are you in your current life struggle—the wise soul, the sleep-walker, or the cynical scared non-believer?

Sincerely,
Stephan Brett

"Start from where you are—not where you wish you were!
The work (healing) you are doing becomes your path."
—Ram Dass

Section I

Your Successful Failing Process— Your Awakening From Within

*"Ego says: Once everything falls into place,
I will find peace.
Spirit says: Find inner-peace and everything will fall
Into place."*
—*Ram Dass*

*"If you want something you've never had, you
Must be willing to do something you've never done."*
—*Dr. Wayne Dyer*

*"Pride is blinding...Humbleness is the open gate through
Which the divine flood of Mercy and Love flows into
Receptive souls."*
—*Paramahansa Yogananda*

Chapter 1

How Did I Ever Get Here?
Your Descending Path

"We must be willing to let go of the Life we've planned,
so as to have the Life that is waiting for us."
—Joseph Campbell

Who is This book For?—My automatic knee jerk response is: You and only You! The next question is: why you are holding this book, looking at it, or perhaps pondering whether or not to read it? My own personal response is I had to write this book, and you have to read it. We are going to be friends for a period of time as we walk through some tough personal stuff and right into the next chapter of fulfillment in your life. Yes, things are going to be interesting, challenging and significant. Lasting change is within you. Okay, now that we have this adult understanding, let's keep going. It's no accident or random coincidence that this spiritual experience book is in front of you. I am an adult man sharing for men/women alike who may outwardly look a certain way, but inside have a whole lot going on that seems and feels unexplainable and in need of desperate clarification. You know that something is much bigger than your own world, more meaningful, and you know you're part of it—but how? If that's you, keep reading. We are good to go forward, knowing that you want to get to that inner part of you. Even if you doubt your inner wisdom, intuitive nature, and brilliant mind, they are all part of your personal awakening.

Before we discuss Joseph Campbell's quote, let me introduce myself—I am Stephan! I want to start off by extending my sincere appreciation for your interest in this timeless transformation subject—your successful life journey. Thank you again for picking up this book. Hopefully, the following pages of our discussion will help you begin to make sense out of the seemingly random, perplexing events, challenging circumstances, difficult relationships in your present-day life. I promise we are going to have quite a ride through the challenges of accepting, changing and allowing your new insights to become your new life experiences with lasting inner peace. Don't we all want lasting peace, calmness and fulfillment? Yes is the automatic answer. You're currently on the path to maximizing your life in ways you could only have remotely dreamed of. But now it's time to move forward and do it.

Your New Road Map—We will begin our discussion when things were peaceful/calm in your life and some thing or many things began to happen. It's your road to the Valley of Despair (we all have one), which is the beginning of your personal transformation (it always happens) and all the stops and starts in-between. This entire book/discussion is all about expanding, experiencing, creating, and transforming your new life perspective on all levels (emotionally, relationally, spiritually, physically, economically, and personally). We are going to focus on your ability to experience and develop your inward journey going forward.

Many times it seems that the forces of your life combine to "explode" at the perfect time. The varied circumstances and relationship disappointments all have the sole purpose of grabbing your inner attention concerning the deeper untapped issues buried within you. It is these "dark nights" of the soul-filled moments that cause you stop and take a serious, honest, non-defensive, non-blaming look into your life and what is happening (your Valley of Despair). Your moments of brilliant insight might be rare, but can be profound beyond words, description or knowledge. You're forever changed by your "successful failures" in how you walk down the road of your life. Everything (your ego) is different, including how you feel and think about yourself, life, your destiny and life purpose, and your soul. As Joseph Campbell states above, we all have to adjust, amend and open up our heart to the new possibilities that await us. Thomas Merton's quote below is a reminder for us to explore and accept (understand the larger unspoken purpose) that your life is critical to your larger and more meaningful purpose. This internal cognitive shift from defensiveness, fear, hopelessness, and resistance to *acceptance* is the theme of Section II in the book.

"In a world of tension and breakdown it is necessary for there to be those who seek to integrate their inner lives not by avoiding sorrow and anguish and running from their problems, but by facing them."
—Thomas Merton

My Life isn't Working—*You know when you know* that your life isn't working the way you had hoped, wanted or dreamed. It is at these precise moments of clarity that time stops and you acknowledge that there is something bigger and more meaningful to your current life circumstances. Your new insight is driven by the extreme emotional pain that you are feeling. The problem is that the emotional distortion of your fears can be paralyzing. When we are panicked, psychologically terrified and/or emotionally reactive, we have zero-to-little clarity or perspective. The deep unspoken fear, for example, that you might end up homeless and penniless, or that the person you love will walk out of your life, seems inevitable. Everything feels like it is slipping away, and you can't get a grip on any of it. The truth is, your old ways, and patterns of life are slipping away, dying and taking you to your own personal hell. The emotional desperation and panic running throughout your life is palpable and frightening. It's difficult to believe, but all these heartbreaking occurrences and situations are purposefully designed for your personal inner awakening. Five fundamental basic paths will expedite your personal awaking, and they will begin coming to you: money/career, love relationships, childhood family, parenting, and health challenges. These awakenings are as varied as the men and women experiencing them. You might find yourself living out one of the themes of what feels like a death march to an unknown place. It is this process of descending to your timely transformation that we are going to explore in great detail.

New Openings for You—Unfortunately the process of making these life-altering internal changes isn't as nice, painless or as pretty as we would like or choose. Your transformation might appear tragic and feel awful, but underneath the disastrous circumstances, all things are working together for your destiny. *The most profound and powerful changes of the heart and soul are directly correlated to the most painfully profound experiences in your life.* There is a clear-cut mathematical connection between your significant life changes, perspective shifts and the desire to reduce and stop your emotional pain. The balance between your emotional pain and ability to activate change is always an ongoing process. *Your spiritual awaking is like gravity. It's always a constant principle/force regardless of the elevation your life or the places you go to literally and figuratively.* The nuclear power of a wounded ego (emotional pain) is always the "grand opening" for your transformation and expanded personal/spiritual journey. Your life path always will be calling you to move forward, regardless of how difficult the circumstances may appear. The question is, "In what direction are you moving—forward or backwards?" Neither direction is without personal pain and personal change.

Moving forward will help create lasting relief and permanent change from your painful life lessons, self-defeating patterns and spiritual frustration cycles (where and who is God?). Resisting your personal transformation process (acceptance of your life lessons) only guarantees the chronic reset of your repetitive painful life experiences. *No one is exempt from the process of personal growth, change and their own personal spiritual awakening.* Men of all ages can say they don't believe in God, but their heart will betray their ego (self-importance) when they begin to consider their higher life purpose. Women can say that God had abandoned them when they were mistreated, but their heart/soul knows it's only an excuse for procrastinating to leave a bad relationship. All these terms, concepts and processes of your personal awakening will be explained in great detail throughout the book. The soulful dynamic of finding your inner passion, purpose and spiritual connection are all invaluable pieces of your life today and not something to avoid, resist, or be afraid of. The short- and long-term goal of our journey together is to move toward and embrace your spiritual side. Saying all that, let's continue our informal introductions on this matter of change.

Your Starting Point—We all have a point on our time line where the whole thing just blows up like a fireworks show in July. My emotional roof came crashing in when I was sitting with a dear friend, Kye, explaining my own current personal horror movie, which I was trying to downplay. We were smoking a cigar together, sipping on a scotch, and watching "March Madness" (college basketball playoffs). Kye looked at me and said, *"Your life is a successful failure."* I could not argue with his statement. The impact of my highly emotional breakup with the love of my life, moving from her house to a hotel with my beagle, Ricardo, having very little money, and needing hip replacement surgery, had left me feeling devastated, defeated and dejected. The backdrop to this story is that my ex-wife had married my ex-best-friend just a few years prior to this. I had introduced them years earlier at a book signing for my book about fathering. To further exacerbate the situation at the time, my kids apparently thought that her new husband was a better father than I. No longer was I needed in their lives—a nuclear missile to my heart and soul. I cannot adequately begin to express the epic explosion that hit my life—I was a displaced father, boyfriend and person. Parenting was my express lane and the non-stop pathway to my Valley of Despair. I did a full face plant in the ash pile of my lost dreams, lost hope and my lost precious angels/children. I wasn't feeling or thinking that this wasn't the life I had envisioned for myself back in high school or college. Rather, all I wanted to do was to seriously disappear into a cloud of dust and hit the "restart" button on my life from about the age of one.

I was incredibly depressed, but I couldn't allow myself to get too "down" because there wasn't much energy or cushion left within me for any degree of self-pity. I was terrified that if I really let go of any small ray of hope, I might never return from my ash heap. My sense of shame and lack of self-acceptance was my cup of water to drink. I could vaguely feel within my heart that there had to be a spiritual pathway out of my hell. I not only felt like a total loser who was on the edge of complete and utter humiliation and despair, but my kids seemed to have the same opinion of me. Even the fantasy of something like moving to Australia with my beagle or to some other foreign country and becoming a farmer didn't seem appealing—it would require far too much energy and motivation. I had very little of either. I was lying face down on the road of my life. I wasn't feeling sorry for myself. I was feeling hopeless.

Removing the Roadblocks—What I soon had to acknowledge was that I had always struggled with a hidden belief that I was a "phony" who was not good enough and was even, deep down, a "bad" guy ("shame factor" is discussed further in Section II). From a nonspiritual self-loathing perspective, I believed that I truly deserved to be loveless and without a partner or children. It seemed that now I was completely consumed with self-doubt, self-loathing and shame. I couldn't even convince myself that my life would ever come out of the ash heap of despair and hopelessness. Things were so painful that I couldn't really take a hard look at the casualty list of my life because my eyes were blurred with grief, anger and despair. The inner war of self-loathing and fear that nothing would ever change for the better was in full gear, and the ride was getting worse every time I looked around. Shockingly, my professional life was growing in spite of my nonstop emotional bleeding. My clients would tell me their stories of rejection by a partner, of kids being jerked around during an awful custody battle, loss of job and home, loss of self-respect. I would nod my head with empathy for their struggle; we were all looking for the keys to unlock the doors in our own lives.

It was difficult to believe that I was the central character in this self-directed personally funded horror movie. I had known since about the age of four that I came to this life to make up for some bad stuff I had done in a recent past life (past lives discussion in Section III). Sounds crazy, but I knew the truth of it the day I first had that thought in the backyard of my childhood home. That thought faded as I got older, but the need to make a positive contribution to the world and help people—especially troubled teenage boys/girls—never left my soul or heart. Sitting there that day with my friend, Kye, it was clear that I was attempting (unsuccessfully) to convince both he and myself that things weren't as painful, devastating and out of control as they felt. As I recounted the events of the recent past, he remarked, without any regard for my fragile, humiliated emotional state, *"You're a successful failure."* As my mouth began dropping on the floor, Kye went on to say, *"You can either look at your life as a failure or see the value in these events. Don't quit, buddy."* I wasn't exactly feeling the love or humor in his words, because his statement hit me in the stomach like a lightning bolt of truth.

Stopping the Pain—Deep within my heart, I had always held a spiritual belief that everything works out, regardless of the circumstances of the given moment. Deep down, I knew things would change for the better. From where I was, standing in my Valley of Despair, to the top of the mountain seemed like an impossible journey—one I couldn't even conceiving of completing. It was now a function of patience and persistence in reinventing my life. But how? I didn't know that my prayer request a few years earlier for a more fulfilling life was ending up as sheer hell and agony. I didn't feel like a saint or have any aspirations to be one, but let's lighten up on the emotional disappointments. I really just wanted to get out of the black emotional cave in which I found myself dwelling. Further, this process of spiritual transformation and awakening was just about to wipe me out. I was very close to quitting on myself and just checking out (going emotionally numb) with a bitter script and limping to the finish line. The Valley of Despair wasn't a joke or a cute phrase or anything to mess with. My current emotional address of failing was beyond anything I had experienced or ever imagined possible.

Maybe There is a Lasting Answer—My emotional discord was in the fast lane for all areas of my life as I faced these disappointments that I could have never anticipated or dreamed possible. My only hope was that I had hit the bottom of my personal Grand Canyon. Hitting the metaphorical rock bottom in life has always been a choice—that much I knew. Whatever life lessons needed to be addressed, I was not going to screw around or avoid the deeper issues of my life anymore. I was fully awake and willing to do whatever it took to transcend this painful and desolate place within my heart and soul (I will explain later what that entailed). I was also aware that so many people have experienced life experiences and tragedies far worse than anything I have seen or known. Yet at that same time, I was feeling deflated and traumatized by this "death-rebirth" process I was experiencing in my own personal life. The old way of conducting my life was no longer a viable option—everything needed to change from the inside out. One of the things I began to do during this crisis was to meditate. Anything that could silence my anger, fear and hopelessness was worth the effort (and I will explain more about this later).

> *"Never be afraid to fall apart because it is an*
> *Opportunity to rebuild yourself the way you wish*
> *you had been all along."*
> —*Rae Smith*

No Blaming—This Rae Smith quote seemed very fitting for what I was feeling—and extremely scary at the same time. Sometimes I felt as if everything I touched only got worse, and sometimes the emotional pain seemed to be escalating with no end in sight. But I didn't want living in despair to be the end of the road for me—or the end of my story. I never truly gave up my hope for better days. I was too scared to admit to myself that all the noise in my head and heart—negative feelings, fearful thoughts, blame, and painful self-doubts could be true. My inner resolve was, "No-way is the goodness and essence of love going to skip my life. If all this 'stuff' about how God/Divine is caring and close to us, then why am I missing this important connection? What am I doing wrong? What is it that I just don't understand?" But I didn't really want to hear from some therapist/psychologist (even though I am one) or have a spiritual mentor say, one more time, "Be patient, everything works out!" Patience my ass, I was dying and didn't know what to do other than try to accept the awfulness of it all. That kind of advice felt like cheap, useless bullshit for someone in a crisis whose ship in life was about to sink. Ironically, they were all correct in the end.

I know that you know exactly what I am referring to—there has to be other ways: realizations and divine actions that can take place in my/ your life. *I wasn't going to be a victim of life, blame others, blame God, blame my parents or blame something outside of me.* Whatever was begging for my full attention, it NOW had it! I wanted to have that inner peace, and spiritual connection to the "greater good." I was tired of being tired, of not feeling good enough, smart enough, wealthy enough, lucky enough or spiritual enough to have my life move forward without pain, struggle, fear and thoughts of impending doom. If this sounds familiar, keep reading, because we can all get out of that black cave and see things that weren't ever visible before.

"In the process of letting go you will lose many things
From the past, but you will find yourself."
—Deepak Chopra

My Full Responsibility—You may be reading this opening and thinking my story is like the proverbial "walk in the park." Maybe your story is so heartbreaking that you can't even believe that God or anything good in the universe could exist because of your personal road from loss to despair. The idea that you have been the object of bad luck, been screwed over, betrayed, or just simply the target of a mean cosmic joke is beyond comprehension. Maybe **you** (this was tough concept for me to accept, but its powerful) have unconsciously created this entire mess to get yourself back to your core life mission and spiritual path? Hmm, the idea that you somehow are actively involved in your *spiritual transformation* is a staggering concept. The main idea that you and your soul (your intuitive nature) have a part in this "death-dying" process of your outwardly driven life is one of the primary operating premises of this chapter and underlying principles of this entire book. We will discuss this idea in full detail in the pages to come. For now, let's just step back from this personal train wreck and get our emotional breath back. Let's attempt to regain your life/spiritual perspective at large. I call this the 10,000-foot overview of your life, current path and life circumstances. With that said, I encourage you to refer again to the Joseph Campbell quote at the beginning of this chapter.

No Religion—The quotation at the beginning of this chapter is an important one because it hits at the core of all of our hopes and dreams. Joseph Campbell is referring to the life that is our spiritual awaking path. ***Your life path will always be your spiritual path.*** There is an internal small voice, feeling, and quiet part of you that knows that you aren't where you should be spiritually, emotionally, relationally and psychologically. *Regardless of your religious or non-religious upbringing, you know that any lasting fulfillment in this life comes from accessing this deeper "knowing" awareness and connection to your true destiny.* Your deeper awareness, understanding and personal experience of the divine" doesn't imply or require that you become a religious person, but rather a spiritually aware person. Remember your life going forward is all about your ever-increasing life perspective. No church, synagogue or temple memberships are necessary or needed. It's simply your personal spiritual enlightenment/realization of yourself. Your inner life (beliefs and experiences) is what will completely transform your life. Reading this book isn't about calling your intuitive self-God or higher power any particular name. Neither is it about attaching any label to your inner awakening. It's your full acceptance of your new insight to your inner self, spirit, soul and whatever language you want to use to describe that life energy within you, me and everyone else.

What Does "Spiritual" Mean?—For purposes of our dialogue, this is a working definition: *Spirituality is realizing the limitless opportunities from within your heart and soul to have the quality life you desire (destiny); it's the belief in something bigger than you in this world/life (Divine/God/Spirit); it is knowing there is a greater reason for your life rather than a random sequences of unrelated events (purpose); it is the process of becoming aware that your higher purpose in life is your Spiritual Factor—it is your positive spiritual footprint on your world and the world around you.*

The concepts of your destiny, life purpose, and spiritual connection to your "higher power" are all parts of your life mission; this is your spirituality in day-to-day action. Everyone has to address, work out and discover their individual gifts, treasures, and purposes on their journey, while doing/living their life. Your spirituality is a very individual experience that doesn't require any particular religious membership, but rather openness to your divine nature. It's a very overwhelming idea that everyone, including you, has something to contribute, learn and give to the "greater" good.

The following short story is a reminder of where your journey will always begin (within you) and always (your heart) has the answers for you. The ideas, desires, dreams and longings all start within you and have to be understood from that perspective. This is your own life journey with enormous amounts of personal information stored inside of your heart/soul to be discovered by You! No one can read or translate your inner soulfulness other than you. Your greatest moments will always start within you and spread to your entire life. This is a very powerful short story that illustrates the many different reasons for exploring, learning and making life/spiritual self-realizations within you:

Look Inside for Happiness

There is an ancient Indian legend about a little-known tribe that was constantly at war with other Indian tribes. They abused their religion and their families, had no morals or feelings for others, laughed at wisdom or any kind of order. Murder, theft, and plundering were a daily occurrence. This violent Indian tribe seemed doomed to wipe themselves off the face of the earth. Finally, an old chief gathered together a few of the least violent of the braves and held a council to discuss how they could save their tribe from themselves. The wise old chief decided the only thing to do was to take the secret of happiness and success away from those who abused it. They would take this secret and hide it where no one would ever find it so it could not be abused again. The big question was—where should they hide it?

One Indian brave suggested they bury the secret of happiness and success deep in the earth. But the chief said, "That will never do, for man will dig deep down into the earth and find it."

Another brave said to sink the secret into the darkness of the deepest ocean. Again the chief replied, "No, not there, for man will learn to dive into the depths of the ocean to find it."

A third brave thought they should hide the secret at the top of the very highest mountain. But again, the chief said, "No, for man will climb even the highest of mountains to find it, and again take it for himself.

Finally, the old chief had the answer: "Here is what we will do with the secret of happiness. **We will hide it deep inside of man himself, for he will never think to look for it there."** To this day, according to that Indian legend, man has been running all over the earth—digging, diving, climbing—searching for something he already possesses within himself.

—Indian Legend
(Speakers Sourcebook, Volume I, pages 207-08)

The Moral to Your Story—Regardless of your belief or disbelief of a personal higher power (whatever name you like is fine) that resides inside your heart and soul, there is a secret that is only for your life/spiritual path evolution. The discovering of your personal secret within your heart is one of your primary tasks along your life/spiritual path. The seemingly illusive intangible feeling of completion, inner fulfillment, success or failure that transcends the material level is part of the untapped secret/happiness potential within your heart. The Indian legend is timeless and powerfully accurate for this time and place in your life. You could be like the people in the tribe that keep running around their world looking for something that is already inside of them. Or, you could decide to stop running, avoiding, hiding from what's within you. Surely you are weary of looking everywhere, hoping to find that everlasting happiness, inner peace, and personal success in your work, wealth, marriage, relationships, family, kids, and accomplishments. *It is within you—the last place anyone ever thinks to look or seek!* All the answers to all your questions about your life, your life purpose, and reasons for all the different events in your life, lie right inside of your soul—your inner energy source that is infinite and unchangeable. We have all been conditioned to believe that through hard work, persistence and being "good," we will achieve happiness. This is a truism if we start from the correct place (our soul/spirit). Our heart is the doorway to our inner/outer journey, not someplace outside of us.

Sunglasses Analogy—If the idea that your inner success, happiness and life/spiritual path is all within you seems a bit overstated, consider this idea for a minute. How many times have you started to panic about finding your sunglasses or reading glasses? You start racing around your house looking everywhere, only to discover they have been on your head the entire time! You just forgot that you put them there! Hmm, this is no different than what you are wanting for your life today. *Stop running around looking for a miracle! YOU are the miracle! It's already inside of you!* Take a moment to remember that it's been within you this entire time, even during your despair, severe pain, fear, loss and despair. The "it" is lasting inner peace, sense of purpose, feeling of connection to the greater good, and a divine perspective for your life and all your challenges.

It is the acknowledgment that what appears to be, at face value, superficial random disappointments, great accomplishments and/or tragic events in your life, all serve a significant purpose. There is meaning and purpose to all of it! There is absolutely no failure in your life! The only failure, if you will, is to not see, resist, dismiss and/or deny the inherent value of these meaningful events in your life. Understanding, accepting and absorbing these life-changing lessons that are staring you in the face is the first step out of your Valley of Despair. There is absolutely nothing random, useless or unrelated to the primary purpose of furthering your personal growth along your spiritual factor/path. Nothing is excluded, it all matters in your life. It is as if you have two lives now: *your worldly life and your spiritual life.* Keeping this new perspective in the forefront of your mind is paramount for avoiding and chronically repeating many of the painful life lessons that have brought you to this point and time. There are more aspects to your life than just the material level that we all live and function on daily. There is a whole other world within you that has been attempting to grab your undivided attention in the midst of your job, family, finances, relationships, health issues, and your "life" for many years. A client of mine, in a moment of clarity, recently made this statement when she accepted the bigger purpose: *"My life is more than merely paying bills and going to work every day. What a relief to know I am part of something bigger than me."*

No Failures: You Are Fine Art—The "no failing" concept isn't a polite way of white- washing your screw-ups, impulsive choices, self-centered decisions or unforgivable acts. This isn't a "skip jail" card or a sloppy deathbed declaration of forgiveness for a reckless life. Rather, it is the heartbreaking perspective that there is inherent value, purpose and meaning for you in all of your experiences. Lodge this new concept in your heart and soul: ***Your losses are as important as your gains.*** The disappointments, rejections and seemingly bad luck themes are of tremendous value and purpose in shaping your destiny and your soul's journey. The process of heartfelt soulful understanding goes all the way back to your early childhood and up to this present-day moment. One of the biggest challenges along your path to genuine spiritual enlightenment is accepting the "learning" value of your current situation(s). The betrayals, resentments, seemingly unfairness of life, poor choices, and self-defeating behaviors, are every bit as valuable as your accomplishments. Your life journey is about your life being transformed from the inside out with a new depth of compassion, love, gratitude, and understanding that transcends all prior versions of you. This is exactly what Joseph Campbell is referring to in this quote:

"We must be willing to let go of the Life we've planned,
so as to have the Life that is waiting for us."
—Joseph Campbell

Okay, now the great debate and argument is on between your head and your heart. When I refer to "higher power," what I mean is your intuition, your sixth-sense, your positive inner voice that embraces love and the greater good of life. You can use whatever your comfort zone tells you when it comes to terms like god, spirit, divine nature, soul, intuition, etc. It isn't the time to argue about semantics when your life is hanging in the balance and something within your heart is begging for your full attention.

Personal Questions—It is always important to do a self-temperature check and find out what is going on in your life. Try answering the following questions with the first response that comes to mind; don't edit or change your mind.

- What is one issue, thing, action, or behavior I'm resistant to accept about myself, or my current circumstances and relationships?
- What is going on with my life on the inside? (You already know the answer, but it is worth asking the question.)
- What is the potential meaningful purpose of these events?
- Why is there a recurring theme to all these events in my life?
- How and why do these things keep happening?
- Why do these events and situations seem so emotionally painful?
- Am I crazy for thinking about wanting to quit the personal growth process and just "numb" out?
- Why has my life been so difficult and/or challenging?
- When will the pain stop?
- Do I have the courage to go through all the changes I need to make?

We could keep asking these questions for the rest of time, but the underlying answer will always be that you can change the course of your life—from the inside. Regardless of the "mess" that you are experiencing, you can create a new path. It is never too early to make the changes you have always wanted to make and/or have postponed. In the next chapter, we are going to address your questions and your possible answers.

> *"We are not human beings having a spiritual experience-*
> *We are spiritual beings having a human experience."*
> —*Paramahansa Yoganada*

Closing Thoughts—The idea that we all have a spirit within us that is universally connected to everyone and to everything is mind-boggling. Your life isn't about your body comforts, but rather about nurturing the spirit within you. Your spirit/soul that is within you has a definite purpose for you in this current life. The idea that nothing is random in your life up to this very moment is a concept that lends itself to the urgency of discovering your destiny, path and/or mission in these challenging circumstances. Paramahansa Yoganada's quote points out that your priorities may be out of order, with your emphasis being first on your body and materialism. It's an old and new idea that maybe your highest goal, priority and purpose is to connect with the intention of the intuition-spirit within you for direction and guidance. For a few minutes consider switching your paradigm from being solely outwardly motivated to becoming inwardly motivated. This shift is the lifelong goal, task and purpose of all life-spiritual paths.

You are on a life path that is disguised as a spiritual journey specifically designed for your highest and best good.

The emotional pain, suffering and heartbreak that you have experienced and are feeling today is all designed by your soul for your eventual spiritual awaking and fulfillment of your intended purpose in life now and going forward. This shifting of perspectives to being inwardly driven is one of the biggest challenges facing you on your path toward heightened awareness and lasting inner peace. All the great saints from all walks of life acknowledge the tremendous emotional pain that is created by going from a human perspective to a spiritual perspective. You are undertaking this life/spiritual shift by reading and considering all these ideas today. Keep going . . . this will make more sense to you as your story unfolds before your eyes.

The following two quotes illustrate the start of our journey together. They focus on something I have always felt and knew, but tended to forget at critical times. The universe has excellent and brilliant ways of creating circumstances that win our full, undivided spiritual attention again and again.

"The goal of the human experience is to transform ourselves
From beings who long to attain power in the physical world
To beings that are empowered from within."
—Caroline Myss

"True happiness comes from within and when you're in alignment with your truth and purpose for being here in the physical—no money, material wants or relationships can ever affect this place of harmony.
Be true to yourself and follow your heart."
—Bill Phillips

Summary Points: Something New to Ponder—

- Your life is your spiritual journey. Everyone is on their path regardless of their belief, lack of belief, or disbelief in a higher power.

- Spirituality is like gravity; it applies to everyone regardless of circumstances or challenges—it's always in effect whether you believe in it or not.

- Your losses are as important as your gains! Loss is never a wasted experience or useless element in your "awaking."

- There is a purpose, reason, life lesson buried within the depth and breadth of your current crisis. Keep looking within, and you will find the purpose, meaning and value—because there is one, if not many, pending lessons.

- All the answers to your life questions lie within you—no one holds the keys to your future, your healing or your mission except you!

- You are living two lives simultaneously—worldly/ego and spiritual/divine. The challenge is switching from an externally driven life (ego) to an internally driven motivated (spiritual) life. This is the struggle and duality of your life.

- Successful failure means that there are no failures, mistakes or missed opportunities if you have a spiritual perspective for your life purpose/journey. What appears on the surface to be a major setback in your life is usually the opening of your heart-soul connection to a deeper, more fulfilling life experience/change.

- You can't fail in life! You can resist the process of change inside your soul and in your emotional and relationship world—but that's just frustration. *Failure is an ego term, not a spiritual or divine concept.* Personal and spiritual change is the result of acceptance—that is your journey. Souls don't fail, they wait for the opportunity to change, evolve and love. Your soul will always evolve!

"For a soul/life to evolve, it must learn lessons, a myriad of issues in each lifetime—including lessons of love, forgiveness, and gratitude."
—*James Van Praagh*

Chapter 2

Five Different Ways to the "Valley of Despair"

"The cave you fear to enter holds the treasure that you seek."
—*Joseph Campbell*

"While the crisis stage of grief/loss does pass in its own time—and each person's grief has its own timetable—deep feelings don't disappear... ultimately you come to the adage...love is stronger than death."
—*Ram Dass*

What is the treasure you truly want? What is it that keeps eluding your grasp? What relationship are you avoiding? What part of your personality do you not accept or resist? Why the does the same thing keep happening over and over (i.e., job loss, relationship heartbreak, addictive behaviors, money problems)? What project, career choice are you avoiding? What do you fear might to be true or needs your attention concerning your romantic relationship? What about your family do you ignore, avoid or deny? What is happening at work that you would prefer to sidestep? What personality themes keep reappearing in your life? What secret about you or someone else is bothering you? Why do you have chronic money issues? These questions are what the above quotes and the quote from Chapter 1 are asking you to ask yourself. Everyone has several deep personal issues/ questions that must be resolved in this current school of life. *No one is exempt from these life/spiritual lessons and losses.* Many people choose to be in denial of them until the issues bring them back to that same cave/ issue that they keep avoiding. Your personal cave is the metaphor for the unexamined parts of your life that you avoid, dismiss or diminish. The timeless purpose, impact or value in your life can't be understood from outside of you—only from within your heart and soul.

> *"There is a battle of two wolves inside all of us.*
> *One is evil. It is anger, jealousy, greed, resentment, lies*
> *Inferiority and ego.*
> *The other is good/spirit. It is joy, peace, love, hope, humility*
> *Kindness, empathy and truth.*
> **The wolf that wins—The one you feed!"**
> —*Native American Cherokee Proverb*

No Exemptions From Learning—The native American Cherokee proverb points out that the need to develop your "good/spiritual" self has always been a challenge. The process between your pain, suffering and life is a constant state of tensions within you. Looking inward and asking and examining your life is one of the quickest ways to feed/nurture the loving caring soul within you. Neglecting your inner feelings, emotions and intuition leaves you hungry, and feeds your ego, not the spirit/goodness within you.

What is one question that you think about asking yourself but never really do? What would it take for you to emotionally stare down and fully address that nagging issue or doubt about yourself? Don't allow yourself to say, *"I don't have any unanswered questions about my life—I am good—I got this!"* If that is your knee-jerk response, go walk around your inner wall of defensiveness and take another look inside yourself. You will be the most surprised and relieved when you stop and walk into your personal cave of enlightenment and transformation (we all have one). The issue isn't asking yourself a rehearsed question, but asking yourself the "real" question that sits at the periphery of your conscious awareness. What is that shadow of doubt in the corner of your mind about? Could it be your current life circumstances and/or the uneasy inner feeling that never goes away? We all need to take a step back occasionally and check on what's going on in our inner circle of life. Now is the time, while your heart is open to new ideas and changes as a result of some extreme traumatic life events, suffering and losses.

Remember, there are many parts to your life in that cave that are waiting for you to embrace, accept and explore. You are in the process of self-awaking, self-discovery and lasting positive change. Your life will expand, change and completely transform as you enter and claim these unclaimed parts of your soul. You will exit the other side of the cave (your cave is the place or activities that numb you out, cause you to avoid or ignore the feelings inside of you) with a completely different perspective about your life, your passion, your direction and most importantly "You!" There isn't enough paper or time to explain the incredible value to you of allowing the process of natural spiritual change to be part of your life today.

What's Going on Inside My Cave—Many times, we begin asking the important questions long after we have descended down into a full-on spiritual crisis that is commonly referred to as a mid-life crisis. The repetitive nature of asking yourself "Why does this painful event, issue and/or problem keep happening?" is absolutely the wrong question to ask at this point in your crisis. All these personal events/crises that lead you to becoming more aware, awake, and mindful of your greater purpose are critical for your mid-life shift toward greater fulfillment and inner driven purpose. Knowing the "whys" will never substitute for the heart/soul changes you can and need to make or do. *Information is never a replacement for action.* Important paradigm shifts in our thinking about our own life and the greater good are all crises that bring change and internal expansion. You want to be in crisis to get out of your narrow comfort zone that has been increasingly suffocating your growth and restricting your insight.

One of the important issues throughout our discussion is the incredible secondary benefit of expanding your comfort zone in every area of your life. Your life isn't about exclusion, restriction or greater limitations but rather the acceptance of the ever-changing flow of expanding your thinking, functioning and "being" in your world. The process of change includes tapping into your own spiritual capacity and developing *your potential for self-acceptance, love and forgiveness.* These human/spiritual values of living from within get refined in the traumas of our life and relationship struggles. It is through five typical portals (discussed below) of growth opportunity that our personal and spiritual awaking (these terms are interchangeable) will be very apparent and necessary for moving our life forward. The repetition of despair, hopelessness, loss of self, chronic physical and emotional issues all have their recurring roots in one primary area of your life. Yes, there is a big purpose to these misunderstood and traumatic experiences in your life. Nothing is ever wasted or lost in your life experiences, heartbreaks and personal losses. No loss, heartache or suffering is for the sake of recreation and recklessness. There is always a purpose—even when it isn't readily apparent.

Where Does it Hurt?—In order to help you refocus on these probing soulful questions above, consider what area of your life has the most emotional and traumatic energy and concern. What thought, person, experience or event is an immediate emotional trigger of anger, rage and a desire for revenge? There is no wrong answer or off-limits topic. There should be no editing of your answers to be politically correct, nice or proper. The answer to the question(s) is the key(s) to opening the door(s) of your psychological and spiritual awareness. It is critical to consider the possibility that there is an ongoing theme to your current core psychological and emotional concerns. Metaphorically, you don't want to keep repeating middle school or the first grade because it is related to your painful life repetitions. The question issue or concern within you isn't going away. You might be able to avoid it for years, but eventually it *always* reappears with more energy and force than the last time you looked at it. Ouch!

Many psychologists (myself included) believe that unless a person's answers, resolves and addresses their core questions, they will spend a lifetime attempting to cover them up. The amount of emotional and mental energy that one must continually burn to avoid, procrastinate and deny is extensive and exhausting. If allowed to remain unchecked within your life, these unresolved unexamined issues can ultimately result in severe and chronic life-altering physical problems, psychological disorders and tragic choices. The universe, higher power, or any word that you are comfortable using, has a perfect way of getting our inner attention, or the inward pressure will continue until we do listen, begin to enter our cave, and start to resolve our life/spiritual journey plans/purpose.

You're Fully Involved—It's always a startling idea that at one time you were fully involved on some level of consciousness in how these events or situations defy your life mission and path, or how you thought your life was going to be at this point on your journey. It can be mind-numbing to realize that you can truly make "lemonade" out of the bitterest, most heart-wrenching, situations without a bitter aftertaste about life, God and yourself. Further, there are five common ways your life will keep taking you to the same unexamined parts or unacceptable, unexploded and/or repressed parts of you.

The ongoing painful reruns of your own personal movie are getting very old and exhausting for you, right? Financial strain, teenage daughter pregnant for the second time, third romantic heartbreak, recurrent health problems, relapses in sobriety from drugs/alcohol, and chronic feelings of suicide are all symptoms of something much deeper than the surface problem. You could simply slip into a very deep depressive bitter attitude and negative perspective on your life. The circumstances surrounding your life are pushing you to the edge of breaking on all levels. The confusing issue is that many times the circumstances of your life seem unrelated, random, and mirror a result of so-called bad-luck. First of all, there is no such thing as bad luck; rather, there are purposeful events. From a superficial view of your life, it is psychologically, emotionally, and spiritually confusing that there is an apparent theme, meaning, or thread that connects all these events.

All you know is that you feel awful, scared and very desperate to do things differently. The key is to begin to realize and accept that everything in your life is connected, related and directing you toward your own life/

spiritual self-realization. After all, how could a loving Universal Spirit, God, Jesus, Higher Power, Loving Guru or Angels allow these awful things to happen to you? All the answers lie in your life's learning process on the inward journey home. It is at this point of nearly losing your mind that new information, insights and change begin to appear on your path. You are about ready to step out from the old ways of doing things in your life. It's the right time for you to begin to look at the new possibilities of perhaps doing things in a different, more purposeful loving way. The old saying that lightning never strikes twice in the same place isn't true in your case. It feels like lightning has repeatedly been shooting through your life and leaving you in an ash heap of despair, confusion and disbelief.

Five Different Paths and Ways to Your Cave—

> *"New beginnings are often disguised as painful endings."*
> —*Lao Tzu*

The top five life changers we all face:
Money/Finances Issues (values/generosity vs. greed/dishonesty/emotional deprivation)
Family of Origin Issues (individuality/passion vs. enmeshed/abused/addiction)
Love/Marriage Issues (self-acceptance/esteem vs. inferior/shame/dismissed)
Parenting Relationships (competent/self-worth vs. people-pleasing/unlovable)
Health Issues (trusting life/passion vs. resentment/entitlement)

These five issues cover many of the interpersonal dynamics within a person's life (there is a sixth issue that appears in the epilogue). Your life will tend to focus on one area at a particular time/phase and then shift emphasis to another area at a later age/circumstance. Each area has a valuable lesson, message, and soulful gift for your life lying deep within the complicated circumstances of your personal experience. These five areas are imbedded with life lessons, challenges and inherent value in your personal transformation and evolution through all the stages of your life. It's understandable that as we grow up, we all encounter a variety of challenging issues and concerns. Many of our early life experiences become the backdrop of our adult day-to- day life struggles. These early challenges can be a combination of many things that are positive, traumatic and/or beyond our childhood ability to comprehend.

No Blaming—There are particular recurring themes and inner struggles that have to be addressed by you. The only approach that has any lasting results is to go beyond blaming and finger-pointing at parents, partners, siblings, children, ex-wife/husband and the important people in your world. For many, this new approach (self-acceptance vs. blame) is nothing you have ever done or even considered before. The courage to look into your personal cave is motivated by the extreme emotional pain and suffering you have today. The best solution to your current crisis is going into your Valley of Despair cave (your heart) and find the missing pieces of your heart/soul.

> *"Nothing ever goes away until it has taught us*
> *what we need to know."*
> *—Pema Chadron*

The basic five areas of our life all possess different challenges and features from multiple levels. We are going to explore why each area is relevant to your current life journey. We need to discuss each particular area of life and explain some of the things necessary to complete/resolve that phase. *It's important to remember that the timing and healing of these issues can take years upon years. It doesn't mean that it (your life or a healing issue) is hopeless, but rather a **process** that you want to embrace rather than a destination to be reached.* Remember your personal transformation and spiritual evolution is the end goal of these new insights for your life. Wherever these challenges have taken you emotionally, physically, psychologically and spiritually are very important to your inner awakening and transformation. Going into your "cave" isn't a weekend retreat project, but rather a new heightened state of awareness and compassion for your life and others. The Pema Chadron quote is a great reminder that your journey is all about acknowledging the events in your life and approaching them with the utmost care and concern. Like the Fram oil filter commercial says, *"Pay me now or pay me later,"* it is cheaper (in all senses of the word) to pay (deal with something) now, than it is to pay later. Paying later (avoidance) is much more costly.

What is the primary issue that you can currently learn from? Underneath all the different circumstances, what are some of the repetitive themes and/or feelings that keep reappearing in your relationships? What is the issue or concern that seems to keep reappearing in your life?

Money/Finances Issues

Money is a very hot topic and a very common measuring stick for most men. Unfortunately, now a lot of women are also dragged into this endless treadmill of emotional deprivation. In spite of the economy, "money" is emotionally, spiritually and psychologically significant in its ability to break or crash through people's lives like a freight train traveling down the tracks of life at 100 mph. Yet, many of us will resist the inherent life lessons while losing everything materially and financially. This can include the prestigious job, huge savings account, country club membership, living in the right neighborhood, the trust fund and retirement fund lost, the business deal that failed, bankruptcy, loss of economic power and self-image. Money is a mean taskmaster who doesn't treat its followers very well or with any respect. On the surface, the power of material possessions and walking an enlightenment path tend to be a contradiction in terms and values. This is simply not true, and a very big illusion in the Western world. Throughout all the world's religions, it's always been said that wealth and spirituality are difficult to achieve. Being poor and homeless is not the answer, but the attachment to material possessions and monetary power in the world tends to cover up a person's deeper inner desires (meaningful life). The spiritual path is an inward path that doesn't get much love or respect, but yet it is the only way to become truly wealthy! *Self-worth and your net-worth can NEVER be mixed, connected or confused.* They are not compatible or interchangeable. OK, this is much easier said than done.

No One Wants to be Ebenezer Scrooge—Losing your job, your status in your world, your stunning home, downsizing, scaling back a lifetime of material comforts can be likened to "dying." The stories of wealth to poverty all point to the inherent value of the invisible spirit of generosity vs. holding onto your wealth at the expense of relationships, love, and being

27

of service to your family/world. Greed is never a kind master and tends to rob its followers of wisdom, lasting inner peace and spiritual clarity. Any type of self-centeredness, greed, emotional exploitation or devaluation of others all come from the ego's need to be superior, not humble. Greed and spirituality are incompatible: one withholds, and one gives freely.

The Story of Scrooge—Written by English author, Charles Dickens, *"A Christmas Carol"* was first published in December 1843 and has never been out of print since its inception). The story of Scrooge perfectly captures the picture of an old bitter miser. The story is about much more than simple the setting of the Christmas tradition in London in the mid-1800s. It's about the intrinsic wealth of giving. Scrooge's longtime deceased business partner, Jacob Marley, comes to visit him in a dream on Christmas Eve. Scrooge is shown a frightening vision/dream about his misguided short sightedness, greediness and his inability to share with those much less fortunate. Jacob Marley warns Scrooge of the irreparable damage and dire consequences that will follow him after he leaves this life if he doesn't immediately change his actions/intentions. What is also very interesting about this story is that Scrooge is awakened from a deep sleep (literally and metaphorically) by a familiar spirit, ghost and/or angel. Much of the time, many of us are figuratively asleep with our eyes wide open, not realizing the depth of our spiritual blindness and incorrect belief system regarding money, love and relationships.

Transformation—The message is clear and never wasted when you are wondering why money and your material desires have left you in a serious personal/spiritual crisis. It doesn't need to be Christmas, a funeral or any particular time other than your current crisis for a message of generosity vs. greed-dishonesty-emotional deprivation to be conveyed. Changing your internal perspective takes a second, but that change can take 25 years of suffering before that moment of clarity occurs. Scrooge was clearly that person—alone, miserable and without any spiritual insight to his self-centered destructive ways. When he is shown his eternal future of despair and loneliness, it is devastating. Upon waking, in an effort to mend the error of his old miserly ways, Scrooge immediately tries to help Bob Cratchit, his underpaid and underappreciated employee. No longer a victim of his old dream state of greed, Scrooge immediately shifts his internal beliefs to generosity, self-love and connects to his life mission. Money has the power to blind, deceive and mislead the smartest and brightest souls into the Valley of Despair. Unfortunately, since the beginning of time, money, power and prestige have been the devil's best friend—derailing many a caring soul into absolute spiritual, emotional, relational and financial ruin, poverty and death.

Money is Energy—The money issue in your life is much more than your lack of cash flow or current credit rating. Rather it is loaded with spiritual information that has to be addressed from the inside of your cave. Money is an energy that is directly motivated by the core values of how you operate in your world—personally, professionally and relationally. Still wondering how money, deprivation, suffering and your despair are all connected? *Ask yourself these questions:*

- Do I value people/relationships as much as my money?
- What's more important to me: money or people?
- Do I treat better and care more about money than the people in my life?
- Do I give more attention to my material possessions than I do to my relationships, kids, and partner?
- Do I feel that there isn't enough money, things, or resources to share?
- Do I use money to try to fill the hole that is inside of me?
- Do I still believe or try to use money to heal the deeper issues inside of me?
- Have I used money to control my personal/professional relationships?
- Do I rationalize deceiving/stealing from others because I feel it's my right or perhaps I want revenge?
- In the past, have I feared being poor, and do I now?
- Do I withhold, and try to control people in my life with money?
- Do I consider money to be the primary measuring stick of my success with people, in business and my life purpose?
- Do I deserve to be happy with or without money, power and/or prestige?

- Is money my "God," and everything I do in my life revolves around it?
- How would my life change if I loved myself more than money and the material possessions that define me?

These questions point out the powerful reality that material acquisitions will blind you to what is truly your life's mission and passion. Until we begin to honestly address the spiritual/emotional vacuum in our hearts that we attempt to cover up with money, there is no end to our suffering. Consider Scrooge and how much terror and panic he felt when he saw his destiny of eternal despair? One of the hardest and most painful ego lessons to learn is that of losing possessions and professional standing in order to find humility and the greater purpose of your life. *Your life will never be measured by your wealth, but rather what you did with it.* For most of his life, Scrooge did nothing with his wealth except hold on to it for fear of losing it. Losing these material love objects are the universe's way of getting your inner attention and priorities to line up with your soul's purpose in this life. Fortunately, Scrooge was awakened from a deep "sleep of greed," in time to see his destiny. Have you been awakening to your new future?

Money Value Challenge—The issues of greed-dishonesty-emotional deprivation vs. generosity/valuing people and relationships will be elaborated on in the next chapter. All five paths to personal awakening will be explained in their complete context and impact in the next few chapters. Each path has its own inherent life lessons which are deeply embedded in your current experience. It's very critical to be mindful that your emotional, psychological, physical, financial and/or romantic suffering isn't the universe's primary concern or intention. It's solely your awakening to your inner spiritual life and destiny that is the top priority for all these events. Suffering is only for the purpose of getting your utmost inward attention and emotional/spiritual cooperation to your life's purpose.

Family of Origin Issues

*"Three thieves: Fear, Self-Sabotage and Self-Doubt
will rob you of your present and future if you let them;
don't you let them!"*
—Fran Briggs

Families are never a neutral subject or lack a wealth of personal information about your life today or in the past. What money is to a self-absorbed/materialistic person is what a problematic family is to an emotionally traumatized son or daughter: Powerful! We are all sons and daughters regardless of our family history, adoption, divorces and all the other countless family relationship combinations. We all have a family that we came to from the other side, and they are the starting point of this discussion. People know they have family issues when this subject is raised and they suddenly feel emotionally overwhelmed and immediately angry. A hot flash of adrenalin runs through your body when you have to explain how "crazy" your family was/is. Consider that a sign. The topic of birth family, much like the other four issues in this chapter, could be several volumes in length—all explaining how those painful family experiences can be purposeful for your spiritual awakening.

Families and Addictions—The psychological foundation of all addictions has its beginnings in childhood trauma that is severe, problematic and terrifying. It is a widely accepted fact that any behavioral changes in terms of addictive behavior have to include the lesson in the emotional trauma response that the person is experiencing today. Frustration tolerance has to be developed to cope with the early and possible current family trauma. Addictive behaviors are unconsciously designed to keep you from re-experiencing the overwhelming, terrifying and sometimes life-threatening events and emotions you witnessed growing up. All addictions are maladaptive emotional blocks to keep us from feeling powerless or completely vulnerable to emotional, psychological, physical pain and/or injury. Emotional and physical trauma has a very strong and lasting impact on a person's early brain development and ability to handle anxiety in their adult life. Neurophysiology is the study of how our brain chemistry is negatively impacted from long-term anxiety and the brain chemicals produced from childhood trauma. Unresolved family issues often will manifest into chronic anxiety, panic attacks and a host of different types of phobias and personality disorders in adult children of chaotic families. All these issues have their roots in your family history, past and present.

Co-dependence is the Drug of Any Nonfunctional Relationship— Another critical collateral family issue is the relationship style of co-dependence. This is the definition of co-dependence for the purposes of our discussion: *the overwhelming need or emotional value gained in seeking another person's approval through selfless acts—with the sole unconscious/conscious intention of feeling loved, accepted and emotionally safe.* A co-dependent man or woman can't approve, accept, appreciate or love themselves without everyone or a particular someone approving of them. Without your family's approval, your life is in absolute crisis until that approval is given. The co-dependent relationship is never equitable, balanced or results in a positive outcome for the person serving in that diminished role. One person is always saving, fixing, and nurturing the other person in hopes of unconsciously recapturing the lost love from their childhood.

The co-dependent adult suffers from severe feelings of shame (they feel they are defective, phony, an "actor"), lacks self-acceptance, does not value their life or their own thoughts. They are hyper-vigilant of what their partner, friends or children think, and tend to have no idea of how they actually feel. In addition, they struggle with finding the emotional strength to say "no" to anyone or to anything. The opinion of others is more important than their own. When a friend or partner is upset with them, they become terrified that the relationship is doomed. This may sound extreme, but it is a very common issue that is emotionally paralyzing, and it will render someone an emotional hostage until his sense of self/soul is given room to breathe and proper expression. Creating an individual "self" is attempted many times in adolescence, but in enmeshed, traumatic families, there is no acceptance for a difference of opinion or permission for behavior that deviates from the family norm. This type of family— regardless of race, creed, economics and education—is all about controlling an independent behavior in service of the parents and other family members.

No Separation—The chronic sense of responsibility for the family is beyond any manageable level of concern, but rather is the emotional/spiritual hub of your life. The expression of rage and anger is very commonly used as a pattern of control and fear in the family. You are only able to express a difference of opinion or change with extreme behavior or self-defeating behavior. This is the primary way you've learned to have emotional breathing space in your life and relationships. Any independent behaviors are viewed as a betrayal of the family unit and lapse of responsibility on your part. The amount of emotional energy that is spent on maintaining, soothing and placating your family is all-consuming. The emotional cloud of fear of abandonment or the fear of losing your family's love is truly your full-time occupation, regardless of your "day-job."

The relationship dramas, power struggles, disappointments, and fear for your emotional safety are all the ingredients that fill up your life. Your sense of individuality has never developed to the degree and capacity it could. The inner desires for your personal freedom have never been actualized or developed. The reaction to such an overwhelming family history lends itself to any type of addictive behavior—avoidance behaviors, self-sabotaging choices, and the fear of rejection. The level of frustration in your life regardless, of your age is very high, and is a major roadblock to your inner spiritual path.

Stopping to inspect the inner relationship you have with yourself in spite of your family and how it directs your behavior is a very powerful journey to take. Finding your own opinion/voice is the beginning to finding your spiritual path and destiny in your life.

Family Questions for Emotional and Spiritual Clarity—

- Do you struggle with saying "no" to people in your life for fear of not being accepted or loved?

- Do you feel that your life is your family, and you can't have your own life without their approval?
- Does your family have addictive behaviors that are dismissed as unimportant issues?
- Do you struggle with intense feelings of guilt, fear, and/or remorse for your conflicted feelings about your family?
- Do you believe that you can't have your own independent life without losing the love and support of your family?
- Do you spend large amounts of your emotional energy worrying about all the different family relationships?
- Does your life revolve around your anger, resentment or hatred of your family?
- Did you or do you periodically cut-off communication with your family?
- Does your family form negative non-supportive alliances against each other and against you?
- Do you talk to your family members excessively for fear of being left out of the family information loop?

Love/Marriage Issues

A broken heart is the worst. It's like having
broken ribs. Nobody can see it, but it hurts every time you breathe.
—Wayne Dyer

In my practice, I repeatedly hear people say they have resolved their entire emotional traumatic childhood history. The painful issues of shame, self-loathing, and self-acceptance seemed resolved, settled. After all, that was then and this now. You were convinced that marriage and/or your life partner would help heal the old wounds—not create new ones. You moved forward with the commitment to do everything differently in your adult romantic life! Then, many years later, you find yourself sitting in a family law courtroom fighting over the custody of your three children, and your ex-partner of 18 years looks like a complete stranger to you. It is at these precise moments of clarity that our past relationship issues (with ourselves and with others) come flooding back into our heart and soul. Unfortunately, the underlying issues stemming from our role models for love, communication style and intimate relationships were often less than satisfactory. *Then what begins to happen is all our unresolved emotional pain from the past is directly placed onto and into our romantic relationships/ marriages without us consciously knowing it.* This heart-wrenching realization occurs as a result of a painful romantic breakup, divorce, and shattered relationship. Any type of love relationship breakup can be a life-changing "trigger," regardless of its duration, sexual orientation, or your age.

Love Hurts—All breakups, regardless of age or life experience (especially divorce), have the uncanny ability to pull up every self-doubt and personal issue that has been dormant in your life (your cave). The overwhelming sense of loss characterized by the "broken rib" quote above is often indescribable; it feels like you're going to die a slow death from heartbreak. People do become very sick when their soul, heart and sense of self feel devastated and unlovable. An emotional and spiritual broken heart can literally kill you unless you intervene on your own behalf. It is at these moments of complete emotional devastation that our shame, guilt and despair from losing our friend, lover, romantic partner of many years is weighted down with this incredible sense of rejection. We may look okay on the outside—going to work, smiling and saying the right things to our friends and family—but emotionally, we are bleeding profusely. The pain is like the broken rib analogy, it hurts to breathe but no one can see it. If you aren't careful with the severe emotional pain, your life can come to a complete stop. The pain, despair and incredible hopelessness can often cause us to react in ways that are far from appropriate or positive for us or for others in our lives.

Purpose of Pain and Love—Divorce, romantic betrayal and broken trust all expose our underlying fears about ourselves and being alone in life. One of the keys to coming to terms with your destiny, regardless of your relationship status, is knowing that you can be okay being alone. You begin to realize that you are connected to your inner-self/soul even without a partner. No one is alone! It is an outdated emotional perspective that being single, divorced, or not in an intimate relationship is a negative reflection on you. Unfortunately, it usually takes a severe emotional crisis to push people past the illusion of separateness from themselves and their world without a significant someone.

We are all connected on so many different levels in life. The emotional pain question is: Are you connected to your own life? The fears, self-doubts and emotional emptiness that this generates will be discussed in great detail in Section II of this book. Heartbreak is loaded with more personal unexplored information about your "cave/inner-self" than at any other time or personal event. It is critical to examine your inner life from a higher perspective than the same level or approach that you've used previously. You want to heal your intimate relationship issues, improve your communication style, have a secure attachment style, have the ability to handle conflict and be open to accepting love. All of these factors are part of your spiritual awakening and connection to an inner sense of self/soul. Severe emotional pain can be the door to expanding your capacity for self-love, self-forgiveness, and meaningful loving relationships.

The Purpose of Loss and Loneliness—Many times our romantic loss, divorce or betrayal exposes our deep sense of feeling alone and the lack of concern in our world. These deep feelings of having no lovable value, being invisible, dismissed, rejected, and abandoned are often labeled as our "inner child" or "wounded child." It is our deep soulful longing for a significant emotional and psychological connection to us, others, and the universe that is really the underlying issue. Your new insight about yourself begins to address these lifelong cravings from within your heart/soul. No romance, marriage, love type relationship will ever fill the empty void in your heart—that is a spiritual issue not a relationship issue! A marriage relationship might help cover up some of your spiritual emptiness for a while, maybe even years. Unfortunately, it is only when these deeper issues are exposed that you can properly address your own sense of self and spiritual path concerns. *The positive effects of a crisis in a failing love relationship and all types of romantic breakups is they get your inward undivided, soulful attention.*

Another powerful benefit of a broken heart, emotional loss and your sense of emotional disconnection/loneliness is that these emotional experiences expose our deepest fears and inadequacies. Addressing your perceived weaknesses can lead to your greatest strengths being developed. Our deep sense of wanting to feel loved, accepted and forgiven is natural and a universal need. Our spiritual awakening answers these deep needs with the power of a loving self-acceptance. Your expanded insight on love and loss allows you to see the value of your own self-realization. This inner awareness is your soul's inward path that has been begging for your attention for years.

One of your new insights is that the pursuit of perfection, in yourself or lover/partner is a powerful form of self-loathing. Your romantic mission isn't perfection, but rather developing compassion for yourself, your partner and your world. The healing process of your broken spirit is that your value doesn't come from your relationships, but from within your own self-acceptance along with a fuller understanding of your life purpose. Potentially, romantic pain opens up your thinking to considering that your life has a connection to something bigger than to your daily world or to that former love.

Romantic/Love Questions for Consideration—

- Are you afraid to be alone/single?
- Do you get your value as a man/woman from your partner?
- Do you over-give in your relationships in hopes to be loved and accepted?
- Can you accept love and support from your intimate partner?
- Do resent the opposite sex?
- Do you secretly worry that you are a phony and your partner will discover it?
- Do have bouts of uncontrollable anger, rage and disappointment in your relationships?
- During a breakup do you resort to being aggressive and emotionally abusive or disconnected?

- Do you feel unlovable, or like damaged goods?
- Do you believe someone can truly love and accept you?
- Do you believe that love relationships are too much work and pain?
- Do wonder if you will have a partner who truly understands and adores you?

All these questions are directed toward helping you find that "pearl" of great price in your heart that has never been fully understood by you or within the context of your love relationships. The priceless pearl is your ever-increasing loving self-acceptance of your life and all the different pieces, experiences. Your pearl (that hidden treasure within you) is the passionate connection to your destiny, divine nature and higher-self. The experience of love from your partner is a wonderful gift when it is incorporated with your inner connection of divine acceptance. Love is the most powerful force in the universe to change, heal and create the life you have always dreamed of and desired. Allowing love to flow through you requires that it comes from the limitless source—your soul/spirit!

Parenting Relationships: You and Your Children

"The world as we have created it is a process of our thinking. It cannot be changed without changing our thinking."
—*Albert Einstein*

Parenting is one of the most underrated challenges, tasks and responsibilities in life! You can be married for years and then become single, but you're always a parent for life—that fact never changes. The title of mom/dad (step-parent applies) and sense of parental concern never diminishes with your children's age or their life circumstances. The mystery of being a parent, regardless of your marriage status, is a challenge that can reveal more things about your life that were dormant prior to this parenting chapter in your life story. Today, more and more "blended families" (not living with both biological parents) exist; the title of parent doesn't change or is diminished by the biological/legal relationship to your son or daughter. *If you have a step-daughter/son, your role is that of a parent; you're a parent regardless of any legal titles.* The responsibility, role and relationship bond as parent/child has all the emotional and psychological effects that make this a unique "spiritual" path. Parenting opens up doors in your soul that many times were undercover until your child (regardless of age—it always happens) kicks open the door to all your personal doubts, vulnerabilities, shame and insecurities. Children have the innate ability to touch on a parent's deepest insecurities and unresolved emotional and spiritual issues.

My Inner Child—One of the most fascinating things about being a parent is the way in which your "inner child" is awakened. We all have an inner child that is as much a part of our adult life as oxygen is to water—inseparable. The term "inner/wounded child" has received a lot of mixed reviews over the years. The spiritual dynamic of your sensitive inner child emotions has its roots in your own childhood. That is why the term "inner child" is used to describe your wide range of feelings, needs and unmet desires that many times reappear with becoming a parent. Often the emotional pain between your adult feelings and your inner child feelings seems paradoxical. *The paradox is feeling unlovable while having the responsibility to love your children.* Being a parent allows for these deep unresolved issues (unmet emotional/spiritual needs) to reappear with a new face (your child as the trigger), but with the same old pain and frustration. Typically, your unresolved issues will resurface when your child is at the approximate age that triggered your original wounding. You're no longer able to avoid these old painful feelings and suppress the desire for acceptance. All of your childhood trauma can be dormant until you begin to feel a sense of vulnerability with your child that sparks your old repressed memories of not feeling loved or accepted.

Conflict is Natural—Many times the conflict between a parent and a teenager isn't about adolescent rebellion, but rather the unresolved rebellion in the parents' heart about their own parents. Your child can be the "lightening rod" that reveals your wounded neglected inner child. *Your developing son/daughter wants the same love and acceptance you might never have received growing up.* Further, your teenager, young adult isn't psychologically equipped to be your emotional support, live-in therapist or a fill-in for your ex-partner or spouse. Yup, parenting always has your parents in the background, even if your children have never met your parents or they've been deceased for a decade. Your parents can be literally cut-off/out from your life, but they are a silent influence that has to be reconciled within your heart. Their presences have to be acknowledged in how you view yourself both as parent and adult child. This can be a very slippery slope into denial and anger if compassion, forgiveness and self-acceptance aren't part of your emotional parenting approach.

Your Parents and Your Kids—Your parents are always a factor in how you're going to navigate a relationship with your children. How could they not be a factor? The conscious decision to be a better parent than your own parents can easily become an emotional minefield that explodes with your children. Wanting to be a better version of your mom or dad is appropriate and very important. *The downward turbulence in your life starts when your unconscious needs and desires for love, acceptance and being valued get mixed in with your children's own developmental challenges.* This lethal combination of needing to be loved and trying to be a loving parent is the basis for all types of child abuse, parent/child alienation and chronic teenage runaways.

The desire to be a good parent and to feel love from another person (your child) gets immediately lost when the child rejects (natural event) a parent. The need to want and seek love was created long before your kids were born, before your marriage and it has its roots in your childhood. The more you become consciously aware of your unmet emotional and spiritual needs in your childhood, the easier it is to heal today. Parenting on the spiritual path requires that you resolve and heal your wounded feelings within you. Healing your neglected inner child allows your children to have a less complicated life. *Your inner-child/wound issues were never touched on to this degree or magnitude until your child found them.* Regardless of age or legal status, children have the gift of knowing your vulnerable issues and can expose them to you better than any social media tool ever can. It is the core feelings of rejection, failure, and not good enough that impair our present-day ability to be the person, parent and partner we want and deeply desire to be. Our complete spiritual/emotional healing starts with uncovering these feelings and allowing our soul awareness to change our inner perspective. You want to see your children as separate functional young people without your overlap of rejection and anger on them. Consider the following questions as part of the process of your inner healing as a father or mother:

Inner Child / Inner Parent Ideas—

- Do you believe you are important in your children's life? (*father*)
- Do you resent that your children will never appreciate all that you do and give to them? (*mother*)
- Do you resent that no one in your family (kids-partner/ex) knows how much you care about them? (*father*)
- Do you wonder if you will be loved and respected by your kids? (*both*)
- Does your adult daughter/son reflect well upon you and your efforts to be the primary nurturer? (*mother*)
- Do you believe that in spite of your childhood you can become the parent you always wanted? (*both*)
- What is the one thing that you resent about your parents growing up? How has that issue shaped you as a parent currently? (*both*)
- What is one thing that you craved from your parents growing up that you never received or still might crave today? (*both*)
- What is one thing you desire from your children? (*both*)
- Do you ever behave or react to your children in an abusive or shaming manner? (*both*)
- Do you seek your children's approval and acceptance? (*both*)
- Do you criticize the other parent regardless of the impact it has on your children? (*both*)
- Do you ever gossip negatively about the other partner in order to gain your children approval and support? (*both*)
- Do you expect your children to never move away or be distant from you? (*both*)

All of these questions illustrate the underlying unresolved wounded child that might be directing and limiting your effectiveness as a mother/father. Don't be critical of your past mistakes with your children or partner. Focus on your present-day issues of love, self-acceptance and self-forgiveness. The best style of parenting is healing your wounded child; this becomes an example to your children of the powerful transformational divine nature within you. Children know if God/Spirituality is real by an eyewitness experience of the divine/intuitive nature in your life. Your kids at any age know whether you like or dislike yourself.

Health Issues

"I was playing tennis, and suddenly I began to lose all the movement
on the right side of my body. I was having a stroke.
I knew I was dying and asked God to spare my life. Laying in the ICU for
eight days allowed me time to see what was killing me.
It was my fears and spiritual disconnection."
—Stephan (Author)

Your body has a brilliant and powerful way of getting your attention like nothing else in your life. The chronic issues of physical pain, suffering, disease, physical appearance, drug/alcohol addiction, food/weight/body issues, cosmetic surgeries, and challenging physical disabilities can become the sole focus of your life. Your body preoccupation can very easily become your primary connection to your world. The idea that you are more than your body is a concept that might not ring true or have much of an impact on how you *feel* regarding body image and physical appearance. It is very difficult to think of anything other than your body issues when physical challenges are real or imagined—especially when you're suffering from chronic pain, addictive cravings, eating/food issues (anorexia or bulimia), distorted body image or any long- term disease (such as cancer). There is a lot of popular press literature (see bibliography) about the connections between the mind, body and our spiritual journey. Whenever I read these articles, I am usually fighting off a chronic illness (like sinus issues) or recurring pain and being told about the direct connections between my health and unresolved emotional issues! What is upsetting is that the correlation between my physical well-being and my emotional/spiritual well-being is intimately linked much closer than I want to acknowledge. Your emotional state, feelings, body and soul are all part and parcel to the same package: You.

Your Body and Feelings—It is very difficult to trust the greater good of life and feel physical pain or that your body is failing you regardless of your choices. It is also very difficult to like yourself when you look in the mirror and genuinely believe that you are unattractive/not pretty enough when your body is changing because of age, pregnancies, surgeries and the natural flow of life. The term "body hatred" (dysmorphic disorder) is an issue that is rarely discussed, but it is one of the core symptoms of a much deeper spiritual crisis. Your deep disapproval of your physical looks and body is a spiritual issue that from a surface level seems ridiculous or unrelated. Your body, mind and soul are all connected and housed in your physical body. Rejecting any element of your life dramatically affects the other areas of your life and well-being. For example, it's impossible to feel good in your body when you dislike it. Your body is always talking to you in a personal manner, offering you the opportunity to learn from the cues and signs. Whether your body is failing you or you're failing your body, either way it's the right time to change your life. The best body medicine is changing your perspective to the inside (beliefs—soulfulness) going outward. Your emotional/soulful heart feelings have the greatest impact on your physical body than any other single element or factor.

You're Not Your Body—Your health is all yours, and no one can ultimately control it for you. No one can control how you respond to your life and the feelings you attach to it. It's a complete myth that the medical community or a prescription or something outside of you can magically change your soulful body. *You and your body have a long- term exclusive relationship.* All the concerns are yours to address, discover and maintain. Your physical body is part of your spiritual path that is solely your responsibility and a reflection of your choices. All your body, soul and emotional choices can easily be traced back to your childhood. It is very difficult to continually blame your parents, partner, God when you have present-day choices and decisions to make your body cooperate and function with you or not. Many times all the self-loathing, anger, rage and unexpressed emotions spill into your body like an oil tanker spilling into the Alaskan ocean. *You either clean up the mess or it will spread into every area (cell) of your life.* It's dangerous when our bodies become the emotional containers for our unresolved toxic issues and relationship concerns. Holding onto your anger and resentment is no different than being exposed to nuclear radiation, only this radiation is coming from your self-perspective and beliefs about your life today. All the different messages and meanings of your physical issues are very delicate and important areas to explore if this is where the majority of your energy goes.

Your Soul/Body/Mind Relationship—Rather than become completely overwhelmed with the vastness of the mind/body dynamic, consider all these aspects of you to be your allies not enemies. It is imperative to not minimize your feelings about your body and sense-of-self (emotions) associated with your body perspective. Everything in/or about your entire life is interrelated and connected to every part of your body functioning today. The importance of the mind/body/soul connection and developing mindfulness is paramount for all of us to embrace. No one is exempt from understanding the multiple connections between their soul, body and emotional reactions to their life path challenges and lessons. *The underlying issues between your health, unresolved anger, resentment, disappointment and bitterness are alarming and something none of us can ignore or pretend doesn't exist.* The holistic approach to our life is seeing and accepting all the different interconnections within that life.

Your body will let you know if you aren't dealing with your personal issues in an appropriate manner. The key is to accept or at least be open to the idea that many of your physical illnesses are valuable pieces of personal information that you must decode and interpret, and then take appropriate action. What's interesting in this school of life is that we all have a body that contains our soul/spirit which is an energy that only changes forms with time. *Your soul is never destroyed, never dies; it only changes forms pre/post life on earth.* Our bodies do pass away over time and aren't eternal. We unfortunately get this dynamic mixed up and try to live eternally through our bodies while neglecting our soul/spirit. The perspective shift that our body is only a container for our timeless soul immediately changes everything about how we feel about ourselves and life's lessons. You are much more than your physical body, and your true value as a man or woman is always within your heart/soul—not in how you look. The powerful illusion of life, "Maya," would tell you the exact opposite—that you are your appearance, and that looks matters more than the content inside of your heart/soul.

Personal Information: We All Have a Lot Information—There is nothing that is written in this chapter that is from the perspective of the ivory tower, or third-party observer. This isn't an academic dialogue or research analysis. Nothing wrong with those, but this discussion is something else. Rather, I have suffered through all five of the of those life changing issues and know first and foremost that my attention has to be on the pressing issue that is revealed to me through each of those five highways to the Valley of Despair. For some reason in this life, I thought it was necessary to take all five highways at different times to get to my current death/birth experience. Each experience of being struck by "lightning" ran me into the next one with no relief or reduction of fear/panic. I have lost so many things in the last seven years, and it wasn't due to the economy but rather my co-dependent approval-seeking behaviors that landed me face down in the Valley of Despair. I am embarrassed to explain all of the events that led me to this point, but they began at about the age of 13. My ego has had to take a backseat to my soul's journey for the purpose of finding inner peace and connect to my destiny. My ego was of no help at all for spiritual transformation.

Your Downward Path—Just like you, it has been a spiritual path that I knew I needed to walk in order to get where I need to in this life. I knew at age 4 that I had a mission to fulfill in this lifetime and the path way wasn't at all clear. These five areas of awakening are powerful and have no limit or lack of intensity to be what our soul/spirit needs to wake us up. When the pain of your life awakens you from your daily sleepwalking, then your life-changing challenges begin to make more sense. I asked God to get me where I need to go, but forgot to mention to spare some of the heartbreak and outright despair and hopelessness. Nothing was spared in order to wake me up from my illusions to the fact that this current life is a "learning tool." Your life is and will always be much more than this material physical moment. In spite of tons of self-imposed limitations, the graciousness of the divine allows us all to share our collective spiritual path together. Remember that we all are much more similar in our spiritual journey than we are different. Also, there is no such thing as separateness from our personal world and the people in it. You are divinely connected to the important people in your life even if there is strain, tension and conflict. The illusion of the ego is that we are all separate, when in reality, we are all connected together far beyond anything we can imagine, believe or understand. Throughout this book, I will give personal stories that show that we are all human and in need of divine guidance at all times. I am clearly humbled by the process of my spiritual awakening that is a never-ending process throughout the course of life. It's all about walking on our path; the process is not getting somewhere or gaining something because the real destination is on the other side of this life.

"People take different roads seeking fulfillment and happiness.
Just because they're not on your road does not mean they are lost."
—*Dalai Lama*

Summary Thoughts— Consider the following summary thoughts and questions as reminders for focusing on your life journey at this time. In the next chapter, we are going to explore the various life lessons that are embedded in your current circumstances. All your vast challenges have latent gifts waiting for your acknowledgment, acceptance and awakening. We are going to address the different lessons awaiting each of us in the next few chapters. Read through these statements and questions with the perspective of wanting to gain clarity in the midst of your current spiritual status.

- What presently is your greatest personally challenge?
- You aren't your body. You're a soul having a human experience!

- Look beyond your current circumstances for your life lessons lying between the lines of emotional pain and despair. There is always a message within to be decoded.
- What is your own spiritual path's awakening experience?
- What theme of Scrooge is related to your life?
- What life lesson are you resisting or struggling with?
- Do you accept your body, appearance and physical gifts?
- What is your emotional relationship to food?
- What one of the five paths speaks directly to your heart/soul?
- How connected are you to your body, mind and intuitive/soul nature?
- How does your body talk to you about your stress, fears and despair?
- How often do you seek people's approval (i.e., kids, parents, partner, and colleagues)?
- What's your emotional relationship to money and wealth?
- Do you believe that your life has a purpose and a plan?
- Do you sincerely believe that you helped design these various life transformational events for your spiritual awaking?
- What person do you hold the strongest emotional resentment towards?
- What people in your life do you love and adore?
- Do you believe that your higher-self/power has your best interest in mind?
- What is one issue, concern or personality challenge you'd like to heal within you?

"I cannot tell you any spiritual truth that deep down within you,
you don't already know.
All I can do is remind you of what
You have forgotten."
—Eckhart Tolle

Chapter 3

Everyone is on a Life Path
What's Your Path?

*"Religion is for people who are afraid of going to hell.
Spirituality is for those who have already been there."*
—*Vine Deloria, Sioux*

*"God never said the journey would be easy, but He did say that
the arrival would be worthwhile."*
—*Max Lucado*

Where is God?—Countless times, I have been told by clients, friends and family that God doesn't exist, and all their pain/suffering is more of a random collection of events rather than a designed purposeful life lesson. What strikes me is that the person speaking would prefer to avoid the subject of spiritual purposefulness and instead blame all of their seemingly fragmented life events on a random "shit happens" philosophy.

The other protest that I frequently hear in my office is that the person isn't sure if there is a benevolent loving spirit/God. The fact that people, situations, plans haven't turned out the way you envisioned doesn't imply that you and your higher-self will exit in an empty black void in the cosmos. My first response to this statement is explaining the analogy of gravity: It doesn't matter if you believe in it or not, the law of gravity is always in effect, and the process impacts you regardless. Jump out a window and check out the results! It doesn't matter where you are standing or sitting in your life, gravity is always present. The same truth applies to your spiritual/life path: Just like gravity, God is always present in your life whether you believe it or not. We are all on our own individual spiritual path regardless of our awareness, acceptance and openness. As ***all rivers lead to the ocean, so do all life/spiritual paths lead to God.*** Countless spiritual teachers, past and present describe our journey here as a walk back to our true home where we all originated from God. The events, people, and circumstances that brought you to this point all support your personal reawakening in this life, in this body, at this time. Nothing is out of control or lost along the way of your life. Nothing is ever lost; there is no failure, just your personal process of awaking. The promise of life is that you will learn and develop as a soul having a human experience. The process might be hell along the way. The key is to remember that suffering doesn't imply or mean you're on the wrong path, but rather that it is part of your soulful process. The second quote by scholar Max Lucado is a reminder to keep moving forward. All of your life events are taking you to places, people and destinations designed for your highest and best good.

Your "Perfect" Game Plan—The specific events in your life have all been designed to create your spiritual and personal awakening. The key is to stay on your path and not resist it. Resistance only creates more pain and suffering in every area of your life. The "it" is the people, betrayals, on-going issues and suffering that have caused you to go inside your heart to discover what your life is all about. Accepting your challenges and your mistakes allows you to assimilate new information. *Acceptance— it's the only way!* Learning how to respond to your painful experiences without fear and avoidance is freedom. Listening and trusting your inner intuition about your present challenges will create new insights and lead to breakthroughs that allow you to get where you need to go in this life. The confidence to keep moving forward often takes all the internal strength that one has to keep from sitting down and calling it quits on their life. Quitting isn't a long-term solution, but just a very painful detour off the road of your life. Eventually, you will reappear in your own life and face your challenges or take them with you to the other side. Regardless of how many times you metaphorically sit down and begin engaging in any type of avoidant behavior, there is always a moment when the courage to address your core issues will push you back down the road of your own life. Those five elements (finances/wealth, childhood family, love/marriage, parenting and your health) in our life play a significant role in getting our inner attention off of the physical world and onto our internal spiritual world. *There are many promises to be fulfilled about why we are here today, and you're on the way to deeper discoveries of what your life means.* Deciding not to avoid, dismiss, run from or ignore your soulful life lessons is the beginning of your spiritual awakening (See Chapter 4 for an in-depth look at your acceptance process). How you come to this awakening is the first part of this book. What are some of the pearls of wisdom that are hidden inside of your heart/soul? Think about what is a gift, talent, quality or endeavor you would like to pursue, develop or enhance.

It's Your Own Spiritual Path—You're quickly realizing that the difference between religion and spirituality is an issue of the heart, not a particular belief system. The first quote above applies to your heart/soul connection to your own self-realization and individualized journey. The Dali Lama (see quote at end of Chapter 2) encourages all of us to be nonjudgmental of other people's journeys and their unique paths for their own spiritual awakenings. The biggest challenge isn't judging someone else's path, but to not be critical of your own spiritual path and the repetitive lessons that you (we all) seem to re-experience because we refuse to learn what needs to be learned. It's frustrating, and it causes many of us to dismiss the value of our own inward journey. This dismissal can become a powerful emotional disappointment that then turns into unmet expectations. These negative reactions begin to take control of our inner happiness and can quickly turn into bitterness and self-loathing. These negative emotions can spread like cancer within our soul and dramatically skew our personal perspective on the "fairness" of life. But it's not about fairness, but rather about gaining your inward divine attention to your life purpose. The ego demands fairness or at least revenge, and your higher-self demands your loving attention to your life's spiritual journey. This is quite a difference here, to say the least.

Your "Hell" is a Temporary State—The first quote at the beginning of this chapter is a very powerful admission in accepting your path's lessons and where the journey in your life is taking you. Don't ever forget or assume that the direction of your life path isn't important or valuable. Your entire life is impacted by your deeper conscious awareness of the new emotional, spiritual and psychological geography of your life. The second quote is a reminder that there is value, lasting meaning and soulful purpose to the things that you encounter which seem heartbreaking and without meaning. There is and always will be meaning in everything that is happening in your life yesterday, today and tomorrow—that's successful failure.

In Chapter 2 we discussed at length the five common pathways, super highways, and circumstances leading to your Valley of Despair. This is a critical piece of your personal awakening. Many times your personal traumatic events are minimized as a passing phase. *Nothing is passing or going away until we accept, apply and take loving action with ourselves, God and the people in our lives.* These events are described as a mid-life crisis, but they have been building for years until they finally come to create the burning ash heap that is your current life. Each of the five roads has specific lessons that you are dealing with, resolving and accepting in order to move on and become the person you have always wanted to be. Your long-term happiness is directly connected to addressing your challenges and living your life from the inside out rather than the outside in. The concept of being inwardly driven is a *completely different life approach with completely different outcomes for sustaining a timeless connection to your soul's journey.*

A Better Plan: No Ego—The generalized circumstances surrounding the five lessons/paths that led to your awakening were explained in some detail in Chapter 2. We are going to explore some of the deeper underlying themes, messages, and pearls of wisdom that can be learned from your personal hell. Developing insight into your current situation will help you transcend it. What once appeared as overwhelming circumstances and impossible events shift when seen from a higher perspective. From this viewpoint you can begin to look between the lines of your circumstances to clearly see your soulful struggle without personal judgment or bias.

One of the primary goals of your journey at this time is to move your ego out of the control center of your spiritual path to allow for the emergence and recognition of your intuitive soul's influence in your life. Changing the programming of inner emotional/spiritual "software" isn't always as smooth and easy as we would like it to be. The human ego (i.e., old computer program) is highly invested in keeping its entire belief system and control in place.

The ego demands perfection and the soul requires awareness. The grids of right/wrong, good/bad aren't spiritual concepts, but rather ego measurements of perfection. Your soul is perfect. We will learn how to apply these truths (these soul qualities in our human experience are described later in Section III) within our current human experience. Our ego is the part of us that is doubting, critical, depressed and at times feeling completely hopeless. The ego believes that nothing can or will ever change in your life for the better, including your important relationships, without you keeping "score." The score is the ego's metaphorical "balance sheet" for greed, revenge, envy, and powerlessness. The ego doesn't see or know how personal issues will ever get resolved or healed. Your heart/soul is the only part of you that can stand back from your fearful self-talk (ego) and offer a positive loving and meaningful perspective on your life. Let's explore the opportunities within each of these painful lessons that are fully designed for your highest good and fulfillment. Changing your perspective from hopeless to hopeful requires your full inner attention to the missing pieces of your current learning curve. This inward shift isn't minimizing or downplaying your broken heart and sorrow but rather taking a new, loving approach to your inner healing and self-transformation process.

Five Key Obstacles for Your Awakening
Money/Finances Path
(Values/generosity vs. greed-dishonesty-emotional deprivation)

Emotional Deprivation—The fear of never having enough can apply to money, sex, emotional attention from the opposite sex, social status, power, control and material possessions. The sense of materiel, emotional or financial deprivation has its roots in your early childhood experience. The concept of emotional deprivation is one of the least understood, and the spiritual or psychological issues that drive well-meaning people into making horrible choices with their money and life are the least discussed. All compulsive behaviors are driven by an emotional emptiness that feels bottomless and can be likened to a black hole in space. *Greed in all its forms is rooted in emotional deprivation.* The emptiness feels like there isn't enough of what you need to adequately address the deep emotional hunger within your heart and soul. What happens with the lure of money is that it will only be a temporary emotional "fix" for the deep internal emptiness that you have felt for as long as you can remember. Money isn't wrong or evil, but it *never* can be a substitute for your spiritual path and inner relationship to your higher power. Many have tried to use money as their god/higher power, and the story always ends the same way: *spiritually bankrupt and internally empty!* There are many, many different roads via "money matters" that lead down the path of spiritual poverty/emptiness and material wealth emptiness.

I've had numerous clients who firmly stated that their "god" was their bank account, wealth and/or enormous cash flow. Regardless of their accumulation of financial wealth and material possessions, social status, *the deep nagging need for lasting inner peace was never achieved.* Addressing the emptiness within your heart/soul is to acknowledge the need to look at your values and hesitation to be generous. Choosing to be actively generous with your emotions, feelings, time, actions *and* with your money is one of the ways out of your Valley of Despair caused by money obsession and the fear of losing everything (deprivation). As a wise scholar once said, "Everyone's grave is the same size so don't over estimate your worth."

Never Enough—The idea of hoarding and holding onto your wealth is counterproductive to viewing it as an "energy" that can't be held. Money and giving in all its forms are continuously flowing. This is an important distinction to understand. For instance, when you go beyond your comfort zone and are generous with your time, you begin to change your core value system from deprivation to emotional and spiritual abundance. Wealth, prosperity and abundance all begin within a person's heart and soul, and from there on proceed out into their world. Material possessions, wealth and positions of influence/power are double-edged swords. They can be used to better the quality of life in your world (generosity) or used to hold onto it (greed) for fear of losing it. Feeling satisfied and emotionally/ spiritually fulfilled starts only within the heart of the individual with wealth or loss of wealth. A powerful internal leap to overcoming your emotional emptiness and fear of loss is to *realize that everything that you have is on loan to you, and ultimately belongs to the universe.* We come into this world empty-handed and we will leave it empty-handed. What we accumulate will be given away when we go to the other side of life. *The paradigm shift from scarcity to abundance is the fast track from despair to immediate fulfillment and purpose.*

The concept that we own nothing and therefore have lost nothing over the course of our journey is a new perspective that releases us from fear and emptiness. The idea that everything in our life is loaned to us for our brief stay on earth is a very liberating feeling. *It's one of your responsibilities to give when much has been given to you!* This is a timeless universal truth and key element to furthering your own spiritual awakening. Your attitude of generosity doesn't begin with money, but rather with your insight into the needs of others in your immediate world. There is plenty of "need" that can be addressed without you ever having to reach into your wallet.

There is Always Enough vs. Scarcity—If you have lost everything of material value, consider it the ultimate gift of grace. It is only in our "losing" that we will truly find our purpose and our spiritual path at this moment. *Over-attachment to money, prestige, power, and control is all gasoline for the fire of transformation in your life.* The universe is ingenious in how it constructs our money circumstances for losing what we hold dearest in order to get us to change our grip on our life. *Your awakening will always be connected to what you consider a tragic loss, but it is rather a great gain from a spiritual perspective—not from an investment portfolio perspective.* Embracing things in your life isn't the same as holding onto things. Your life going forward is all about how you're going to use your energy of love and how you give it to yourself and others.

Values of Love/Generosity vs. Greed-Dishonesty-Emotional Deprivation—An important spiritual lesson about money and the key to your healing is that your emotional emptiness can only be filled from the inside going outward. As you ponder your life purpose with regard to money, career, and positions of power, they are all only truly fulfilling when you see the greater purpose of your life (generosity) rather than a short-sighted and self-serving approach (greed/withholding/accumulation). Your life is all about giving so that you can genuinely experience the power of receiving unlimited love and lasting inner peace. The value of money is replaced by the priority for the value of love and the purpose money can give in serving/helping the people in your immediate world.

What are you willing to part with in order to heal that deep longing in your heart? The degree to which you release your hold on your material world is the same degree to which you will enjoy the deeper more meaningful things in your life. *The things that we all crave and desire are intangible and priceless: intimate love relationships, deep friendships, loving family, service to others, and giving without expectations.* Sharing your emotional, spiritual and soulful energy with those that need your love and attention is priceless. When in doubt about what to do for the loved ones in your life, focus on what your money can't buy: Love and Time.

Childhood Family Issues Path
(Individuality/passion vs. enmeshment/abuse/addiction)

"The Universe is made up of experiences that are designed to burn out our reactivity, which is our attachment to pain, to fear, and negativity...the universe will find places to confront us with these issues...for our healing"
—*Ram Dass*

New Perspective on Family—As we all know, our childhood families and the stories surrounding them tend never to be neutral or unemotional. Our childhood family is where we come into this story/world and joined a group of souls designed to help us achieve all that we want to in this current life. The concept that we picked our family before coming here is a tough one, especially when your family was anything but calm, emotionally stable or psychologically safe. There is nothing random or haphazard about the family you grew up in and from which you learned to view yourself and your world. Accepting the notion that you had/have a role in your destiny (childhood family) in this life automatically breeds personal responsibility and freedom from any addiction or deep-seated anxiety disorder. You picked your family, and they are part of your transformation process. Your parents were selected by you to help you to achieve and become the spiritually awakened soul that you desired to be on the other side of life prior to your physical birth.

Your family is not a case of bad luck or unfortunate circumstances, but perfect for your inner development. Past life beliefs and reincarnation ideas are interesting because they sometimes help explain and make sense of the difficult family issues we encounter growing up. The concept of having many previous lifetimes has been part of human history since the beginning of time. The Christian/Catholic church in the third century removed the theory of reincarnation from their theology and teachings. Western theologians have dismissed these (past lives, past karma debts) as non-valuable concepts and part of pagan mysticism. Eastern and Indian spiritual scholars acknowledge the personal value in considering another preexisting perspective to your current life. I encourage you to entertain the idea that you picked your parents and siblings prior to this life. Your family isn't a random group of colliding personalities with no purpose or meaning for you.

It's Your Own Team of Souls—Before you throw this book out of your house or delete it off your electronic reading device, please consider the following ideas below. Consider also the ideas in the quote by Ram Dass at the beginning of this section as part of your current life project. Remember that you picked these other family souls to join you on your current life lesson course. Any type of past life ideas can shed another insight into your current struggles and emotional pain. Past lives thinking doesn't erase your suffering, but rather helps to give it a bigger context to understand from within.

New Ideas for Your Consideration—

- Your family helped to foster some of the issues that you need to address in this current lifetime.
- You soul can't develop completely on the other side; you need to learn certain life lessons within the context of your family relationships-enmeshed or isolated.
- Your family is perfect for your current spiritual transformation.
- You wanted/selected your family prior to this incarnation to move forward in your soul/spiritual enlightenment.
- Accepting responsibility for your need of your family's life experience allows you to go from blaming to accepting the inherent gifts within these complex relationships.
- Your family is the learning laboratory for resolving, healing and learning your current soul lessons.
- Your family is part of the group of souls that you partnered with on the other side to come to this life to work things out and transform.

Family Selection Process—I remember when I first heard the concept of the family soul selection and thought: *"What the hell is wrong with me? Why did I pick my parents, ugh! Clearly, I was drunk while dialing God and wasn't paying attention when I picked my family."* There was an immediate paradigm shift in my head. I went from being angry and resentful to considering the inherent value in the traumas and disappointments that I experienced. The family selection process idea/concept has taken years for me to fully comprehend, appreciate and wrap my mind around. Now, more than 20 years later, acknowledging that I truly needed my parents as soul guides has helped to reduce the underlying anxiety and compulsive behaviors I developed in childhood. Most anxiety behaviors are a child's attempt to manage the unpredictable events in their life. I am painfully aware that many of you have suffered horrible events at the hands of your family that can't be described adequately on these pages. This discussion is not intended to minimize or dismiss your trauma, but rather to get you to step back from it and consider some other perspectives/options. There is the possibility that something positive could and did come from those early years in your life. Your childhood isn't a waste or a mere collection of emotionally traumatic events; rather, it has deep significant value for your long-term growth.

The key is to begin looking for some of the hidden value in your chaotic, dramatic childhood events. We all need to heal and develop the strengths that come from the early childhood emotional/spiritual impasses. Otherwise we become developmentally arrested, psychologically and spiritually paralyzed with anger, first in our childhood and later as adults—not a good situation! For some people, their childhood doesn't hold much energy or residual trauma—while for others it is a lifetime struggle to overcome those early painful messages, scary events, and neglect of all types, abuse and terrifying emotional experiences.

Many times your siblings don't view or agree with your perspective and experience growing up in the same family, house and community. There are no psychological reasons why children from the same family view their childhood experiences completely differently, as if they lived in different homes. Yet they do, for reasons that aren't readily apparent to the casual observer. Under the surface of your life, there is an important soulful purpose in choosing your childhood family of origin. It's one of the greatest miracles of the universe to connect and direct you toward your ultimate life purpose via the path of your childhood. *What seems like a complete dysfunctional family mess always has something very positive and powerful emerging out of those ashes:* You!

Family Trauma—You evolved out of your childhood family with a life direction and path to walk. It's important not to label your childhood as good or bad, but rather as a process of your early years of learning. You can (and many do) spend several lifetimes arguing about how awful their family was/is, but in the end it is all about you stepping forward over your emotional and spiritual roadblocks. Try viewing that there is no right or wrong about your internal struggle with your parents and siblings, but rather that it is your pathway of healing. It's the pull of your early family who are still very present and a powerful roadblock to your self-awakening that is the primary focus. Many times the family selection process concept can serve as a personal awakening when your adult relationships begin to mirror the same problematic issues that existed in your childhood. It's the repetitive anxious nature of our self-defeating behaviors that has its roots in our primary years of life.

The challenge to exploring, examining and processing your deeper fears and anxieties is uncovering these very painful and repressed emotions that got buried years ago. It is only when our adult relationships become a re-run of our early disappointing childhood experiences of love, understanding and forgiveness do we stop and consider the possibility of the core issues which are directly connected to our family. There are relationship themes about your sense of self, your independence or dependency, self-acceptance, your opinions, your core values of feeling loved and cared for that all started at day one and continue to this moment. Can you see the common threads, themes in all your important relationships? Don't block your own opportunity to see the similar patterns of disappointments, not feeling loved, valued, cared for, and feeling that you aren't good enough.

"You can only succeed, you cannot fail. Failure is impossible; it's an illusion. Nothing is a failure. Nothing. Everything moves the human story, and hence the process of evolution. Everything advances your journey, including your family."
—*Neale Donald Walsch*

Challenge—Before we get too far in over-explaining our family lessons and their residual influence, value and importance, your journey is always a process of successful failures through your increasing new spiritual insights via your family. Consider some of the following questions for further clarification:

- Do you feel that you struggle with chronic people-pleasing tendencies?
- Do you fear being emotionally suffocated in your intimate relationships?
- Do you prefer to be the helper/rescuer in your intimate relationships?
- Do you have intense resentment toward a particular parent living or dead?

- Do you feel that you never get the love or emotional support you crave in your marriage or love relationships?
- Do you find that you need other people's approval of you more than your own approval?
- Do you struggle with addictive behaviors or self-destructive tendencies (drugs, alcohol, gambling, sex, work, anger, excessive mobile device use and/or television viewing)?
- Do you often struggle with feelings of being overwhelmed, or feeling powerless?
- Do you have bouts of strong fearful feelings of being alone or abandoned by a close friend or lover?
- Do you have to be in control in your personal and intimate relationships?

All these questions stem from our childhood selection process and the inherent lessons that accompany each of these questions. Do these questions trigger some type of emotional energy (anger, resentment, avoidance, sadness, grief and despair)? If they do, then your particular spiritual/life path could possibly be to choose this time to go through your childhood family lesson plan. *The primary lesson with our childhood family is developing self-acceptance with the ability to forgive ourselves and our parents.* Don't underestimate the value of true self-acceptance and its life-changing powers. Many anxiety issues stem from experiencing a very deep rejection. Feeling safe in the world comes from being accepting of your entire life and all the cargo that goes with it. If your current challenge is self-acceptance and being peacefully aware of your own life, we will discuss in the next chapter how that process of "self-acceptance" leads to your own spiritual acceptance and journey.

Love-Marriage-Intimate Relationships Path
(Self-worth/self-esteem vs. inferior/unworthy/dismissed)

"Is suffering necessary? Yes and no. If you had not suffered as you have, there would be no depth to you as a human being, no humility, no compassion. Suffering

cracks open the shell of ego and it has served its purpose. Suffering is necessary until you realize it is unnecessary."
—*Eckhart Tolle*

The sudden unexpected loss of a romantic partner, betrayal by your lover or grave disappointment with your romantic love life is the fast track to your inner awakening. It is an amazing discovery that when your heart is emotionally bleeding, other things in your life suddenly come into perfect focus. Many times we don't give the issues of our life a chance to be expressed except in times of personal pain and tragedy. The common gift of a broken heart is seeing clearly your soulful purpose going forward after a painful breakup/loss. Nothing cracks open the hard shell of your heart/ego like the loss of your wife, boyfriend or the ultimate betrayal by your partner (an affair with your close friend). Another type of heartbreak is the on-again/off-again seven-year dating relationship that always seems to stall out at the commitment point with no further movement forward. Your 27-year marriage ends abruptly (it is never abrupt for the person leaving, only for the partner being left) after your dream vacation or after the youngest child graduates from college. All of your deep desires, wishes and dreams are left suddenly exposed—resulting in a deep pain that exposes the underside of your heart/soul. The padding and cushions are all gone when a love relationship is ripped from your life. But, it's the peeling away of your outer shell, tough covering and layer of emotional defenses that suddenly makes room for your soul's passion to come out. Losing the love of your life, breaking up or divorcing rips at your heart in such a manner that you can't ignore your unresolved personal issues that are screaming for your time and full attention. A broken and grieving heart is one of the biggest challenges any adult will ever face. Your emotional heart can literally and figuratively kill you if you don't handle it with care or try to gloss over it! Your physical body always reacts to your emotional status with no regard for your ego or outward appearances. Your heart, soul and body all feel your love loss, disappointments and unmet desires.

Love Always Prevails—Romantic relationship loss creates an immediate space in our consciousness for us to look within and find out what is really going inside of our heart and soul. The space, hole and/or ripped open emotional heart is a place where your life is now finally fully exposed. There is no more emotional or spiritual hiding from yourself or your "ex." All your issues of trust, fear of intimacy, self-doubt and fear of shame are set on the table in front of you for better or worse. The loss of romantic love can be likened to getting struck by lighting and wondering why the pain is so severe. Often the immediate emotional fallout of a broken heart leaves you feeling hopeless and asking the same old personal question, "Why me?" Hoping for new answers to these old nagging personal questions requires a new look (wide-angle, telescopic, panoramic, etc.) into your soul. The story of love throughout history, literature, music and movies has always been the unseen mover to change a situation instantly from despair to hope or from safety to rejection. Love changes everything and everyone involved in a relationship.

The crisis of love is that the seemingly rejected lover (anyone with emotional heartbreak feels rejected even though that isn't correct) is facing their own inner demons and unresolved emotional lessons. The empty space created by your former partner's exit is now an opportunity to gain new information about yourself. Your open heart has the chance to create new spiritual insights and spiritual shifts within you. The top priority during a breakup or separation of any type is to view your broken heart as a prime opportunity for genuine introspection and change. If you keep your mind open, your painful circumstances will lead you to new possibilities and information about your life, partner selection and purpose in life that lends itself to resolving your core issues. Now is the time to answer some of your core questions about your purpose and goals. *"Love" has said that he/she is a messenger of God, or the angels and/or your higher self to get you to remember your real purpose in Life: Love!"*

Ego Woundology—One of the biggest challenges to tapping into your heart and all your deep spiritual and relationship needs is not allowing yourself to be consumed or distracted by your ego. Your ego during a relationship loss is always looking for someone to blame and pin this loss on. The key to discovering your new heart and future is emotionally separating from your former partner without playing into either a victim or a bad-guy mentality role. There is a term that best describes the cement roadblocks on the pathway to healing your broken heart and learning your life lessons from these love relationships: *Woundology. This term is best defined as the chronic need and resistance to let go of old wounds, hurts, betrayals, or inner personal violations in order to keep alive your past in spite of the opportunity for change and transformation in the present.* Further, blame is one of the strongest emotional glues that hold the mind-set, belief system, and the power of Woundology together. Resisting the natural changes and the divinely driven events in your life while holding a death grip on your past and revenge or vengeance toward your "Ex" ultimately short-circuits your psychological ability to see your bigger purpose/picture. Your personal sense of Woundology has no forward vision, no insight and no understanding of your life-long intuitive purposes or the valuable life lessons in your present and former love relationships: None! What gasoline is to fire, blame is to your Woundology. It is an explosively powerful combination. If you continue to resist the possibility and option that there is something of personal and spiritual value in your ex-romantic relationship, you will continue to drive down that dead end street where there is no outlet or relief from your suffering.

Revenge, passive vengeance (i.e., negative gossiping about your Ex) and wanting to even the score are all forms of developing a strong emotional bond to your own personalized form of Woundology. Feels powerful, but keeps you in the victim role, where nothing changes. Some people might call what I am describing a strong resentment or form of disdain: that's absolutely correct. It's developing and maintaining a whole life story solely based on your Woundology and all the infractions you have suffered in life. This perspective isn't limited to just negative emotions or events, but to the entire emotional fabric of your life and soul purpose. The unfortunate side effect of this painful ego issue is that the core belief system of your life and view of God is distorted and misunderstood. These types of beliefs (life isn't fair and love is cruel) stall men and women from overcoming and moving past these old events. A Woundology perspective makes it almost impossible to address or reason with your past or present relationships. The emotional wall of protection surrounding your heart is dense and without any give. The universe is the only loving force that can open, heal and mend this type of heart/soul injury.

Blaming Love and Others—I have people in my office every day of every month of every year who can litigate their reasons for holding onto their resentments and blame—constantly retelling their story of being wronged in life. It is a tragedy when a person decides it's easier to live in the past and ignore all the recurring life lessons that are pending, waiting and needing their immediate attention. The mystery is that the very thing that any angry man or woman really wants is understanding and acceptance. Yet it is the very thing that will elude their emotional understanding until they release their score sheet of wrongs. These fundamental human needs (love and acceptance) are all within reach when their barriers to a deeper spiritual life are addressed and challenged. One of the primary psychological reasons people have a death grip on their negative personal story is an undeveloped sense of their life purpose. Detaching from the familiar story of anger and refocusing on your inner drive of self-love and compassion allows for endless personal possibilities. Often it feels easier to hold on to resentment and build a life around that story than it is to release it and move beyond the disappointments and wound of your life. The power of familiarity isn't always helpful in the process of self-acceptance, self-forgiving and letting go of the past to make room for the new in your life.

> *"Growth is painful, Change is painful.*
> *But nothing is as painful as staying stuck somewhere you don't belong."*
> —*Caroline Myss*

Challenge and Questions of Love—Consider the idea that maybe there is another reason or perspective to your divorce or betrayal and valuable life lessons for *which are buried deep within your greatest disappointments and heartbreaks.* There is a direct correlation between heartache and willingness to change our life: the degree to which you are suffering is the same degree to which you will change. The only lasting and permanent solution to your nagging self-doubts and resentments for feeling dismissed is to connect with your inner self/soul. Changing your emotional, psychological and cognitive approach so you can go from the inside (heart) out to your world (new romantic relationship) creates what you have always craved: *love and acceptance.* Your outward personality then stops needing attention as a walking advertisement for the emotionally wronged or wounded by an ex-partner. Consider these few questions to properly evaluate your role, responsibility and unspoken purpose in your romantic story.

A Few Questions About Your Love Relationships—

- What is the one issue, concern that you resist or will not even consider as an option for your healing or forgiving?
- What is the one quality or trait about yourself that you don't like or struggle with?
- What role (everyone has a role regardless of how the relationship ended) did you play in your divorce, breakup or end of relationship?
- Does blaming your "ex" remove your personal responsibility for your role?
- What role does blame have in your life?
- What do you sincerely want (qualities in your partner) in your intimate relationship?
- What is the one ongoing theme, issue or emotional challenge in your romantic relationship?
- What role does Woundology play in your marriage/relationships, career, and parenting style?
- Would you consider replacing your Woundology with loving acceptance of your journey?
- What do you emotionally hold back in your romantic relationships?
- What quality or personality trait do you resent or despise in your "ex" or former romantic partners?
- Do you fear romantic relationships or being emotionally vulnerable again?
- How would you make your next intimate/love relationship different from your prior romantic pattern/history?

The issues of the heart/soul are always centered on forgiveness, self-acceptance, acceptance of others, empathy, understanding and new actions of love. All these variables are keys to opening your heart and soul to your higher purposes. Your heartbreak experience is a gift that will keep recurring until you accept the lessons within each of these relationship crises.

Parental Relationship Path
(Empowered/competent vs. people-pleasing/
unlovable/wounded child)

*"The best day of your life is the one on which
you decide your life is your own.
No apologies or excuses. No one to lean on, rely on or blame.
The gift is yours. It is an amazing journey
and you alone are responsible for the quality of it.
This is the day your life really begins."*
—Bob Moawad

One of the biggest secrets to parenting is finding who and what you are on your own spiritual path. Helping your children find their path is secondary to you finding yours and removing your own roadblocks. The biggest roadblock to parenting is the wounded child within your heart and soul. Your inner child is seeking to be loved, accepted, and acknowledged as an important vital adult man/woman. Having children will force you to come face to face with who you are in your family, in your relationships, and with each child regardless of their age. The nagging underlying issues of people-pleasing, approval-seeking and wanting to be loved all come to the forefront with parenting. The pathway of parenting requires that we stop and heal our own wounded child as the only way to effectively guide and empower our children. *If you reject your own inner child, the parenting process becomes the beginning of a very turbulent and painful season in your life.* As stated in the last chapter, having children—regardless of being a blended family or a step-parent— is an absolute guarantee that all of your unresolved spiritual/emotional issues will get pulled out of your cave and revealed in front of your eyes, and your kids will be the ones pointing them out. It never fails to happen, and it always transpires in the most unusual way with a perfect spiritual purpose/lesson in mind—*always!*

We all have an Inner Child—Our own wounded inner child is the major challenge to becoming the effective father or mother you always wanted to be. Why? At some point in having children, your unresolved and undeveloped psychological parts of yourself will get touched, pushed on and exposed by your relationship with your kids. It's inevitable and will happen; the question is when? Many adults will spend enormous amounts of time and energy to avoid having their wounded child exposed or seen. It's an impossible task and a complete myth to avoid your own personal issues within the context of creating a family. Families expose everything in each other's emotional closet, unknowingly or not. It is your childhood issues coming out in the context of your relationships with your kids that trigger your own unresolved and unmet childhood wants and needs. The conscious and unconscious resistance, denial or avoidance to healing your wounded child automatically creates a negative emotional atmosphere within you and your kids. *It is impossible to see your children clearly if you can't properly see your own inner child issues clearly!*

It All Starts With You—If you aren't mindful of your own resistance to healing, you will begin to use your children to help cover up your issues and make their issues your excuse for not changing. Your child's, teenager's or young adult's developmental issues will become a great smoke screen that keeps your wounded child covered up. This type of limited insight is absolutely impossible to maintain with your kids. Your inner child is already out of the closet and demanding your full attention—and your kids know it. Remember that kids know everything about you but don't understand the why's and how's of their intuitive knowledge. Parents are the ones who typically underestimate their children's wisdom and insight. All types of compensatory (denial) parenting behaviors are counterproductive to you and your children's evolution and create severe emotional blocks for each of you. Embracing who you are is the quickest way to teach respect for yourself and others. Children don't respect a father or mother who avoids their own emotional issues. *It's impossible for kids of all ages to understand why their mom/dad accuses them of avoidance when they watch it happen every day at home!* This type of parent-child relationship is the beginning of a very painful path that neither will enjoy. It's important to remember that it is never too early as a parent to start addressing your emotional issues of love, self-acceptance and purpose.

Your Kids Know You—*The primary task of parenting is healing your inner child so you can allow your children an unencumbered path to finding their* *own spiritual passion and purpose in life.* Remember what I said earlier about the family selection process—you and your kids are all connected prior to coming to this current life. Yes, it's an incredible thought that you and your kids picked each other to be a family in order to evolve spiritually. It's critically important that our own natural childhood issues of wanting to be loved, cared for and needed don't become our unconscious preoccupation instead of a focus on developing a loving parent/child relationship. It is obvious that all parties involved will be adversely impacted when we use our children as emotional supports. I can't begin to explain how many teens and parents I work with, whose primary issues at home are the mother's/father's wounded inner child screaming for attention and not their rebellious 15-year-old. It is never the teenager smoking pot or failing the ninth grade that's the primary issue. The crisis is just a cover up for something much deeper within the parents' lives. Rather, it's the child's attention-getting behaviors that are their unconscious attempts to grab the attention off of you and on to them. What happens in these tension-filled relationships is that the unmet emotional and spiritual needs of the parent and child become a tug-of-war for control, power and position in the family.

Now is Your Chance—It is never too early or too late to address your wounded unloved inner child. I will explain pragmatically in Section II of this book how to strengthen, embrace and ultimately heal that adorable, lovable wounded five or six year old in your heart. For purposes of not being repetitive, the issues of shame, anger, addiction, forgiveness and co-dependence will be extensively explored. All of these emotional variables are part and parcel to your personal/spiritual transformation. Healing the child in your heart is the doorway to embracing your spiritual path and passionate life purpose. All the relationship and parenting issues of emotional enmeshment, people-pleasing behaviors, wanting everyone's love and acceptance in the family, are all connected to your wounded-neglected inner child/self.

Acknowledging your own wounding is the key to healing from the inside out and embracing all of your life long needs and desires for love, acceptance and forgiveness. *You can't change what you are resisting or blaming on your children or parents.* No longer can hiding from your unspoken inner fears of feeling unimportant and valueless become inroads to finding your spiritual connection and personal awakening. Your children, starting from birth and continuing all the way along the journey of their life, will only benefit from your spiritual work and emotional growth. Your spiritual development is the greatest timeless legacy a parent can leave their children. The sooner you stop resisting your deep feelings and needs, the sooner you can appropriately see and guide your children on their life-spiritual path.

Health Issues
(Self-acceptance vs. resentment/entitlement/self-hatred)

"You can't change what's going on around you
Until you start changing what's going on within you."
—Tom Ziglar

Our physical health isn't an issue until it's an issue. This discussion is about the invisible and visible bonds between your mind/body/soul. All three components are intimately connected and make up your current incarnation. When our health begins to break down, it often times related to our unresolved emotional, life, and spiritual concerns. Our bodies are biological miracles, and they never betray us! We tend to betray our bodies by not addressing the emotional, psychological and spiritual challenges in front of us. Our bodies only relate information on how they (personal pronoun he/she) are being treated. Many times the physical information is ignored and the degree of attention escalates until it then has our full attention.

Everything is Connected to You—A physical breaking point can range from a chronic sinus condition to a life-threatening illness. The warning signs, symptoms and illnesses keep developing until the issues surrounding your whole person are addressed. It can be a complete lifestyle change from sedentary to vegetarian, from sobriety to the winter flu, from pulled back muscles to something more serious. The spectrum of mind-body interactions is limitless and is always directly related to your heart/soul.

Regardless of the situation, all the physical warning signs are all within us. In my clinical practice, I have seen men and women developing all types of cancer after a very emotional hate-filled divorce/breakup. The incident rate for this group of people is stunning, and also the rate at which their bodies break down with all the stress hormones and anger flowing through their weakened immune systems. Once their immune system is compromised, the range of illness is limitless. It's not a random act of God that our bodies break down, but rather a valuable road sign of information on our journey for change. If we listen to our bodies, the insight and information is invaluable and a powerful motivation for change and personal growth. If we ignore the subtle hints, signs and cues, then the physical intensity will increase until proper attention is given to the underlying concerns and emotional/physical issues. Your body will always get your attention regardless of the circumstances surrounding the wake-up call.

Your Body's Information—There are illnesses and physical challenges that people experience which are far beyond this current mind/body discussion. It's not difficult to figure out how our bodies work, but rather how we can work better with our bodies. This discussion is more focused on the sudden onset of a serious adult illness that could have a direct link to an emotional upheaval. It is imperative that you become mindful of your mind-body connection when a sudden illness follows a traumatic event in your life within three to five years of the event (divorce, loss). It's not a random event. Birth challenges, long-term physical issues are difficult, and there is no simple answer or explanation. Most importantly *don't blame yourself or believe you're a bad person or being punished physically.* The universe or whatever you call your higher power doesn't operate that way and clearly isn't the God we are connecting to within this discussion. Your goal is to gain as much information as possible about your spiritual journey through your mind-body connection. Please never allow anyone, including you, to blame God as punishment for your health and well-being. It simply isn't true, and that way of blaming is a very serious personal misunderstanding of you and your higher power. Unfortunately, many well-meaning people will assume you are to blame for something physical that is simply unexplainable. This discussion is to raise question about the invisible or visible connections between your current health issues and your emotional and spiritual issues.

Body/Mind/Soul Are All Connected—The old Western medical model looked at disease separate and apart from the emotional and psychological life of the person. People don't exist in a vacuum, nor do their bodies. Everything is connected, related and balanced together. The sterile approach to emotions, health and living is no longer the predominate norm but rather an outdated preference in the medical community. The whole man or woman is comprised of more than just their physical being. The role of emotional and spiritual health all factors into understanding the complete composite of your current daily life. All the parts of you have a very powerful interplay that can't be examined or fully understood in a vacuum. In order to gain a comprehensive picture of your health, your entire emotional and spiritual life has to be involved and considered.

"We don't always fully appreciate our health until we are without it.
The human body can only do so much on its own. We need to assist it."
—Horth H. Gunther (Relki Theory)

The Next Level of Insight—*Anger, resentment, disappointment, fear, self-loathing and feelings of rage are all issues that can't be solved on the same level on which they were created or experienced in your life.* The physical breakdown of our immune system caused by any of these toxic emotions is immeasurable and very powerful. We all know people who have an angry personality or temperament and who are a physical energy drain to be around. We also know people who are high-pressure "Type A" persons who are aggressive and relentless. These are the same people who then suffer a sudden heart attack. No one, including the sufferer is surprised when these types of personalities experience serious physical problems/illnesses. The interesting question is: why aren't we surprised? It is very big challenge to ask and require our body to combat and resolve the ongoing emotional/spiritual problems we all face at times.

The metaphysical sciences are experts in documenting and explaining the delicate balance between our body, emotions and mind. The need is to effectively understand the powerful interplay with all the parts of your being. The imbalances between the different parts (physical, emotional, spiritual, and relational) of our life will eventually cause a breakdown. For example, any degree of long-term immune system suppression (stress) will eventually cause harm to your physical being, deterioration of physical capacity and possible premature death. You're the primary source of prevention for any serious diseases and for keeping interpersonal issues from becoming physical problems. Dr. Louise Hay and Dr. Wayne Dyer are two of the foremost present-day experts in the cause and treatment of many physical problems that are a result of a lack of self-love/acceptance (see bibliography for their brilliant works). The power of the mind-body connection has been understood, accepted and practiced in Eastern medicine for centuries. Today, Western medicine is beginning to acknowledge this powerful interplay of emotional energy with the physical body's systems.

Perfectionism Isn't Healthy or Safe—It is a powerful concept to trace our current physical illnesses back to our core emotional/spiritual issues of self-acceptance and being perfectly imperfect. The removal of the need to be perfect is a primary component for developing emotional and physical energy equilibrium in your life. Perfection is a man-made concept that will always be created from a lack of self-acceptance. We all know that things happen physically that seem completely random, but consider for the sake of this discussion that maybe sometimes *there is a link between your physical body and your spiritual body.* It isn't a far reach to consider that your life is more than your body, and that the on-going physical challenges could be a result of an inner emotional belief and/or a sign that something is very wrong in your life on all levels.

Your Body Feelings—If there was a possible connection, for instance, between your chronic lower back pain and your fear of never having enough emotional support or that you don't deserve to have a peaceful life or feeling appreciated—would that correlation make sense? Consider the following mind-body-soul connections for healing your whole-body:

- Could your nagging self-doubt, guilt, shame, anger or resentment have an impact on your body?
- What if you contracted a serious illness or developed cancer after a very traumatic divorce or the death of a loved one?
- Where in your body do you feel excitement?
- What part of your body is your gauge for feeling, scared, stressed or shamed?
- What if you allowed yourself to feel good about your personal relationships, and forgive your ex-partner or parents? How would that change your emotional energy and perspective?
- What would it feel like to be emotionally pain-free?
- What if you let go of the resentments, betrayals, and disappointments that seem to never really go away or fade into the background of your mind. What if for five minutes right now, you allowed yourself to be psychologically pain-free, resentment-free and fearless, and forgave your ex-partner/lover?
- What would that do to your body, mind, emotions and inner peace?

"In order to stay healthy, we must fully go through the experience of feeling. Our feelings are our barometer for living."
—*James Van Praagh*

Consider all these questions as "pokes" to start moving the emotional blocks out of your life pathway. Your health is as connected to your emotional life as the breath in your lungs. You can't survive without oxygen or without awareness of your feelings. Both are necessary for the completion of your journey. Your feelings are valuable to understanding the process of improving your overall health.

Literally Taking a Physical and Emotional Time-Out—For the next few minutes, try this very simple exercise of releasing all your emotional baggage (anger toward self/others and resentments). Take several slow, deep breaths right now, closing your eyes. Breathe in peace and exhale anger, fear, anxiety or whatever is bothering you at this moment. Do this several times and begin to notice the physical change in your body. Picture in your mind that you are emotionally and psychologically relieved of your current struggles. Allow the feeling of ease to fill your mental picture of you and your body. It is a very powerful exercise and reinforces the unconscious power of our mind-body connection. Secular thinkers for centuries have argued that the mind is the most underrated power tool all humans have at their disposal. I fully agree and want to add that the most powerful tools that we all have at our disposal are our self-love and self-acceptance within our heart-soul. The feelings of health that come from a peaceful mind, soul and loving heart are the body's best medicine against any and all disease, illness and physical challenges.

> *"Remember you are a spiritual being having a human experience, not a human being with a spirit. Knowing the difference is life changing."*
> —*Wayne Dyer*

You're a Spiritual Being—How would the simple act of self-acceptance of something that you feel awful about, which seemed so shameful and heartbreaking, make any type of difference in your physical body? There is so much medical evidence on the long-term benefits of a peaceful, self-accepting mind/soul that it is shocking we all don't do more with these untapped resources. The science of Eastern medicine, such as acupuncture, is based on energy blocks in the body that cause a chemical and physical imbalance. Spirituality, regardless of your personal expression, consists of your body housing your infinite soul. The psychological/spiritual emotional shift in perspective from anger to forgiveness is a complete game changer for your body, mind and soul/heart. I don't want to alienate people or over-simplify physical circumstances that seem beyond this discussion of the mind-body connection. The point of this very controversial discussion is solely to increase your personal awareness of your own mind-body-soul connections. This is entirely for you to explore and ponder, while considering your quality of life. Health and well-being is a topic that will never be lacking with valuable information about you and your inner world.

These closing thoughts about our health, mind-body-soul connection, and ultimately our higher purpose in this life, are by Neal Donald Walsch and Guru Yogananda. The themes of inner peace and listening to your intuitive nature are all developing within you as you read this page. We will explore all these ideas fully in the pages to come.

"Good health is not the absence of symptoms, it is the presence of peace...your
body is a magnificent tool, for sure, but nothing
more than that...your body will
wear down completely but your soul will never do that. Not now, not ever.
Listen, therefore to the whispers of the soul, not the cries of the body."
—*Neal Donald Walsch*

"Your part is to awaken your desire to accomplish your worthy objectives.
Then whip your will into action until it follows
the way of wisdom that is shown to you."
—*Paramahansa Yogananda*

Chapter 4

The Acceptance Process of Your Life

"The wound is the place where the
Light enters you."
—Rumi

"The two most important days of your life are the day
you are born .... and the day you find out why."
—Mark Twain

The Power of Self-Acceptance—One of the biggest steps in moving forward with your transformation process is beginning to accept all the wounded, sensitive, powerfully personal parts of you. This idea allows your life to go on with a new purpose and passion. There is an old adage about "who" is that standing in front of the bathroom mirror: It's you! Take a long hard honest look at yourself and who is staring back at you (how do feel about that person looking back at you?). The challenge is to look into your eyes without a judgmental attitude about yourself, your current challenges and your overall life journey. You're done feeling bad about yourself; it's a black hole of wasted energy to keep doing it. Let's be sick of feeling sick about our life.

So, you are tired of being tired of your chronic self-criticism. Any type of self-rejection is psychologically pointless and leads you nowhere and changes nothing. You have walked far enough down the road of your life to know that you want things to become dramatically different, better, purposeful and more fulfilling. You are painfully aware that change is in the air for you and all your relationships. No unturned stone, avoided issue, relationship concern is beyond your unbiased examination now. The quotes by Rumi and Mark Twain capture the process you are currently in and the wave of new self-discovery you are experiencing. How the universe has finally gotten your full undivided attention is where your insight has started to come to you. Rumi reminds us that the wound or losses are truly our unwrapped gifts—open your present: it's time! The betrayal, loss and/or heartbreak are where your ego has lost control of you and your new intuitive awareness has appeared. Unfortunately, we just don't realize the gift that comes through our deep emotional grieving at the time. Who doesn't truly love a surprise, even when it involves accepting your personal life? As we discussed in the prior chapters, finding yourself in the Valley of Despair is your own personal wake-up call that you can no longer ignore or avoid. Your immediate response and full attention is required. Avoidance, denial and blame no longer work or serve you well in navigating the next chapter in your spiritual/life journey. Accepting that your old ways of operating in your world no longer work is mandatory for your personal change!

Your Phone Call—Metaphorically speaking, the inner phone call in your life isn't going to stop dialing you. The circumstances and situations that trouble you will keep happening, coming at you until you stop and accept what the underlying issue is: *You!* ***The greatest battle you will ever face in your life is within you.*** Nothing compares with the internal struggle and resistance we all have with our own challenges, fears and doubts. Your deepest issues aren't your failed marriage, your adult children, negative cash flow, your parents or your cancer scare: *it's all You!* Remember you are the problem and the solution to discovering the gifts within you. No one is to blame or is responsible for your current status or challenges. Yes, blaming others—your parents, ex-partner, circumstances or God—isn't going to do anything other than prolong your emotional and spiritual suffering. Lastly, blaming yourself is ultimately the greatest form of self-loathing/rejection because it is blocking you from accessing your inner potential, intuition and personal power.

Your life is the "perfect storm" of circumstances specifically designed to open your heart, soul and mind. Answering and/or accepting this call (life purpose is further explained in Section III) is step one in your self-acceptance process. The caller is waiting for you to say something like, *"Hello, let's work together on this issue (my life) and get to the real purpose of my life,"* or *"Okay, I want to finish what I have started with my family, friends, and children and do it differently."* Answering this call is literally your awakening, and it can happen at any moment under any conditions. There is no script or preplanned tragedy to get your spiritual attention and focus. The caller is merely following up on the prior commitments the two of you made before this current life. Your higher self is taking responsibility for following up with you on what you set out to do in this life. Denying or avoiding what's inside of your heart or what is buried inside of you is no longer a life strategy that works or is worth following. Consider the simplicity of this quote and how it answers the inner calling from within your heart-soul:

> *"Sometimes the smallest step in the right direction ends up being the biggest step of your life."*
> —Lao Tzu

No More Missed Calls—What is going to surprise you is that the universe has been waiting your entire life for this opportunity to finally reconnect with you: seriously, your entire life! There have been missed calls attempting to bond with your current inward/divine relationship for years. Now isn't the time for regrets and looking at missed opportunities, but rather it is the time to maximize the new beginnings that are in front of you. There is a new opening in your heart and ego for your soul to speak with you directly. The caller (your intuitive voice—we all have one) is connected to your soul and knows exactly how you can start picking up the pieces of your life that seem beyond repair or healing. There is absolutely nothing in your life, career, family, finances, childhood, retirement, adult children that is beyond the reach of the universe's loving plan for you—*nothing!* It's all doable, and nothing is lost other than your ego's control. Your current situation, whatever it looks like, is changing and moving along with your self-acceptance process—which is a lifelong journey. Personal change is empowering once it is accepted. The changes that are happening inside of you are timely and necessary for you to continue along your life path with a deeper purpose and meaning.

Why the Phone Call? The caller, aka Spirit (or whatever name you are comfortable using), has only your best interest in mind and knows how all these seemingly fragmented parts and relationships will work together to propel you forward. One of the biggest secrets and unspoken hopes is: *Nothing in your life is beyond the forces of the universe and the power of self-love.* There isn't any circumstance that can't be reconciled within your life and within yourself. *The power of self-acceptance is your greatest untapped potential and gift, and it has no expiration date.* I know personally and professionally, that one of your deepest dark negative thoughts or unspoken fears is that your life will never change and things will only get worse. This is one of the most erroneous, far-reaching, and damaging psychological beliefs anybody can hold onto when in a personal crisis (remember our successful failure concept?). The root of all emotional depressions is the fundamental belief that you don't matter and that your life is only getting worse day by day. The truth is, you do matter regardless of the old negative self-loathing and shame-based looping tapes playing in your head.

Your depth of despair and fear that nothing is going to change for you is why the caller is calling. Your divine intuitive nature isn't part of your ego, self-loathing, or fear of failing dialogue. The powerful depressed feelings of wanting to die, disappearing or contemplating suicide are all signs of how psychologically disoriented you have become. None of these self-destructive options will ever take you to a better emotional and spiritual state/place. Our ego always beats us up with the past and with the belief that nothing matters going forward. Nothing could be any further from the truth and the true soul purpose for your life. Everything matters, especially your transformation.

The truth is that everything is changing as you read this book. You're pondering how to allow yourself to look/experience your life differently from a new higher perspective. Nothing ever stays the same, and significant life change starts first within your heart and soul. Once changes start to transpire internally, then outwardly things will begin to evolve in your life. You are the change that can't be ignored any longer.

> *"Accept yourself as you are and that is the most*
> *difficult thing in the world, because it goes against your*
> *training, education, your culture."*
> *—Osho*

One of the five life paths has become your emotional, psychological, relational and spiritual burden that is now demanding your full and complete attention. The caller wants to discuss with you how to heal your current crisis. Pick up your phone and answer the call. Beginning a dialogue with the caller is surprisingly easy. Yes, the dark ages are over where the Spirit only speaks to certain ordained spiritual leaders. Now as always throughout time, the universe is speaking to all of us (all the time) and we can't refuse the call or the caller. When you pick up your direct messages and process what's happening in your life, you begin a new path and direction. Merely being open to addressing your deeper, long-term life/spiritual concerns moves you immediately down the road of your own enlightenment and toward positive lasting change. Remember, the caller is always seeking your attention and wants to assist you on your life journey. It's that simple, really—no one is against you, including God! No more shame, guilt, denial or fear. The caller is more committed to your evolution than any other factor, force, circumstance or person in your life. The caller will create opportunities for you to recognize and access your potential. This allows you to begin to better understand why you are here with these specific people (romantic partners, kids, parents, friends) and circumstances (your current despair) in your life at this time.

Answering Your Own Call—Once you answer/accept your metaphorical phone, you might want to scream at the caller, *"What am I going to do?"* or *"What are you going to do?"* These are always excellent questions to begin any type of crisis intervention on your own behalf—seriously. Some other questions that might be applicable to your current situation for you to consider:

- How do I put things together with this huge mess of my life spilling over into everything and everyone I know?
- How do I stop repeating these painful life lessons?
- How do I get out of the way of my own personal growth and spiritual change?
- How do I begin to connect (God/intuitive self) and relate in a very positive way?
- Why do the same relationship issues keep repeating in my life?
- Why have you, God, allowed me to suffer so much?
- Why didn't you, God, stop this (…..you fill in the blank…..) from happening?
- How am I going to properly understand what to do next or how to be?
- How can I allow you, God/Spirit, to help me?

These types of questions are the beginning of your own self-acceptance process. The irony is that the caller wants to remind you that *you have already been accepted into the school-of-life, and classes are currently in session.* This might sound cute and nice, but the circumstances of your life are begging for your new insight. Opening up your heart and mind to your spiritual purpose is the larger foundation of your life path. The important element to understanding your bigger purpose usually comes to you through your school-of-hard-knocks education. No one is exempt from suffering, but many refuse to attend their classes or to do the necessary homework. It's a human condition (avoidance) that has no regard for gender, wealth, social status, education, marriage status or zip code.

"Self-acceptance is the difference between inner
peace and despair. If you have
developed your self-acceptance, you value yourself as worthy, and you feel that
you can accomplish what you desire."
—*Ram Dass*

Interestingly, all of your desires will begin coming into conscious focus as you begin to take inventory of where you are at this present moment in your life. The Ram Dass quote is a reminder that your emotional/physical pain, struggles and suffering aren't wasted but are rather part of your school-of-life education. Your emotional/soul pain is a window of opportunity for you to change and evolve. Mark Twain is also reminding you that your transformation is in discovering your life purpose, and that is achieved only through soulful introspection. It's nearly impossible to fulfill your life/spiritual journey without developing a loving sense of self-acceptance. Everyone has a life purpose and it's your sole responsibility to follow it. No one can do it for you. People will love and support your life/spiritual path, but you are the one who has to walk it. No one can walk or do it for you. There are no replacement players or substitutes in the game of your life. None—it's all you! Accepting yourself is the bottom-line for fully engaging and fulfilling your life purpose. Remember that the immediate emotional and spiritual by-product of self-acceptance is lasting inner peace—who doesn't want that? You wouldn't be holding this book if you weren't already well on your way on your own self-acceptance highway.

Making the Connections With You—Nothing has happened in your life or will happen that isn't of value and without the expressed intention of your higher soulful purpose in mind. This conversation isn't about predestination or the theology of free will verses God's will. Our discussion is much more personal. The concept that you have the power of choice/free will is what sets us apart from all other creatures on this planet. Your willingness/choice to accept what's in front of you and inside of you is the primary issue at hand. The deliberate choice of evolving, changing and accepting starts and stops with you. For instance, what are some of the recurring spiritual/life themes throughout your life? Why do these seemingly unrelated themes keep occurring? The same issue about forgiveness keeps appearing in all of your close friendships. Maybe the issue of love and being more accepting keeps happening with the same types of irritating male bosses or bitchy clients. How was I so stupid to not see the problem with this relationship, business deal, and my kids or with me? Why does God keep punishing me? Don't be defensive (I got edgy when I was first confronted with this acceptance process) that your current crisis doesn't make sense to you or seems unnecessary—it will in time. All of us can only absorb so much insight at a given time. Insight and wisdom are developed through overcoming our internal struggles via accepting our current life condition, circumstances and feelings/beliefs.

> *"Self-love, self-respect, self-worth. There is a reason*
> *they all start with "self." You cannot find them in anyone else."*
> *—Ram Dass*

Listening to Your Higher Self (Inner Self)—The quote above points out the path your life has taken you—to self-acceptance! Your new internal road map going forward is going to take you to places of acceptance that you have possibly never experienced before. Your life is unfolding in a manner that is moving you down your life path with direction, purpose, meaning and a destination that is coming into focus. Eventually, all the pain and noise in your head and heart will quiet down so that you can begin to hear your inner voice, intuitive self. The crisis will pass. The money will come and go. The kids will be fine. The divorce will be final. The lawsuit will be resolved. The surgery will be complete. You will calm down. The job offer will be great. The parents will be happy. The storm will pass and the sun will shine again in your life. You can then begin to listen and finally hear what the caller has been trying to say earlier this year, week or morning. Even though you have historically hung up on the caller many times before, for some reason today, you choose not to put the phone down and go do something else. Maybe you will start a dialogue that could be the beginning of a very exciting new relationship with yourself? Maybe there are things about yourself that you are now willing to consider?

> *"To the mind that is still, the whole universe surrenders."*
> *—Lao Tzu*

Learning to hear, listen and understand your spiritual self opens direct access to your unlimited potential. All of your gifts and dreams hinge on your ability to open your heart and mind to new possibilities. These possibilities are miles beyond your old comfort zone. There is no going back to your old ways or ignoring what you now know about yourself and relationships. You can try to regress, try the old behaviors, but it never works and feels awfully uncomfortable. The path and process of your current awakening has taken quite a sudden turn and is now seriously requiring your full attention.

The Story: "Your Hut is on Fire" is a very powerful story (metaphor) about how your current circumstances, marriage, finances, kids, health, in-laws, legal problems can be likened to your life being completely "burnt" down, bottomed out, and where everything is seeming hopeless and beyond repair. Your last good effort for change has turned out to be a bust and things are only getting worse. In fact, your closest friends and ex life partner are all wondering what is happening to you and why? Maybe your job, health, romantic relationship, children, business ventures aren't working out the way you had planned. You are literally and figuratively bankrupt and emotionally exhausted. Your life feels out of control. You're scared that you don't have any idea of what to do to stop the pain, the ongoing trauma, and sense of despair from completely overrunning you. Consider this story as a reminder that things will change for the better even in the face of seemingly utter personal disaster. There is always divine providence/guidance in your seemingly non-spiritual life path. *The spiritual connection is like gravity; it is always present whether you believe in it or not.*

Your Hut is on Fire!

The only survivor of a shipwreck was washed up on a small, uninhabited inland. He prayed feverishly for God to rescue him. Every day he scanned the horizon for help, but none seemed forthcoming. Exhausted, he eventually managed to build a little hut out of driftwood to protect himself from the elements and to store his few possessions. One day, after scavenging for food, he arrived home to find his little hut in flames, with smoke rolling up to the sky. He felt that the worst had happened, and everything was lost. He was stunned with disbelief, grief, and anger. He cried out, "God! How could you do this to me?" Early the next day, he was awakened by the sound of a ship approaching the island! It had come to rescue him! "How did you know I was here?" asked the weary man of his rescuers. "We saw your smoke signal," they replied.

—Author Unknown
("Got God," page 111, Julie Bovines)

The Moral of This (Your) Story—It's easy to get discouraged, hopeless and even considering death when things are going from bad to disastrous, but we shouldn't lose heart because God is at work in our lives, even in the midst of our pain and suffering. Remember that the next time your little hut seems to be burning to the ground; it just may be a smoke signal that summons the grace of God! The grace of God is something that can be likened to the air that surrounds the earth. It's always there holding your life together without a sign of anger or need for repayment. We will discuss these powerful topics of virtue, grace, compassion, patience, and hope as all parts of your self-acceptance process throughout this section.

Looking at Your Self-Acceptance Process—"Your Hut is on Fire" has multiple meanings and present-moment applications for your life. A personal question that stands out: *Has your Hut burned down?* Do feel like your life has been washed up onto a deserted island? Do things feel hopeless? You're the only one who can answer these questions. It doesn't matter if anyone else agrees or disagrees with your spiritual insight or answers. These types of insight-oriented questions can only be asked and answered by you. Your honest and non-defensive introspection of your current life lesson, purpose, direction, and love relationship is the opportunity to shift you forward. The immediate result is that you begin to open up your heart, ego, mind and soul to a new perspective and inner peace about your life today while walking down your life/spiritual path.

One nagging question that has to be asked is: What's keeping you from maximizing your life? The answer isn't a stark comparison of you to a colleague, or to a close friend or to your professional peer group. Comparisons have nothing to do with the topic of your self-acceptance. The simple and complex answer is *you!* The answer to any of your probing life questions will always start and finish with you. There are many different components to your spiritual life path process that always lead you back to your learned resistances. Remember that everything you want and desire starts within you. It's all there within arm's reach of you changing the entire the landscape of your life situation. How do you get there from where you are today? One of the ways is your personal acceptance of you, your circumstances and appreciating the value of your current challenges. Regardless of the emotional or circumstantial pain involved with your journey, it's all purposeful and necessary in the bigger picture of you.

Self-acceptance is the fundamental prerequisite to moving forward with a fuller grasp of all that you are and are becoming. We don't need to spend any more time discussing the painful side effects of a poor self-image. The ongoing power of self-acceptance is one of the most overlooked psychological steps and developmental phases for adults (myself included). It is generally assumed, and wrongly so, that everyone likes, cares and feels good about themselves. Without a balanced sense of yourself, it's literally impossible to move past your old recurring issues and move toward fulfilling your life and spiritual purposes.

What is Self-Acceptance?—I get asked this question all the time. You would think as a psychologist that I could fire off an automatic answer, but it's a process of ongoing definition. The general premise of self-acceptance is as follows: *It is a comprehensive spiritual, psychological and personal karma (discussed further in Section III) developing within you throughout your life journey. Your self-acceptance at age 8, 18 or 56 is at different stages of completion, varying degrees of insight, experiences, depths and understandings.*

Each stage of your life requires an on-going fuller, wider, deeper appreciation of your purpose and life mission. Your personal awareness/ acceptance is not a fixed event or static process. Your self-acceptance can be likened to a flowing river that moves throughout your life. Many times how you see and feel about yourself gets blocked by past events, traumatic situations and limiting beliefs. It's the situational blocks, emotional injuries, incomplete stages of psychological/spiritual growth that impede your ongoing self-understanding/acceptance process.

"We are all here to learn love. The first lesson is learning love of self.
Without love and awareness of self,
we cannot know how to love others."
—James Van Praagh

It has been my personal and professional opinion and experience that most adults (myself included) don't fully understand or truly know how to keep developing an ongoing healthy high-functioning sense of self. The quote by James Van Praagh reinforces the fundamental emotional, developmental and spiritual necessity for self-love/acceptance. The ability to incorporate and expand on your feelings of love, self-forgiveness, and empathy for yourself and others on the journey of life is one of the necessary steps for your inner spiritual self-awaking. We are all included in this timeless process of evolving deeper personal insight on our life/spiritual path. Your entire healing process and personal growth all start and stop with your varying degree of self-love. All significant personal insight and spiritual connection to you and your soul *requires your personal acceptance of You. It's a life course requirement!*

Working Definition for Self-Acceptance and for Moving Forward—
Gaining personal insight and acceptance is a critical life step that begins to clear your road of emotional debris, fallen trees and washed out pathways. The net result is that many more self-discoveries that you never imagined possible will come saying "yes" to you and your life. We all agree that a healthy degree of your "self" is never based on devaluing others or having a self-adsorbed opinion of yourself. The self-acceptance/love pole has at one end ego-self-centeredness and at the opposite end self-loathing; the middle balance is self-love.

In summary, the working definition of self-acceptance that we are discussing is as follows: *An understanding of your life purpose, ability to feel compassion, empathy for yourself and others; the ability to see yourself as separate from others; to understand that your life experiences are unique and individual; accepting that everyone has their own path, including you. Your life/spiritual path is for you to understand; it is knowing that you are imperfect, lovable and capable of receiving and loving others as much as loving yourself.*

Your sense of self is an energy that is expanding throughout your lifetime; it is a fluid process with no limits on changing or healing.

What this definition means to you at 22 years old is very different than what it means to you at 48 or at 72 years old. Each stage of your enlightenment is important and necessary for continuing to fulfill your purpose and positive intention for your life today. **The endless experience of your self-acceptance is an ongoing process. It's never finished!** You will continue to develop more and more insight and compassion for yourself and where your life is at this moment. Your journeys with all the different elements along the way aren't finished until you leave your school-of-life session. You will finish your present-day journey with having developed a deeper spiritual sense of your life that is connected to your loving sense of self.

Painful Roadblocks Within Your Life—The undeveloped parts of our inner self (low self-esteem) are one of the primary causes of the painful experiences that now serve as awakening events and crises. No one is exempt or finished with the ongoing process of self-discovery and developing a greater capacity for love. There is no personal theme or relationship challenge in your life that will not require you to express love. In the final analysis, your life will always be shaped by your ability to love and to be loved. *All the different factors that "Spirit" uses to get our attention have the direct or indirect message of self-love as part of the healing medication for you.* Low self-esteem, poor self-image and/or lack of confidence are all facets of you working on your self-acceptance process. Your inner sense of self is an energy within you that knows what you think and feel without the overlay of outside influences, fears and unmet emotional needs. Unfortunately, our life can cause us great trauma, which then becomes an emotional block of our natural internal energy. It's the unresolved feelings about us that cause so many problems in our life.

One major piece of your healing process is examining your sense of acceptance, liking yourself and embracing your current life lessons. People argue that they have a strong sense of "self," but meanwhile they are plagued by shame, addictive behaviors, people-pleasing tendencies and/or waves of self-doubt. *Developing a loving sense of self-acceptance is one of the biggest adult life challenges and secrets to lasting happiness.*

Every day of every week in my practice and in my relationships, I see the results of not accepting your own life and self. It is never easy to start exploring your beliefs, self-imposed limits, fears of failure, and core issues of love. The alternative to your spiritual awaking is continuing to remain in a chronic emotional state of despair and hopelessness, with no clear direction for your life. Your awakening can be likened to digging up your personal underground Internet system. The older system is slow, functional and familiar, yet continued expansion is always a challenging yet necessary task.

Why Don't I Have a Stronger Sense of Self-Love?—The short answer is that we aren't taught that liking yourself is one of the foremost requirements or necessity for any life/spiritual path, relationship, or career. Rather, the myth is that outward accomplishments of achievement will result in your inward growth. Wrong! The assumption in Western culture is that outward achievement is superior to inward awareness. Wrong again! Nothing could be any more erroneous, and it leads many well-meaning adults, young, middle-aged and old, into complete and utter despair. Without the inner tools of our ever-expanding self-liking process, daily life is akin to walking uphill with a 200-pound backpack on wondering why life is so difficult. All religions, psychologists, and spiritual masters teach that self-love/liking is the front door to spiritual enlightenment. Unfortunately, all of us spent little time cultivating the inner gifts and purposes that are now most needed in our lives. The primary focus has always been on the outside/external accomplishments of life to the detriment of the soul.

Your Four-Step Acceptance Process

"Live life as if everything is rigged in your favor."
—*Rumi*

Step One: No Perfectionism—Your acceptance process is allowing yourself to be *perfectly imperfect* with the insight to know that self-love is a necessary ingredient for you and the people in your life. Perfectionism is a severe form of self-loathing, self-rejection and the root of many obsessive behaviors and irrational beliefs. The underlying assumption is that if you aren't prefect, then you aren't lovable, good enough or valuable. This is a never-ending crisis in a perfectionist's life and relationships. First no one is perfect. It is an impossible task to attain perfection in a perfectly imperfect world. *Your spiritual path is full of ruts, turbulence and detours specifically designed to expand your capacity for self-compassion, not self-perfection.*

Perfection is an ego issue, not a spiritual virtue, and it is the major roadblock to your inner self-acceptance and lasting peace of mind. The fear of not being good enough is a scary idea for many people. Realizing that you are perfectly imperfect with unlimited potential in your life path is transformational and emotionally liberating. The pursuit of perfection is the pursuit of an endless black emotional hole with no completion ever being achieved. All the different spiritual themes across all cultures are based in the principle of self-love, which is self-acceptance of You! Perfection is not considered a spiritual quality. It's all about you in a loving way, and Wayne Dyer states it so well.

> *"Happiness starts with you—not with your relationships,*
> *Not with your job, not with your money, but with you!"*
> —*Wayne Dyer*

Step Two: Acceptance of Your "Burning Hut" Experiences—In order to fully complete this part of your school-of-life course, you need to accept the events, situations, and emotions that are the lightning rods of your awakening. What breaks your heart? As we've discussed in previous chapters, it can be any combination of the five different paths to the Valley of Despair. There is ultimately one primary issue, a challenge that underlies all the circumstances of your life. It is always one of the five core issues of the five spiritual tools being used for our development/transformation. What comes to mind right now? What is the fear that might keep you from embracing this part of your life? What personal issue seems unfair and beyond your control? In the burning hut story, the survivor accepted with great disappointment that his life was ruined (an incorrect assumption although understandable). He sat in his misery, went to sleep (metaphor for all of us) and then something happened!

The miracle will always happen within the ashes of your crisis of complete despair and hopelessness. The survivor incorrectly blamed God for this ending to his life crisis—yet it wasn't the end, because there is no end. That's the wonderful irony in your life and in all the stories where you allow love and your divine nature to work in spite of your feelings, circumstances and incorrect spiritual assumptions. Things will work out, heal and come together for your highest good and for those involved in your life. The situations, relationships, and crisis surrounding your burning hut will be resolved in ways that you couldn't have ever dreamed or imagined possible. This isn't a sacred wish but a journey that you will walk, know, survive and come to realize your higher purpose. You will live through your personal burning hut crisis and resolve all the different relationship problems (personal, romantic, family, self and spiritually) surrounding it.

Your Situation and Self-Acceptance: The Dual Combination! The process of your personal self-acceptance and situational acceptance are different sides of the same coin in your life. You need to do both. They are interchangeable and overlap with everything you are doing and feeling today. Your life journey isn't in a vacuum and your inner world is shaping your outer world. Both facets of your life hold very valuable information for you at this very moment. For instance, it's impossible to develop a stronger sense of self and keep doing your people-pleasing behaviors; to continue to reject your imperfections and still have a loving, supportive relationship with your partner; to continue viewing your shortcomings as bad rather than issues to heal; to feel valuable and good about yourself while remaining in an abusive relationship; or to continue to abuse your body with excessive drinking or drugs and wonder why your life isn't improving.

The power of your self-acceptance and your current struggles are interrelated. The complex connections sometimes are subtle, but very important to understand at this juncture in your journey. You will begin to see that the Wayne Dyer quote above points out that the recurrence of your personal struggles have their roots in your resistance to the concept of personal and situational acceptance. Take a step back for a moment and consider what is happening in your life from the view from 34,000 feet.

What's Your Crisis—Personal and Situational? What is your current struggle involving? Is it money concerns, a romantic partner, health issues, children, divorce, career, marriage, and/or depression about your life? Take a moment to open your spiritual eyes to the pressing issues, purposes and gifts within you—we all have this inward pressure. For me, it was my kids. It was the parent-child bond that was my soul window's opening to a much deeper wound of despair. Nothing hit me harder, faster and cut through all my defenses than my two kids. My kids have always been the fire to my heart and soul. Sometimes they have warmed my journey and at critical times they have been the fire that completely burned my hut down. My parenting dynamic was the window/heart-soul opening to continuing and driving my journey forward with purpose and clear intention. Through the heartbreak of the child custody process, my heart and soul felt absolutely terrorized and crushed. Prior love relationships didn't get my full attention. Neither did money (loss of it) nor romantic disappointments. My kids were the 10,000 volts of lightening to the hard ego shell covering my heart/soul.

The underlying issues surrounding the parent-child path for me was not feeling like I was good enough, along with my wounded child and lack of self-acceptance. These issues had been with me all my life to a greater or lesser degree and were now clearly impairing, impeding and stalling my life/spiritual journey. I knew it, but I didn't quite know how to resolve these painfully active issues/problems. It was like swallowing chunks of gravel for me to fully accept that my people-pleasing tendencies were a major part of my crisis (co-dependence—see Section II). It wasn't about being betrayed, wronged or misunderstood in my love relationships. It was my lack of fully completing my self-acceptance process that was the heartbreak and doorway to healing/transformation. I had to accept the totality of my despair and my powerlessness to change anyone other than myself. This is *Step Two*, which is fully accepting your current journey/life lesson. What is demanding your full acceptance and attention? What's burning your hut down? This step of acceptance is your life changer!

> *"Anything that hurts you can teach you, and if it keeps*
> *hurting you, it's because you haven't learned it yet."*
> —*Stephan Speaks*

Step Three: Your Resistance to Change—Your ego's resistance to change is the ultimate deal breaker for any degree of significant and lasting inner change. The emotional energy drain caused by fighting and/or anger is for most people the primary root of their chronic dissatisfaction with their life. There isn't a single factor along your journey that can derail your life for years more than your emotional, spiritual and psychological resistance to self-acceptance. The psychology of resistance is your ego's strongest hold on you, blocking the changes you want naturally to take place. Many times people feel that if they let go of their anger or notions of how things should be that they are giving in to the enemy. The enemy is and always will be your ego and its self-serving practices. *There is no "losing" on your life path—only your ego's loss of you!*

One of The Greatest Days of Your Life—Spending your money, time, and emotional energy trying to make your life (or a situation) the way you want it to be is a complete waste when it involves resisting self-love/acceptance. If your personal choices aren't aligned with your soul purposes, you are on a dead-end emotional street. It is useless to resist the fact that you can't change your ex-partner into who you want them to be, or avoid the bad business deal or erase your past impulsive decisions. These are all part of your self-acceptance process and continued inner peace. *Surrendering to your life path, to the lessons you need to learn, and to developing self-love is one of the greatest adult decisions you will ever make.* As Mark Twain said at the beginning of the chapter, that day of accepting your life purpose is the beginning of living from the inside of your heart and soul and going into your world. Your ego will fight you all the way to your grave in attempting to keep you a slave to fear, self-doubt and hopelessness—this is the way of the world (see a further discussion in Section III of "Maya," the illusion of life).

The road to continual unhappiness, emotional emptiness and hopelessness is lined with your belief and need for control. One of the big secrets you discovered along your journey is that your sense of control is enhanced by acknowledging your lack of control over events, people and yourself. Your greatest act of control is accepting your life lessons and painful circumstances as gifts for your spiritual development and greater good.

Many great spiritual masters have written that your ability to accept the circumstances of your life allows for immediate inner peace and lasting comfort. When you no longer fight with the people in your life, especially ex-partners (business, romantic) and stop resisting the changes happening in your life, you open yourself up to incredible inner and outward opportunities. You have no idea what your life can look like without the active resistance to your spiritual path and allowing your life to unfold organically.

> *"Grant me the serenity to accept the things I cannot change,*
> *the courage to change the things I can,*
> *and the wisdom to know the difference."*
> *—Niebuhr (Serenity Prayer)*

Step Four: Acceptance of a Higher Calling and Path—The quote by Niebuhr is called the serenity prayer by many people. This lovely prayer points out the gift of acceptance and surrendering to your higher calling and path. Surrender, resignation and letting go of your way are the final stages in your acceptance process. The quote above describes one of the greatest decisions you will ever make: *acceptance of your life!* The irony is that this powerful step can take years to develop, and yet it can be resolved within a second. The internal shift away from all the things you have been fighting within you is over! ***The war within is over, and has ended with the unconditional surrender to your life path.*** Accepting the limits of control and embracing your destiny are so powerful that you will never again be the same man or woman inside or outside. Your entire life has been building for this moment of complete and utter surrender to your higher-self and the life lessons pressing within you to move forward. All the acts of acceptance breed a deeper and more comprehensive sense of responsibility and passion for your life and the life of the people surrounding you. *It isn't about giving up, but rather about getting up off the ground of despair and walking out of your burning hut.*

What Would the Phone Caller Say to You? ...."Glad you answered the phone, and it's good to hear your voice.........?" You finish the sentence and the conversation! The discussion will take many different routes, but it will always lead to you and your spiritual-self working together on this joint project called Life. It is the ultimate love relationship you have been looking for and craving: *You and your divine nature!* The love, acceptance, compassion that you have always wanted have always been within you waiting to connect with you. Now that the caller has reintroduced this concept to you, let's get on with clearing away all the roadblocks, irrational personal beliefs and fears in your life and relationships. There is nothing that has happened thus far that hasn't pushed you to embrace all the awkward, uncomfortable, unpleasant concerns and issues about you and your life. Allowing yourself the opportunity to experience the sense of nonjudgmental unconditional self-acceptance and self-forgiveness is your heart-held roadmap out of any crisis, conflict or challenging situation in your life.

> *"Letting it go and it all gets done."*
> —*Laz Tau*

> *"Sometimes letting things go is an act of far greater power*
> *Then defending or hanging on."*
> —*Eckhart Tolle*

It is now your time to let go and allow your journey to unfold—let's move any and all debris off your path. The next section of the book (things are going to get really good for you now) is all about "resolving" your inward emotional-spiritual blocks, resistances and self-doubts. Letting go of your resistances to whatever you need to accept is your next step to moving on. It's your time to move forward!

The following seven ideas are reminders about how to continue to develop your soul, and inner self-acceptance process. You're evolving inner confidence, intuitive voice, life purpose, inner peace and spiritual awakening all starts within you. Self-acceptance is your soul's primary task and is the inner relationship that influences everything else in your inside and outside journey. The amount of personal and spiritual freedom that comes with your self-acceptance process is endless and limitless.

Seven Life Acceptance Ideas: Consider these ideas as you journey on your self-discovery path which will always include your complete and utter surrender of your old personal beliefs about yourself, your relationships and your purpose in life.

- Anger and self-loathing are all symptoms of resisting what you need to let go of and try not to control. The acceptance process is all-inclusive of every area of your life. What are you still fighting within yourself?
- Personal judgment is no longer an option or good choice for feeling better or emotionally safe about yourself or others. The chains of a judging attitude instantaneously derail your emotional, psychological and spiritual progress.
- Self-acceptance, self-love, self-forgiveness and self-worth are all about you and no one else. Your inner self demands that you look inside your heart and soul and allow the natural by-products of your spiritual awakening to direct you going forward. All the important "self" qualities start and end with you. No one can do the work for you.
- Self-acceptance is a lifelong process with many turns and detours along the way. Your inner self-acceptance journey will ultimately lead you to a higher, more peaceful perspective than you've ever imagined or thought possible. Everything you want and crave is within you! Acceptance of your entire life is the royal road to bypass your ego, irrational resistances and sense of failure.

- There is no losing, failure, or waste of time (choices) on your life path; it's your ego's loss of control of you that is the only issue. Resistance, denial, anger and self-doubt are all characteristics of your ego directing your life from the outside, rather than your life being directed by the intuitive nature within you.
- Your personal burning hut crisis isn't the end of your life but rather the beginning of living your perfectly imperfect spiritual journey. No matter what has happened, you will survive it.
- You can't fail. You can only learn to love and accept yourself!

Section II

Clearing Your Inner Pathway

Your Awaking is More Important than Your Emotional Pain

"When one door of happiness closes, another one opens;
But often we look so long at the closed door that we
Do not see the one which has been opened for us ..."
—Helen Keller

"You must first recognize that there is a journey. When you begin
To awaken to your predicament—there is something that begins to
Change within you and illusion starts to fade away ... there is a purpose
Within you."
—Ram Dass

"Each of us comes to this planet with the intent to learn about ourselves
through interacting with others—treat others
how you would like to be treated."
—Jeff Van Praagh

Chapter 5

Your Shame Factor—Exposing the Big Secret

"There is no separation of anything, from anything. There is only unity. There is only Oneness. You aren't separate from each other, nor from any part of your life, nor from God. We are all connected."
—Neil Donald Walsch

"It's like there is a hunter over your shoulder, and the hunter is always coming. And they're going to find out that I am flawed and defective. They're going to find out that I am not what I look like I am. My secret will be exposed."
—John Bradshaw

No mental health professional, psychologist, healer, spiritual master would disagree that there are many different psychological, emotional and spiritual issues, disorders and chronic human conditions in life. None of these disorders have the deceptively negative influence and residual toxic power of shame. *None!* Shame is one of the most universally traumatic emotional states, fraught with irrational beliefs and paralyzing experiences for people of all ages, races, spanning all economic and educational levels.

No one is immune or exempt from the most underrated and misunderstood of all human emotions and states of mind/being. Shame is clearly a taboo topic and is a rarely discussed emotional/psychological condition that remains largely untreated, unhealed and unexposed. Because of its complexity and insidious nature, shame is difficult to discuss or describe. The experience of shame is like trying to nail Jell-O to the wall and wondering why you can't get a handle on it. Before we define the inner-workings of shame, let's first describe in detail the raw, dark experience of it. Both writers quoted above are describing the psychological power of shame in creating irrational personal beliefs that ultimately separate us from the people we love and most importantly ourselves.

Shame is the Emotional Cancer of Your Heart and Soul—The best way I know how to express the power of shame is to liken it to an emotional cancer of the human soul. We all know what physical cancer will do to the human body by attacking a person's health and vitality. *Shame functions the same way on an emotional and spiritual level. It rebels against the heart and soul of an individual in the same way that a cancerous tumor attacks a person's physical body.* Rebellion of any sort against your higher good is never an easy issue to address or to see clearly. Symbolically, emotional cancer can literally kill the holder of it (you) in its attempt to remain in control. Regardless of its insidious and intrinsic nature, shame is an issue that is treatable, but must be addressed head-on in order to move forward on your life/spiritual path.

The lasting legacy of emotional shame is that you are secretly and privately defective, always hiding your dark, personal secret of not being good enough, which is counter-intuitive to your self-acceptance process. The hunter in the brilliant John Bradshaw quote is your shame always terrorizing you and threatening to emotionally blackmail you into remaining a victim, captive and psychologically/spiritually repressed. Shame is an awful taskmaster, ultimately driving you into complete despair and hopelessness. This reaction is in direct opposition to your life's journey which is expansive, loving, accepting, caring, forgiving and compassionate. Two entirely direct paths that have two entirely different outcomes for your life! Shame is incompatible with your divine, intuitive, and loving nature.

Many religious scholars refer to shame as our sinful nature, fallen-self or simply evil. Clearly, shame isn't our higher self or divine nature, it's the ego's control at its worse. Whatever you name you give it, it isn't a positive or life-embracing element.

The "Big Secret" of Shame—One of the salient features of being a victim of this silent but deadly emotional poison is that it always leaves its victim feeling flawed, unlovable, and/or disposable/replaceable. The core belief that you are of no value to the world and to the loved ones in your life impairs and sabotages any significant spiritual and personal development. Another way to put it is that you have a chronic, deep-seated fear that your coworkers, romantic partner, children, neighbors, and clients will discover that you are a "fraud." The nagging voice in your head keeps telling you that *"You really aren't any good. You are incompetent and incapable of doing or being whom and what you pretend to be. Eventually, everyone will find out about your terrible secret."* This isn't an occasional emotional state, but rather the inner emotional geography of your fragmented sense of self and stalled self-acceptance process. The feelings of shame are relentless and chronic, and the emotional intensity can vary from low to extreme.

Shame isn't alleviated by selfless actions or loving gestures. Shame doesn't decrease with any type of outward behaviors, wealth, education, love, sex or relationships. Shame is immune to all outward treatment or healing actions directed at it via drugs or any other mind-numbing behaviors (i.e., alcoholism, gambling, sex, or any addictive behavior). Addictive behaviors can momentarily silence your inner shame critic, but never for very long or without leading to more self-loathing later. Shame can only be addressed, treated and removed from your life with an inward approach that involves self-acceptance, self-love and your newly acquired spiritual awareness.

Not Good Enough—Shame chronically slices away at a person's sense of self-acceptance, preventing them from developing any degree of personal autonomy or sense of competence. It also prevents a person from properly developing inner confidence and the belief that their true self is lovable, acceptable or good enough. How could anyone ever trust or believe in what you have to say or do when you are harboring your big unspoken secret (you're a fraud)? I can't begin to describe how many of my clients over the years describe these exact feelings, and yet still argue that it's their personality that is the problem, and it is their plight in life to feel deficient and a phony.

Most of the shame-based driven people that I work with are some of the greatest souls and individuals I have ever encountered. They are addicted to their shame belief system like a dog is attached to a bone (my beagle Ricardo and a bone—inseparable). They aren't giving it up (shame addiction) until the emotional trauma caused by this shame cycle blows up their life. The huge explosion usually occurs in your relationships, finances, career or family. It is only at this point of complete despair that the possibility of a spiritual awakening begins to reveal the truly deceptive power and nature of shame. Only then will you consider the possibility of healing and resolving these powerful lifelong self-defeating emotions, beliefs and actions from the inside (your heart/soul).

Shame's Super Emotional Glue: Addiction—It's my professional and personal experience that the issues of shame are the most undiagnosed, untreated, completely misunderstood, least-discussed emotional concept in all the various types of psychological/psychiatry therapy modalities, 12-step recovery programs, and peer counseling. The powerful emotional combination of addiction and shame is a force within a person's life that has to be reconciled; otherwise the prognosis for healing is bleak at best. For instance, it's much easier to discuss depressive bipolar issues than the collateral intangible power of self-loathing, self-hatred and addictive behaviors (all motivated by shame). Psychologically and spiritually speaking, shame is a deep-seated belief and feeling that is part and parcel to all maladaptive, self-defeating and self-destructive behaviors. Shame isn't an action-related feeling or event, but rather an *ongoing emotional malaise* that rears its ugly head at certain times in a person's life. It is a paralyzing feeling and a negative thinking process that has no regard for a person's education, intelligence, wealth or professional position. Shame knows no boundaries or limits in our lives.

The Working Definition of Shame—Shame is the primary reason that psychotherapy, 12-step programs and spiritual counseling have huge relapse rates, and recurring symptoms of anxiety, depression and a host of addictive behaviors. For our discussion purposes, I am defining shame as the following:

A primary emotional wound, not a secondary belief based on a particular action. A paralyzing emotional, mental, psychological state of mind that distorts a person's view of themselves in their world and with others, preventing them from developing a loving sense of self; it impairs the man/woman from developing trusting, secure, safe relationships that are based on mutual respect and understanding; it is a chronic fear of being discovered as a phony, a fraud, and an imposter; this person is emotionally incapable of feeling like a valuable and productive adult, has an under-developed inner sense of self and lacks personal self-acceptance, characterized by a negative inner self-portrait and an unclear perspective of relationships with self and others.

This definition isn't out of a book or from a particular theory, but rather from thousands of individuals, clients and friends (myself included) who have struggled with this distorted and ugly blinding emotional state. The far-reaching influence of feeling and being ashamed isn't limited to any particular situation in a person's life. It is simply pervasive. Like physical cancer, it becomes the driving force in all of your decisions— romantic, financial, sexual, health, career, parenting, etc. There is no area of functioning, feeling and living that isn't colored or touched by this silent shadow. Shame in psychological theory is frequently referred to as a person's "shadow side," consisting of unwanted and disowned aspects of their personality. Clearly, if you feel ashamed, you don't want to expose or explore these aspects of your behavior or emotions. Yet exposure of your toxic feelings is the pathway to your transformation and inner healing. If left untreated, shame has the potential to completely and thoroughly take control of any man or woman's life (hence addictive behaviors). The first questions in treatment are: How did it develop? Why did it develop? And finally, do I have it and if so, to what degree?

Shame: How Did it Start?—Your parent-child relationship was the start of this insidious emotional dynamic within you. Please forgive my frankness going forward, but sometimes the best way to describe a painful situation is to simply say what it is. Any parental discussion in this book isn't about blaming or finger-pointing, and isn't intended to alienate anyone or cause any more pain and suffering. The only productive reason for looking at the genesis of your early emotional/spiritual growth is to widen your scope of insight about how your sense of dread and not feeling good enough all started. Secondly, you can stop this cycle of shame from being passed onto your children and the generations to follow with a deeper compassion for yourself and your own parents. All of us are walking our spiritual path with the implied goal of becoming everything we desire in this life without the complication of a shame-based personality. Unresolved shame is a roadblock that tends to only be removed/healed by new spiritual insights into your true loving essence and the development of deeper personal love and self-acceptance. *At first, your feelings, beliefs and emotionally painful experiences of shame are highly resistant to any degree of significant personal change or spiritual insight.* Healing your shame is a reconditioning process that requires your persistence in exposing this insidious emotional cancer. The fastest way to start maximizing your inner intuitive potential and lifelong dreams/purposes is by exposing your shameful beliefs. There isn't an area of your life that isn't negatively impacted by the power of shame—which is why it is such an all-consuming emotion, belief, and lifestyle.

Shame is a Reaction—For the sake of our discussion, I am addressing "shame" as a learned behavior. Shame isn't a genetic or biological disease. We could argue for a DNA shame component but let's not get lost in debate on this theory. It is far more valuable to focus on your emotional, psychological and spiritual healing. My clinical experience is that the *genesis of shame is a compensatory reaction to an under-developed emotional capacity of nurturing by your mother/father (or primary caregivers).* Developing a shame-controlled emotionally driven personality is a direct reaction to your parent own shame and their need to off-set their own awful self-loathing feelings. Your parents unwillingly projected their unresolved feelings of inadequacy onto their child (you). A parent can love a child in many ways and still create a shame- based personality in their son or daughter. In order for the uninterrupted creation of a young child's soul/personality to progress naturally (pre-five years old), a parent has to have developed their own sense of self-acceptance and self-liking, and hopefully self-love.

When parents haven't resolved or addressed their own sense of shame, this trans-generational emotional cancer is naturally transferred and passed down throughout the family tree. The feelings of shame begin to tarnish a young child from developing a secure sense of self, and those feelings begin at a young age with the parent transferring their personal disdain into their child. It's important to understand that shame-based feelings are on a scale from zero (doesn't exist) to ten (paralyzing shame/nonfunctional relationships (see below for the shame scale explanation).

Another Building Block of Shame: Thousands of Unmet Emotional Needs—The young child (you/me) learns very quickly that all of their needs and wants aren't acknowledged, and that some of their attempts to engage their caregiver (mom/dad) aren't successful. It's far easier to explain the parent/child relationship from a third-person perspective for clarification purposes of the shame genesis. The young child re-experiences the emotional injury of not being understood, nurtured or noticed thousands of times over. These residual disappointing emotional misses begin to be associated with feeling bad. We could literally write volumes of books on this empathic emotional breakdown within the parent/child exchange.

Your parent/child bond is a very important topic for healing and creating change. The lifelong impact on this son or daughter of learning to feel bad for wanting to be loved and understood started in the crib and continues on to this present day. If the child's natural cravings for love aren't normalized, explained by the parent as natural, the cravings grow into and become a shame-based personality. After so many failed attempts to feel loved, noticed, accepted and valuable, the young developing child begins to view himself as having a major personal problem (feeling defective). Between the ages of 5 to 8 years old, the child associates in its mind that they have horrible feelings inside of them. What they really have is a natural longing to feel loved and accepted. The distortion of the child's basic human needs becomes their foundation for feeling wrong, inadequate and emotionally insecure. *The young girl/boy doesn't know or couldn't possibly understand that their chronic feelings of frustration, anger and rejection are appropriate because of the inability of the parent to provide a positive feed-back loop for the child's natural wants and desires.*

It's Not Your Fault—To restate the above sentence, your normal, age-appropriate emotional/psychological needs weren't the problem in your childhood. The problem began with your parents' inability, for whatever reason, to understand the basic natural developmental emotional stages all children have and need to progress through. As a young child, teen and young adult, you didn't feel emotionally safe or secure about your own feelings and needs—nor having those needs met or expressed. You learned at a young age from many, many and many more emotional impasses that your feelings weren't an accepted part of your parent/child experience. The lack of supportive parental reactions to your natural cravings to be loved and accepted for your own creative individuality weren't addressed then. The problem is, this self-shaming pattern becomes the center of your personality functioning and the emotional connection to yourself and your world. The lack of nurturing between you/mom or dad is enabled to this day by your own lack of self-acceptance nurturing.

Never Noticed—Unfortunately, your parent's unmet emotional needs superseded and covered up any of your own interests, personal thoughts and developing opinions growing up. This emotional trend of not being noticed by your mother/father usually persists on into the child's adult life (your life today). Your parents weren't emotionally or psychologically attuned to your emotions or basic childhood personal needs of emotional attunement and safety. The bottom line for you and your childhood parenting experience is: *The long-term psychological reaction to this fundamental emotional breakdown in the parent/child bond is the psychological foundation of a shame-driven personality.*

"As painful as shame is, it does seem to be the guardian of many secret, unexplored aspects of our beings. Repressed shame must be experienced if we are to come to terms with the good, the bad and the unique of what we are."
—*Dr. Robert Karen*

Shame Factor: The Classic Symptoms—The list below is potentially some of the more common characteristics of shame-based behaviors and feelings. Take an honest look at how you feel about yourself, love relationships, sexual intimacy, God and your ongoing self-doubts which are all influenced/fueled by the shame-based emotional malaise. Understanding the silent operational ways of how shame lives in your daily life is critical to exposing it, healing it and permanently removing it from your life/spiritual path. Do not lose sight of or perspective of the concept that nothing about you or your life circumstances is unacceptable, unlovable, or worthless. Nothing! Shame is a learned behavior that can be amended, changed and healed regardless of how awful you might feel and think.

Exposure is Really Good—The first step on your recovery journey is that your shame-based feelings, actions and personality patterns have to be honestly examined up close *and* from a distance. It's important to mention at this juncture in our discussion that everyone is in recovery. Recovery is the deliberate act of accepting your personal shame and making a commitment to heal it. If someone isn't in recovery, then they are still looking for their Valley of Despair. Our entire life journey is about learning, recovering and transforming. Shame happens to be a spiritual and emotional malaise that can be left unnoticed and untreated for many years.

Unfortunately, most people stop at this critical point of confronting their shameful beliefs on the road to their enlightenment. Don't stop, no matter how awful or scared you are. I assure you that it is well worth all the effort. The paralyzing fear of revealing your hidden secrets and toxic feelings is absolutely necessary to go past your current shame state. It's a paradox, because the very thing you desire is already within you. Your uncomfortable feelings about yourself are the roadblocks to your immediate fulfillment and purpose. Acknowledging your shame and its incredible hold on you is a major transformational phase in your life. Staring your shame in the face with the limitless power of self-love/acceptance is applying radiation to an emotional cancerous tumor. It all turns your shame-based personal beliefs to nothing and disappears from your consciousness and daily life. Be brave and be honest with yourself. You can and will survive your shame exposure process even though it feels as if you will die exposing it. What you can't survive is another lifetime of living as an emotional prisoner to your shame.

Your Shame Scale and Shame Checklist—Remember that you aren't a "monster." Shame is only a shadow in your closet of secrets. Turn your own light on and look within your closet of old issues, addictions and secrets. Everyone has a closet that needs to be cleaned out and restocked with new items. Before you answer this shame checklist, think about rating your feelings of shame from zero (healed) to ten (worst case). The following scale and brief descriptions will help you focus on where your current shame level is and how extreme it gets when triggered by certain events, feelings or actions. All experiences of shame, whether on a daily, weekly, monthly or random basis, are generally triggered by your distorted personality belief system about your feelings, actions or relationships (love and sexual).

Your Shame Scale: Zero to Ten—

0 – Not your emotional issue.

1 – You understand the concept but don't feel shame.

2 – You occasionally feel shame about certain issues, but the feelings don't last.

3 – Certain events or experiences trigger a wave of shame, but it doesn't last.

4 – Sometimes you are scared to reveal the truth about yourself or a personal feeling.

5 – You have bouts of having shame-based reactions and embarrassment; you are enraged and/or feel like a fraud at work and with friends, and are fearful of being exposed.

6 – You have more days or moments when you feel exposed, enraged and emotionally panicked about being discovered a fraud or reprimanded for something.

7 – It's difficult not to immediately escalate your emotions when you are being accused or asked about a problem. You feel very exposed and fearful. You react with intense anger, and it's very difficult to calm down after being triggered. You become verbally abusive to others and yourself.

8 – People tell you that you have an anger management problem. You get into physical and heated verbal altercations as a means to protect your inner feelings. You're very aggressive toward others when feeling shamed.

9 – Your relationships are influenced and shaped by your powerful negative feelings, beliefs and self-defeating shame driven actions. Your life is controlled by your shame reactions, and you struggle with addiction and feelings of death/suicide. You cannot tolerate any conflict without extreme inappropriate reactions.

10– Your life is consumed with shame-based addictions and behaviors, and you are incapable of functioning at your potential. You consider death as your escape plan or murder as an option; you're a danger to yourself and others. This extreme reaction can be a result of severe drug abuse, and professional mental/medical help is mandatory, even though you are resistant to seeking any type of assistance.

Your Own Shame Triggers—The above shame scale is a barometer for your range and cycles of feeling shame as it flows through your heart, soul, body and mind. This self-reflective personal shame inventory is critical to explore and consider as you answer the questions below. These questions are examples of how you react, what triggers your shame, and how you feel about yourself. The shame scale illustrates how far you allow your shame at times to control all your relationships, including the one with yourself and your entire world. It's important to restate that any degree of shame can be healed within you. Nothing is ever beyond the understanding "hand of the divine" within your heart and soul. Nothing! Your belief system surrounding your shame hinders and impairs your healing. Your personal spiritual transformation is the way out of your current shame cycle maze. In Section III we will explore the direct applications for removing your shame reactions, beliefs and unresolved rage. Now consider the following traits, behaviors, beliefs and personal triggers of how your own version of shame operates in your day-to-day life. Please feel free to add your own descriptions and elaborate on the ones listed. This is your own private personal inventory about the untreated shame in your life.

How Your Shame Can Control You—

- You have an irrational fear of being exposed as a fraud/phony in your career, job and/or role as a manager.
- You don't allow anyone to get be too emotionally close or near to you for fear they might see your awful secrets and constant failings (your true bad self).
- You have intense negative feelings (panic) of being discovered as a really bad person because you feel that everything is your fault.
- You consistently worry what other people think or know about you, and feel that their opinion can't be positive.
- You are chronically worried that someone will discover who you really are.
- You experience (anytime, random events or special triggers) terrifying emotions of embarrassment.
- You resent your short-comings as an adult.
- You privately believe that you are an anger monster, or that there is some type of monster within you.
- You feel like there is a secret inside of you that can't ever come out or are seen by anyone you know or love.
- You tend to do things that are deliberately self-defeating and purposefully try to hurt yourself.
- You are privately convinced that everyone knows that you are a bad and worthless individual, fraud or a phony.
- You blame yourself for anything that happens negatively in your life because you deserve it.
- You have an uncontrollable temper and/or anger management and self-acceptance issues.
- You have a history of physical violence and/or domestic violence.
- You do not and will not believe that anything positive or good can happen for you.
- You become emotionally overwhelmed and feel crazy when you express any of your anger, frustration or aggression.
- You have an emotional blackout with no clear memory of what you said or did (not drug/alcohol related) when you become emotionally defensive or angry.

- Your feelings of anger or rage scare you so much that you will do anything to suppress them—which causes you to feel very depressed and hopeless.
- You feel shame about sex (within appropriate relationship contexts), your sexual orientation, or your sexual feelings, as if sex is a shameful experience.
- You have feelings of rage and wanting to physically hurt or to kill when you feel dismissed, discredited or disrespected.
- You are secretly waiting for bad things to happen to you as punishment from God and/or the universe because you feel that you deserve it.
- You really don't like yourself.
- You secretly feel like a loser.
- You feel like an imposter in your career, relationships, and social life.
- You don't sincerely believe that anyone can truly care for or love you because you're such damaged goods.
- You fantasize about "dying" when you experience high levels of shame.
- You can't and won't accept your strengths, only your weaknesses.
- You feel like a failure in life, love, career, family, and kids.
- You feel this awful emotion (shame) about yourself most of the time to a greater or lesser degree. It is pervasive in your life.

This list has some of the more common shame symptoms, so it isn't remotely exhaustive, but it is a good test sample. Consider this a general emotional and psychological overview of some of the typical traits and typical behavioral response patterns that a shame-based individual encounters. What's your shame trigger? Which question on the list above is your primary raw nerve trigger that floods you with shame-based feelings? Think about the operating core beliefs that are part and parcel to feeling shamed on a daily basis. There are many issues surrounding shame which are valuable sources of insight for your healing and resolution. One of the most commonly misunderstood elements of shame is how it is expressed when you are feeling it surging through your mind and heart. The response shame cycle is typically fueled by anger toward people or yourself or by extreme embarrassment. These are typical emotions that are generally triggered when you're feeling shameful.

These primary emotional responses have layers and layers of collateral issues, feelings and reactions attached to them. For instance, no one would argue that a person who is expressing their shame-driven anger with violence or deadly force is "in control." The person who cannot constructively express their anger/rage feels embarrassed and humiliated that they react the way they do. The problem is compounded emotionally because they then try to suppress their nonproductive automatic behavioral response. The inevitable failed attempt at not feeling mortified cycles into deeper feelings of self-loathing/hatred or, in the worst case, self-destructive actions. The cycle of shame is endless until you finally go beyond its reach. Understanding the cycle of shame allows you to have a better insight into your potential healing and loving self-accepting response. The ending of your shame-controlled life is our discussion in Section III.

The Shame Cycle—This three-step cycle can be immediate or it can take days or weeks to play out in your life circumstances. It is during this repetitive shaming cycle that one of the five transformation issues (finances, romance, family, parenting, and health) in a person's life is adversely affected. Given years of experiencing the emotionally crippling cycle of feeling and suppressing shame, an individual ultimately feels emotionally drained and powerless. This low self-esteem energy causes their life journey to be extremely painful, disappointing, and filled with chronic feelings of hopelessness. The shame cycle is relentless, and it is the primary cause for developing many serious personal problems, life threatening challenges, and despair/suicide.

It is important to mention that any degree of shame-based anger is dangerous for both the holder (person expressing it) and the people yo whom it is directed. Many psychologists call this type of anger narcissistic or infantile anger expression. Rather than differentiate anger with many different sub-types, I refer to any type of anger expression that is being generated from a shaming feeling or emotional defense as toxic and deadly for all parties involved. ***Shame is usually expressed in one of***

three classic ways: anger, embarrassment/self-blame or self-defeating choices. Which one of these three responses is your typical reaction to feelings of shame? We are going to explore all three below in order to help you heal and no longer be a prisoner to this horrible emotional cycle of self-loathing. No amount of personal, professional, social or romantic shame-induced suffering is ever warranted or needed in your life. Shame tends to be the primary roadblock that prevents you from moving forward on your journey at this time and place in your life. Shame and personal change, self-acceptance and spiritual growth are incompatible. Shame is the emotional/psychological root cause of any type of self-doubt, self-loathing, anger management issue, and all types of self-hatred. It's why addressing your repressed, buried and active denial about your shameful feelings and reactions are the pathway to emotionally freeing and liberating your inner divine/intuitive self.

The Big 3: Anger, Embarrassment and Self-Defeating Choices/Blame

Shame Cycle #1. No One is Winning—If a man loses his temper and goes off verbally, he is considered dangerous, violent or a bad-guy. If a woman goes-off and engages her shame-driven anger, she is considered a bitch and/or a very mean-spirited person. The truth is, neither individual is mean or dangerous but rather deeply hurt, misunderstood and feels powerless to stop their raw nerve response to their long- standing wounds. These labels only intensify the anger, embarrassment and self-loathing that a person feels when their shame cycles come to the surface of any encounter or within any relationship.

Going beyond your anger issues, emotional fears and self-doubts are all critical parts to your life purpose and journey. *You no longer have to be defined by how your childhood and unmet emotional needs control your life today.* From this point and time on, you can choose to define your journey without your shame vetoing your choices. One of the challenges to healing your shame is how to manage your angry impulses and random bouts of rage. Many times men in particular are labeled as rage-aholics, when really it is their unmet childhood emotional wounds being triggered. Any type of anger management technique must include information on the development of a shame-based personality. This is the primary root for all types of abuse in a relationship (physical, verbal, mental, sexual and deadly violence). If you're going to sincerely address and heal your anger issues, the process must include insight into your neglected and ashamed inner-child. It's not enough to acknowledge your anger issues, but also pull the emotional roots out of it by resolving your shame cycle.

It's very important to remember that anger isn't a primary emotion such as love, happiness, sadness or fear. Anger is a secondly emotion, reaction to an emotional, psychological and heart-felt wound. Anger is the thinly veiled cover over your most sensitive and vulnerable inner self, or what is more commonly known as your wounded inner child. All childhood psychological, emotional, developmental wounds left untreated or unaddressed will evolve into some form of a shame-based driven adult personality. Any discussion of anger management has to include healing and embracing the unmet emotional needs of your childhood years. Otherwise, the avoidance of the inner child-shame issue is like spraying perfume on a pig and wondering why things still smell. Shame is covered up by your anger defensiveness, not the other way around. The order of importance is critical to gaining lasting relief from your inner emotional terrorist—*shame.*

For instance, when an adult goes off and becomes enraged about a missed airplane flight, the person is immediately flooded with paralyzing emotions. There is an absence of insight and understanding, and the old connection to the man's childhood is lost. The present circumstances of feeling emotionally rejected, misunderstood, powerless or dismissed are all replays of early childhood-parent relationships. The emotional triggers tend to be specifically connected to significant emotional relationship in the person's life (i.e., wife/husband, love interest, family, children, close friends, colleagues). *The neglected little boy or girl inside of any adult will become enraged when the raw exposed nerve of neglect is touched, triggered or reactivated.* Without a deeper understanding of the power of the original wound of shame in a person's life, there is no lasting cure or relief for anger management issues. Ignoring a person's shame is like watering the sidewalk and wondering why the water isn't absorbed by the cement—nothing changes! The cement in this case is a person's operating shame-driven personality that is unreceptive. The resistance to change or healing these deep wounds is understandable. Shame is the emotional illusion of self-doubt that keeps the openings to all other possibilities and dreams of your life frozen.

Shame's Cousin: Emotional Disrespect—The feeling and experience of being dismissed, devalued and overlooked is one of the strongest triggers for a shame-based anger explosion. The person feeling disregarded by a partner, ex-partner and/or family member can many times become so enraged that all common sense and self-control is temporarily lost. The childhood belief that you are disposable is your shame feelings in action today. The root of fearing the feeling of being emotionally dismissed is all connected back to your early parent-child relationship. You're not conscious of the underlying connections that block you from seeing your life from a loving, self-accepting perspective. You just feel the raw emotional nerve having ice water poured on it.

The circumstances can be varied but the overwhelming feeling is anger for not being considered or treated as someone of value or importance. This might sound overly simple or psychologically elementary. Unfortunately, the perception of being disregarded or dismissed is a match on a bucket of highly flammable liquids: *your sense of self.* There is a guaranteed explosion, which in worst cases results in physical harm or death. To be perfectly clear, the power of shaming is the driving force behind all crimes of passion. The person who is full of resentment doesn't understand that the feelings of being dismissed/disregarded aren't a personality flaw but rather an untreated emotional wound. The depth of emotional energy that comes out of the man or woman who is carrying around such a wound is paralyzing at best, and lethal at worst for them and their world.

Shame Cycle #2. Embarrassment Has No Limits—After extreme feelings of anger, rage and frustration have cooled off, the next piece of the cycle kicks in: paralyzing embarrassment. When the wave of emotional embarrassment is triggered, it is like a 100-foot wall of water consuming the victim. The triggers again are generally centered on personal themes of not being good enough, being bad person, awful parent, horrible partner and/or disappointing son/daughter. This very strong emotional response is an internally driven private experience where rage can be both an internal and external phenomena. The victim of shame-driven embarrassment is psychologically vulnerable to any type of circumstance where they feel their world is judging them or discovering their secret. The shaming incident can be triggered by something as simple as looking at a fellow coworker in a sexual way or having angry feelings toward your newborn child. The triggers are highly personal and private. The seemingly neutral events always reinforce the irrational feelings of being an awful, fraudulent, and phony individual. The victims feel that they are containing, hiding, and concealing a monster within their heart and soul. This inner monster, or the hunter that John Bradshaw referred to at the beginning of the chapter, is always alive and well within you. This dark force, this secret about you is always on the periphery of your thoughts and feelings. No matter what the personal cost is, these awful, embarrassing emotions have to be kept undercover at all times. The long-term damaging effect on your soul/personality caused by repressing your natural feelings of wanting to be understood can develop into many different types of mental illness and/or severe personality disorders.

No Lasting Relief—The secondary crisis for the horribly embarrassed man/woman is that they don't know how to rid themselves of their awful feelings. The avoidant behaviors (the endless list ranges from sleeping, drugs, eating, sex, work, etc.) are only a quick-fix to a long-term problem. The incredible inner emotional pressures of these absolutely intolerable feelings of inadequacy are extremely painful to experience. They have learned to rid themselves of shaming feelings at any personal expense. This shame-defensive behavior begins at a young age and can often lead to an addictive or compulsive personality in adulthood. Feeling this paralyzing shaming embarrassment is to be avoided at all costs and becomes the doorway to any type of addictive numbing behaviors. The spectrum of mind-numbing behaviors is as varied as the people experiencing it and doing it. Triggering the sense of inner embarrassment is an experience that is so painful and crippling that one's life is controlled by the avoidance of it.

It is very critical to understand that the cycle of shaming embarrassment is your automatic emotional/psychological response to your preconceived notions of good and bad behaviors. Often your shame-based driven belief system is irrational and goes unquestioned by you. ***You have formed your emotional belief system based on the foundation of feeling inadequate—not an accurate basis for your future.*** Your shame-based beliefs are the primary cause and theme of your present day relationship problems. It's almost impossible to feel good about yourself and have a loving sense of self with an underlying chronic feeling of inadequacy. *Loving self-acceptance and feeling shameful, inadequate and awful are like oil and water: they don't mix and they naturally repel each other.* The best way out of your emotional shame maze is to focus on your inner purpose and passion for life. Beginning to understand and see your cycle of shame allows for new personal self-accepting information to begin to transform, embrace and heal your wounded-neglected inner child. No amount of knowledge will replace or be a substitute for your ability to feel and experience positive loving emotions for yourself and others! Experiencing a different response to your relationships and yourself is a major step toward removing the roots of your old shaming cycle.

Shame Cycle #3. Self-Loathing is an Underestimated Force—All the shame roadblocks, personally, romantically and professionally, which challenge a person are connected to an underlying belief of self-loathing. *Self-loathing is your shame feelings in action.* Self-loathing is defined the same as shame and is the active ingredient the application of shame in your day-to-day life. Another way to say it is that your self-acceptance process has been aborted, undeveloped and stalled. All the various degrees and feelings of shame get played out with many painful life detours, poor choices and regret (self-loathing). Allowing for any degree of self-acceptance in your life will immediately benefit you by exposing this insidious cycle. Slowing down your shame cycle can and will reduce at least 80% of your self-loathing choices. Any degree or action in the direction of the self-acceptance process when addressing this emotionally driven behavior is always worth the effort and struggle.

Self-loathing, low-self-esteem, self-hatred and self-destruction all come from the same well of resisting your self-acceptance process. The emotional poison in your well is your shame. Your personal well of goodness, empathy, passion and compassion might feel contaminated by your current choices and circumstances, but it isn't. The biggest secret on your life journey is that all your happiness, acceptance, love and purpose are all within your heart/soul. Going back to our Native American story from Chapter 1, "Happiness Within," the wise Indian chief says: "*hide it (happiness) within their hearts because they will never think to look there.*" Wow, all the buried dreams, lost desires and hopes are all within your inner well of self-love/acceptance. Any action, feeling or belief that comes from a sense of disliking, hating or punishing yourself regardless of its significance is a classic symptom of your shame. The range of punitive behaviors is endless, and they are all directly connected to your shame- driven belief system. Yes it's all related.

Letting Go of Your "Bad" Self—If your well of shame is full to the brim with sensitive self-accusations, critical personal information (of course it's inaccurate), recriminations and distorted beliefs, then the well needs to be drained, emptied out and refilled with your own pure feelings. Any degree of self-rejection is the ultimate ball and chain holding you back on your journey. Emotionally speaking, you deny your ball and chain of shame that you carry around every day and wonder why you feel inwardly awful. The saddest and most extreme expression of self-loathing is self-destruction—i.e., suicide. Suicide is an extreme reaction to you rejecting your life. Suicidal thoughts, feelings and wishes all come from the untreated reservoir of your shame. The cure to your insidious bad feelings about yourself is all correlated to the degree that you allow and accept your self-acceptance process. It's impossible to predict what, how and where your life-spiritual journey will take you. *What is clear is that when you detox your heart/well of shame and all of its accompanying paralyzing side effects, then you are able to pursue your inner passions and dreams with courage and confidence.*

Stopping and Healing Your Shame Cycle

What is Emotional and Spiritual Sobriety—Developing a loving sense of sober self-acceptance is the ultimate antidote and cure for healing a shame-based personality. When you consider a new positive spiritual/life approach and develop a loving sense of self, you slow the shame cycle down considerably, if not completely. We will discuss at great length in Section III how to implement all of your new life purpose skills, tools and life/spiritual desires for the rest of your healing journey. It is important to clearly define what exactly emotional sobriety is and how it is a cornerstone to your life-spiritual journey:

Emotional sobriety is the ability to respond, ponder and consider the multiple issues when you're confronted with an emotionally charged situation (shame, betrayal, rage), relationships or crisis. Sobriety is allowing for new insights, new information and a higher life/spiritual perspective to influence and guide your relationships, emotional connections, decisions, responses and self-perception. It's the absence of familiar automatic emotional defensive reactions, yelling and abusive behavior. It's the absence of needing to conceal or hide your true feelings and thoughts in any situation.

Your emotional, spiritual and self-acceptance clarity allows you to better understand what you genuinely think and feel about all the things in your life. You will start responding to your inner feelings without the hunter or monster of shame lingering around your heart and soul. Instead, you will begin to experience an emotionally balanced, non-reactive, non-approval-seeking, fearless and empowered point of view about old issues and old challenges. You will view life events with a fresh perspective and with new insights. The need for validation, acceptance and approval from others will no longer be important factors or unspoken forces in your emotional and life/spiritual decisions. You find yourself feeling good about yourself and your life path regardless of your outward circumstances.

It's Not Your Fault—When someone triggers one of your shame issues, such as holding you responsible for their feelings, rather than automatically reacting/resorting to feeling your emotionally painful crippling shame cycle, you can pause and consider that maybe there are other options to your particular situation or circumstances. The ability to pause, breathe, and allow new self-accepting information to filter into your emotions and feelings is emotional sobriety. When people are drunk and/or under the influence of a mind/body altering drug, they aren't remotely capable of responding to any situation with 100% physical or emotional capacity. It simply isn't possible or an option when you're physically numb. The same analogy holds true for you emotional, feeling and psychological capacity. You can't respond or clearly understand any of your life lessons, challenges, or spiritual/life journey situations from a foggy personal shaming perspective. Your emotional clarity is directly correlated and connected to your emotional/mental ability to not react to what triggers your own shaming cycle. The correlation is directly related to your clarity vs. your feelings of shame/self-loathing. The higher the degree of your emotional/spiritual clarity, the clearer your life and responses to it will be (the "it" is your relationship world). The higher your feelings of shame, the less clarity, inner peace and perspective you will have.

Staying Emotionally Sober—Emotional sobriety allows you to consider other points of view or new possibilities that were never imagined or even part of your previous personal emotional experience. You are developing the capacity through your own self-realization-spiritual awaking to recognize/know that your life is going in the right direction regardless of the emotional or physical pain/crisis currently surrounding you today. You find that you are not automatically anxious or reacting with the old shame cycle symptoms or the powerful debilitating beliefs, feelings and thoughts when confronted with your old triggers. You have a sense of comfort in your own emotional and psychological "skin."

Closing Ideas—The two quotes below underline the life journey that you are currently embarking on and moving forward as you grow in your own self-acceptance and increase your emotional sobriety. Your inner challenges, relationship tests, ans life lessons are yours to resolve and move beyond—and you will! Shame is one of the toughest roadblocks to remove and one of the strongest spiritual/life path depressants along your journey. What seems impossible is only an illusion of how distorted our thinking gets with the constant recycling of shame throughout our daily life. Increased emotional sobriety allows you to feel and experience your life without the rapid undercurrent of shame, anxiety and psychological terror. The black inner cloud of impending doom that lingers in your heart and soul begins to dissipate. Healing your heart, soul and mind is a lifelong task, but worth every ounce of effort to reduce all the symptoms and beliefs of shame. The next chapter is going to expose shame's near and dear friend—*emotional fear!* Shame and fear together can create a seemingly hopeless life situation, crisis and "mess" that only the universal Genius of Love can resolve and heal within us.

Lastly, which of the five lesson paths from Chapter 3 are you dealing with? Think about it, and how shame did or does play a role in creating the emotional pain that you are currently experiencing? How did your shame feelings about your life journey influence and shape your current situation? Regardless of your answers, nothing is beyond change or can't be healed. As your shameful feelings decrease, you will open a new chapter in your life and relationships, along with more and more loving self-acceptance.

> *"Life is the most difficult Exam.*
> *Many people fail because they try to copy others,*
> *not realizing that everyone has a different question to answer"*
> —*Deepak Chopra*

> *"As spiritual beings, we are forever learning, developing and evolving.*
> *We pick our experiences on earth for optimum spiritual growth—Everyone*
> *is here to learn something. That's why everyone does things differently."*
> —*Paramahansa Yogananda*

Both of these great spiritual/life teachers are explaining that you (all of us) have many personal lessons to learn on the path of life. Finding your own life purpose and passion will always have challenges and tests, not to mention a steep learning curve. Removing the emotional roadblock of shame allows for your higher education to continue and evolve. Your road trip experience through your Valley of Despair and shameful feelings are all part and parcel of developing your highest and best purpose. Your self-acceptance process is a lifelong project aimed at healing and evolving your inner self. Nothing is ever lost and can't become learning material for the bigger plan for your life. You have a specific journey of awakening that is currently in process. Your experiences can't compare to someone else's because their life exam is an entirely different one from yours. Your only concern is to focus on your inner divine nature and what you need to heal in your relationship arena.

Chapter 6

Your Fear Factor—Where's the Net?

"Everything you want is on the other side of Fear."
—Jack Canfield

"The doors will be open to those who are bold enough to Knock."
—Louise Haye

"Failure is not falling down but refusing to get up."
—Chinese Proverb

*F*ear is one of the most complex emotions, feelings and forces of life to address and overcome on your (our) life path. All spiritual/life paths at some point will take you through the Valley of Fear and Death. It's just part and parcel to understanding the duality of this life. Your pathway only gets fuller, wider and more fulfilling as you master the personal and spiritual issues surrounding fear of the unknown. We are discussing how to reduce your emotional fear of doing, trying or considering something different, taking different actions and becoming a different person. We are discussing your fight-flight fear response. The problem is that our inner safety monitor can't be used all the time for our emotional, psychological, and spiritual challenges. Your inner psychological ego-based fear always demands that you know the outcome before the process or the action has

125

taken place. Irrational anxiety-driven fear requires that you need to know the future while you're still in the present, which is simply impossible. Your feelings of fear are relentless in pushing you out of the moment into the future or your painful memories of the past. Regardless of where your fears take you emotionally, psychologically and intellectually, it's never to a calm or peaceful place. Living in fear is similar to projecting a horror movie into your future and wondering why you don't feel calm! The power of emotional fear is a learned reaction and a major roadblock to stepping into the next chapter of your destiny.

Expanding Your Comfort Zone—For the sake of not being repetitive, one of the major intentions of this book's discussion is to assist in developing a foundation of loving self-acceptance rather than approaching your life with a fear-driven, anxious personality as your guidepost. The three quotes above are all addressing the need to remove fear as a one of the roadblocks for your life and replace it with new insights on your spiritual path. For purposes of clarification, it is important to note the clinical difference between survival fear and emotionally learned fear. A survival fear reaction to a speeding car coming at you while in the crosswalk is appropriate and important. Being that I am a native Californian and a native Los Angelino, earthquakes trigger my fear response. Very few people would argue the concerns surrounding the issue of the earth shaking and your house moving on its foundation. Yet I know that I am not moving out of the "City of Angels" because of the potential for a massive earthquake. *All fear responses and reactions have a balance between protecting you and controlling you.* We are focusing on no longer allowing your fears to control your destiny, choices, relationships, health and career.

Emotional Fear: A Relentless Force—We are discussing and exploring the emotionally driven fear that questions, worries and resists change and personal expansion and frets about dying or the unknown. Fear has no calm or peaceful foresight for your life or future. All the natural changes and transitions that you desire have the inherent challenge of expanding your emotional comfort zone. The tremendous resistance to change, natural human evolutionary movement (age/body changes), and personal growth is the voice of fear and the magnetic pull of self-doubt in your head. Fear can be likened to the slippery icy slope of caution with no regard for the limiting consequences of your safe behaviors or poor choices. Once you are emotionally engaged in an inner fear-based dialogue, the mountain top perspective is lost. You find yourself at the bottom of the icy hill, fearful of falling again and forgoing that challenge, relationship, job or new opportunity presented to you. Fear has the unspoken message: *"If you don't listen to me, you will die"* (symbolically). The problem is the paralyzing feelings (shame) that get connected to your fearful thoughts and anticipations of future events. This emotional link between your fears and the thoughts that trigger them is a very powerful controlling force. Yet with proper exposure of the irrationality of your fears, you can create new connections and emotionally safe links.

Built-in Fear Limits—Your life will increasingly become more and more limited, restricted, and hindered by your need to keep yourself feeling emotionally safe and in control. It's a pure illusion of the ego that avoiding your life path challenges is safe, and consequently a wise decision. Rather, emotional fear is a progressive and debilitating psychological and spiritual condition. Long-term fear decisions have serious life-altering consequences unless resolved. All social phobias, including agoraphobia (fear of public places) are continuously restricting your emotional life experiences. The victim (the sufferer) finds the emotional walls of their life becoming increasingly and systematically smaller and smaller as their life unfolds. The final result of a fear-based personality is complete isolation from the world and yourself. This isn't a desirable outcome (a life of fear) or a peaceful and productive life/spiritual path. You're ready to address your fears and move beyond them at this time and place in your life. If you weren't ready or willing, you wouldn't have this or a similar book in your hands. Exposing the irrationality of your fears is critical to uncovering the underlying reasons, sources and untapped potential within you.

The overarching question is how do you resolve, heal and appropriately handle your emotional fears? I can't begin to describe the amount of energy, time and money that people spend on keeping their fears alive and well. This can range from passing up the opportunity to take a career/life step forward or move out of your childhood town or city. It can be as simple as allowing your children to experience their life without you being the helicopter controlling parent. The unrestrained fear that is a constant personal torture can be activated by any routine daily events and normal life situations. The deep-seated panic that emotional fear feeds off of is always just an inch below the surface of a person's life. For instance, a mild headache can be the misdiagnosed untreated brain tumor, or your stomach cramp is the undiagnosed stomach cancer. *Fear/anxiety and control are different sides of the same emotional coin.* The need for control of the events, people and relationships in your life is a relentless task with a never-ending cycle of new concerns to be addressed. Anxiety and chronic worrying are all symptoms of your fear-based emotional response to your life journey. Fear is a ruthless taskmaster that is never satisfied or resolved by any decision in your life. Some of the six-million-dollar questions facing you today:

Exposing Your Inner Fears/Anxiety/Panic—

- What drives your need to control or chronically worry so much?
- What truly scares you?
- If you weren't anxious or worrying about the future, what would happen in or to your life?
- Are you more concerned about the future than the present?
- What does the voice of fear say to you?
- Do you obsess about how things might turn out?
- Do you spend time thinking about all the different ways something will happen rather than focus on what's happening in the moment?
- Do you ever think about dying and your afterlife?
- Do you have trust issues?
- Do you believe that your ego isn't always correct about you or situations in your life?
- Do you consider yourself hyper-vigilant (focusing on possible disasters with people, places and things)?
- Does the idea/concept of the unknown cause you to avoid those situations or circumstances?
- What emotion, situation or circumstances do you actively avoid?

- Do you have panic attacks when you're emotionally overwhelmed (fearful)?
- Do people describe you as a control freak?
- Do you make important decisions from a fearful perspective or from a positive life perspective?
- Do you deliberately avoid emotional tension surrounding your fear of the unknown?

Anxiety and Loss of Control—I will address the answers to the above questions in the next paragraph, but first a small introduction is necessary before we jump completely into the rushing river of your emotional and spiritual life. Current psychological research shows that effective treatment of any depressive disorder must first consider in the treatment plan the underlying untreated anxiety disorder. New psychological research is considering that all depressive disorders are rather different forms/types of anxiety. People can and do spend a lifetime resisting what lies beneath their greatest anxiety and deepest, darkest unexplored fear. The ultimate source and core cause of all anxiety disorders, obsessive-compulsive behaviors, panic attacks and generalized phobias all have one common denominator—*avoiding death!*

The greatest source of all our unknown fears is related to our lack of insight about our life, purpose and passing. When we begin to accept our life mission, death, the afterlife and our ego-driven fears are dramatically reduced. Appreciating the natural cycles of life allows us to live our life more fully with the absence of fear, anxiety and impending doom. All of these types of dark feelings, emotions and thoughts come from our core misunderstanding of our life, dying and afterlife. The Ram Dass quote below is excellent in stating our obvious need to live our life fully.

> *"Death is a Reminder to live your life fully"*
> *—Ram Dass*

The irrational belief and behaviors designed to keep control over things that far exceed our grasp (such as our birth and death) is useless. This fundamental error of control and false emotional understanding of our life journey is exhausting. Attempting to play God in other people's lives is another classic no-win arrangement at best, and can become a severe mental disorder at worst. Even though people know intuitively that their control issues are about their own life and death issues, this doesn't stop the ego from playing God. It's not until a person embraces their mortality and the concept that their life has natural limitations that their fear of change/unknown will become less psychologically debilitating and paralyzing. The grandfathers/mothers of psychology, saints, and timeless spiritual masters are all in full agreement that *your life starts at your death.*

Your Full Acceptance—Death is one of the biggest issues (if not the most challenging) that demands a reconciliation along your life journey. Grappling with and considering your death opens the doors for you to fulfill your life purpose with clarity and courage. Your acceptance is much more than making a living will or funeral plans. It's looking inward about the infinite impact of self-love, forgiveness, soulfulness and your upcoming afterlife. These are all spiritual issues that everyone has to resolve, act on and choose to live with or not. Acknowledging your fear of not having control of how the big plan of your life works allows you to have more control and inner peace in everything you do and feel. Life is full of paradoxes, and this is the classic one: *Less is more.*

> *"Our journey is about being more deeply involved in Life
> and yet less attached to it."*
> —*Ram Dass*

Loosening Your Grip—Less worrying about controlling life events creates more inner peace and a deeper sense of well-being and purpose—that is the meaning of the Ram Dass quote. Sounds easy, but why is there so much confusion surrounding this natural process of death and rebirth? The answers all lie within your emotional death-rebirth acceptance process. Please try to suspend judgment of your prior religious beliefs about God, heaven/hell, and your current life path struggles. Consider for a moment stepping outside of your preexisting spiritual beliefs (we all have them) and imagining the possibility that you can have all the joy, hope and fulfillment you have always desired by accepting the natural destiny of your own death-rebirth process? Resistance to your own destiny is like putting your hand over your mouth and refusing to breathe. In a matter of moments, you will gasp and then allow oxygen to enter your body. Try to do the same symbolically by removing your mental restrictions covering up your soul and clouding your mind. Much like your body gasping for air, your soul is gasping for relief from your denial of inner freedom and peace. *Death isn't the big unknown restricting your natural life flow! It's You!* We are always the problem and always the solution to any and all of our issues, regardless of their magnitude or seriousness. Understanding, accepting and resolving your own death and afterlife is a necessary pathway that everyone walks down at some point. When you stop avoiding your immediate purpose and accept your learning transformation crisis, you open your life, heart/soul to unlimited possibilities that once seemed beyond your reach and experience. Now, considering your expanded spiritual life perspectives and priorities allows for new options that are now attainable through your inner divine heart self-discovery.

> *"Your soul doesn't care what you do for a living—and when your life is over, neither will you.*
> *Your soul cares only about what you are being while you are doing whatever you are doing."*
> —*Neale Donald Walsch*

Your Death is Your Starting Point—This is the exact place, according to Eastern spiritual beliefs, masters and practices, from which your life starts. The quote reinforces the concept that your soul is only interested in your life lessons, not your bank account balances, wealth or social status. It's the classic idea of "let's look at the end of the book and find out how it all ends" (your story). Please indulge the idea that exploring your death is the doorway to healing the majority of your anxiety issues and fear-motivated behaviors. Embracing your death allows you to live fearlessly, passionately, and purposefully with courage, intention and direction. According to our Eastern spiritual masters, Western thinkers (that's us) spend way too much time fearing our death and never embracing the inherent joy of learning to live. Wow!! You can relax now in this moment because you accepted and know this book (your life) never really ends (your soul never dies); it just changes forms. Now you can keep living until you leave your body, while not leaving or losing your soul. Before we discuss your afterlife, lets focus on living without the fear of life.

Betty Lou—I had a client years ago, Betty Lou, who would continually tell me that she wasn't afraid of dying. Yet her life was consumed with fear and dread of everything. What she was really saying to herself was that she was afraid of living. Dying seemed like an easier way to avoid all her unresolved family abuse issues. Focusing on escaping her life seemed fearless, but was really quite the opposite. Betty Lou was terrified of exploring her traumatic, physically abusive childhood and understandably so. She wasn't embracing her own spiritual path and purpose.

Betty Lou eventually began to accept that her adult life was still negatively impacted by her old childhood fears that stemmed from a traumatic history. Her resistance and avoidance to living was her need to be in control of all the circumstances in her life. Betty Lou's anxiety mechanism of always being in control was a very limiting and difficult life companion. Living required Betty Lou to accept that dying" wasn't an escape, but rather a sense of freedom to live peacefully now in the present moment. Her fearlessness of dying wasn't really about courage or embracing her destiny. Rather, she was using this emotional misunderstanding as a barrier to not relive the terror of her childhood. The spiritual shift of acceptance" of the life/death cycle for Betty Lou allowed her to begin to consider her deep desires and hopes. Looking at her destiny and life purposes required that Betty Lou stop avoiding her emotional terror and see the value in resolving her old childhood issues.

Another type of Emotional Cancer—A fear-driven emotional lifestyle always becomes more and more restricted over time. Fear is like physical cancer; it continually grows, spreads and consumes its holder. The roots of your fears have to be emotionally addressed and resolved. There is no personal expansion or freedom of choice with an emotional terrorist named "fear" directing your choices. Your inner dilemma is that you must always act or behave in a safe controlled way, otherwise your life will blow-up and you're dead! The dread of the unknown is simply not true or remotely accurate when it applies to taking new action along your journey. All fear- based beliefs/behaviors are driven by a strong inner conviction of avoiding dying and utter annihilation.

It's no surprise that the idea of stepping out of your comfort zone is viewed as beyond a reasonable or necessary task. Most people become very defensive and emotionally aggressive when their irrational psychological fears are exposed. Your life purpose should be much more than playing it safe and avoiding new challenges, new relationships and your own personal transformation. The fear of annihilation indicates a lack of understanding of your body-soul connection and the process of your afterlife. You must be exhausted from having your fears hold you captive to very limiting beliefs, actions and behaviors. If you want to live well and peacefully, then fear can't be directing your destiny.

> *"If we wish to die well, we must know how live well:*
> *Hoping for a peaceful death, we must cultivate a peace in our mind,*
> *and in our way of life."*
> —*Dalai Lama*

Inner Peace and Dying—The Dalai Lama, the modern-day Buddhist leader, encourages us all to understand that death in this life is unavoidable. Death seems obvious, but our lives don't reflect this innate knowledge and spiritual passion that cause us to look beyond our current daily circumstances and time-limited short-term desires. The fundamental concepts of death and dying provide a meeting point between the Tibetan Buddhist Eastern views of it and modern Western scientific traditions and values. Both perspectives have a lot to contribute to our individual journey, and the level of acceptance and understanding of our present day life challenges.

According to traditional Eastern spiritual beliefs and mystical teachings over the centuries, the moment a man accepts his death (loss of fear) he is freed from the "Maya" illusion of no afterlife in his world. *Acknowledging your death and how you would like your life to be is a release from the material outer world into the passage of your inner spiritual world.* Accepting your natural world of inner peace (spiritual journey) and passing into your next life is a drastic shift from the panic of the moment (rat-race) to a more meaningful and purposeful existence (fulfilling your destiny). The illusion of life (Maya is discussed further in Section III) is a veil that prevents you from seeing the bigger, more meaningful spiritual/life purpose that all the events and experiences in and about your life represent. Accepting the natural physical ending of your present form and that all the things you do, learn and love matter in your next life is a very calming experience. Your inward acceptance of your death/life now and in the future is a new dramatic vantage point, allowing you to view your life from 10,000 feet. You no longer live on the street level of chaos and despair. Your inner emotional perspective of acceptance of your ongoing death/rebirth cycle allows so many new things to come into your life now and going forward.

Preparation Stage—Accepting and allowing your life journey to organically unfold is all part of your expanding life/spiritual transformation awareness. Emotional and psychological acceptance of your own natural birth/death cycle allows for more clarity and the birth of new fresh spiritual ideas about your present crisis. Many times the answers and solutions to your life challenges are completely different when considering the far-reaching impact of another life. The concept of an afterlife adds a new focus as you move down the road of your life, allowing you to step back from your old fears and consider something bigger: You don't die. *Your life is a current preparation for your next life.* Ultimately, from a higher more enlightened vantage point, all the challenges you are experiencing do matter and have inherent value. The consequences of today's choices exceed this life and pass into the life to come. Your emotional and spiritual heart crisis of acceptance and passion for your journey is more profound than merely a superficial mid-life crisis brought on by losing money or tarnishing your social image.

Power Shift—Your new spiritual awareness of life now is much more than the immediate moment or the collection of past resentments. These types of cognitive shifts from an outwardly driven life to an inward spiritually driven life are limitless. Living and making decisions based on your inward higher-self is the entry point to fulfilling your purposes and desires. *Your ego is going to have an absolute tantrum about being replaced by your soul's decisions.* We will discuss later your ego's current crisis (tantrum) now that it is no longer running your show. Your ego doesn't consider or value your inner divine path or the meaningfulness of your death and afterlife. Your ego is freaked out about being left behind at your death/passing. The ego is your body and its primary concern is to only live on the material level of life. There are so many concepts, information and ideas to ponder with regard to your death, life, afterlife and spiritual journey that this is just a brief introduction. Let's consider how to assimilate this new information without becoming overwhelmed by it.

How to finish your life journey from this point forward raises more questions than it tends to answer. For instance: Why am I here? Do I really have a purpose to fulfill? Do I really believe in a higher power, afterlife and my destiny? Do my actions today really matter now and in my afterlife? Does my passing on earth at this time matter? All these questions are answered in the affirmative with a resounding "YES."

Your New Body of Knowledge—The Dalai Lama, along with Western and Eastern spiritual teachers, all encourage us to view our passing to the other side as changing out of an old outfit and putting on a new set of clothes again. It is a common spiritual principle, concept and belief among Eastern and mystic traditions that *our body is an energy that just changes forms and is never destroyed or dies. Your soul never dies and your physical body is just a covering for it!* Paramahansa Yoganada, a young monk from India, came to the U.S. in 1920 to share the knowledge of the soul's connection in this life to many more lives to follow. He was the founder of the Self-Realization Fellowship, a worldwide spiritual community of all faiths, and introduced the practice of yoga to mainstream America. Paramahansa always reaffirmed that *"the body is simply mud covering up the gold brick inside of you (your soul/spirit)."* Throughout the centuries, the reparative life message espoused by numerous spiritual traditions has always been "don't forget about your soul's development and don't worship your body." The journey of your life is to connect to your soul (your divine nature), and your physical body will cooperate with this mission.

Consider the idea that your life force just changes forms. Your soul never ends; it just keeps evolving. This soulful idea can assist us with continuing to develop a rich and meaningful life as we approach our natural transition to paradise. Consider also that your efforts for your personal spiritual growth transformation are valuable and timeless. What you do or don't do in your life can and have far-reaching consequences for many life times to come. This is a very powerful concept for the "Western soul" thinker, but not a new idea or way of life for other metaphysical spiritual orientations (Eastern spirituality). Afterlife and/or heaven concepts have always had a prominent place in religious literature throughout the centuries. The modern-day idea of the immediate here and now (no afterlife) and the physical importance of today have made the transitory energy of the physical world more important than the infinite energy of your soul. The greatest energy in your life is always within you, and that is timeless, ageless and priceless.

The circumstances outside of you are far less important than the issues and feelings inside of you. Your life is always a process of becoming spiritually engaged while living in your body and world. Your life is much more than your physical body, your looks, your wealth and your accomplishments. All those things in your life (wealth, education, social influence, privilege, business/relationship opportunities) are in service of fulfilling your soulful purpose. Everyone, including you, has a life purpose and something to contribute regardless of your current crisis. The sense of personal failure, fear and emotional disappointment are all important parts of the bigger life puzzle that you are piecing together. The view of your ever-expanding life journey transformation is all about fulfilling your purpose for your time here. It's never too early to focus on fulfilling your purpose, following your passion and uncovering your heartfelt desires. The ideas of failing, of not being good enough or somehow lacking aren't concepts that come from your soul, but rather from your ego. The ego has no intention or regard for your or anyone else's spiritual purpose and path. Your heart and intuitive soul is always connected to all the souls in your life now and the purposes that are all interrelated. The many individual life purposes, soul connections and life lessons are all woven together seamlessly.

Your Cycle of Death and Rebirth: After-Life Question—There is a practice among spiritual masters/teachers, regardless of orientation, that when a person is seeking their guidance they ask one simple question: ***Do you believe in a life after this one?*** The question isn't whether they believe in it as a philosophical idea, but whether they feel it deeply in their heart. The guru, teacher, rabbi, pastor, monk knows that if a person believes in a life after this one, their entire outlook and approach will be drastically different. Having a belief in a life after this one breeds a distinct sense of personal responsibility and morality now for the future. The overriding premise is that what you do now really does matter in the present as well as on the other side of this physical world.

The second part of the life-after process is understanding and fully accepting your own death-rebirth cycle. The death-birth process began when you entered this planet and happens repeatedly during your life/ spiritual journey awakening events, experiences and insights. Your particular death-birth cycle is very subjective and personal to your necessary life lessons and spiritual education. *The death-birth cycle is continuous during the entire course of your life.* The obvious final phase (your passing to the other side) isn't finished until that unknown time when you depart and change "clothes" again.

No More Denial—Along the road of your life, you will go through many perfectly designed death-rebirth cycles that are all designed for your personal and spiritual realization, culminating in your final completion. Fear has no regard for your afterlife and will always argue that you don't have to move forward or change. In the quote on a previous page, the Dali Lama is explaining that your values, morals, choices, life lessons all play a big part in how you enter the other side. This is a very powerful concept with far-reaching consequences in the here and now of your current day. All your struggles in trying to be more loving, accepting, forgiving, generous and even supportive of your enemies have a huge significance in this life and the ones to follow. All of your unspoken suffering, betrayals, and good-will gestures are recognized and work towards you moving through this life and into your next one. *Nothing is ever lost in the cosmic universe of which you're part and parcel. Losing is a human/ego concept, not a spiritual truth or reality.* In a loving universe theology, everyone wins and losing is merely a subjective ego perspective with no regard for the value of change and divine purpose.

It is important to underscore that all of us in the West, myself included, have been formally and/or informally taught to deny, avoid and ignore our death. For many people, psychologically, emotionally and physically, *death means nothing other than pure annihilation and loss.* This prevailing secular belief implies that most of us live either in denial of our death or in absolute terror of it. The emotional foundations of anxiety disorders are all fueled by the mere mental anticipation of "changing forms." It makes perfect sense that the ego or lower thinking part of us is so scared of dying. Its control over your life is over! Your life is never over. You just change forms! Your physical body is left behind along with your ego, but your soul moves on at your life line crossing. Even talking about death in this book seems a bit edgy and provocative. The quote below by Caroline Myss further reminds all of us that the death-rebirth process is part and parcel of our school-of-life spiritual journey. It's very ironic that people (myself included) are so highly educated in every subject except the one that holds the key to the entire meaning of life, and perhaps to our very survival: *your death/rebirth process and afterlife!*

> *"You have to give up the life you have (death) to
> Get to the life (rebirth) that's waiting for you."*
> —*Caroline Myss*

Your Life Always Matters—all your decisions matter. Your spiritual life journey matters, and yes, you matter the most. If this is the only concept you glean from this book, then you have gained a great pearl of personal wisdom. The avoidance of death is a fundamental misunderstanding of your spiritual purpose and life journey. Death, as we all know intellectually, is a natural occurring event that is something to embrace rather than deny. According to Eastern teachers, mystics and spiritual teachers throughout the ages, acceptance of your ending is freedom from this painful world of fear. ***The physical world is ruled by fear, and the spiritual world is ruled by love.*** We all live in both worlds, but which one controls us? The inner struggle between your ego and soul/spirit for control of your life is part of your balancing process of living. A lack of appreciation for your gift of life and your gift of death keeps you isolated from your ultimate inner freedom and purpose (love). It's impossible to assess your inner sense of love and calmness when this current life is viewed as the sum total of your entire physical, soulful and divine existence.

The crisis that all people face at some point along their journey is accepting their own life/death process. How the crisis comes to you is always individual, creative and subjective (remember Chapter 2—five pathways to your awakening). For instance, *the resolution of your mid-life crisis of sorts isn't about buying more, acquiring more, or doing more, but rather it's all about the inner personal acceptance of your destiny (intended life purpose)!* In his quotes at the beginning of this chapter and below, Jack Canfield again reinforces that your life is on the other side of your life/death fear factor. I added the word "your" because your fears are also highly subjective and personal. Fear will always be a major distraction from your higher purposes, along with a misunderstanding of your gifts and destiny. If we are going to embrace our own destiny, let's start with our day of "passing"—your funeral.

"Everything you want is on the other side of your fear."
—*Jack Canfield*

Your Funeral: What's going to happen?—Let's consider how you want this particular movie (your life) to end, and what needs to be healed, amended and forgiven in the meantime. In order to fully comprehend your current crisis, death/rebirth cycle, you must consider your funeral. Many people resist and try to avoid their life/death fear factor to their own peril. Looking at your funeral is a very powerful tool for getting past any denial or avoidance of the unknown terrors of your life. Picturing the setting, location, day and time of your funeral is a powerful image to ponder and emotionally feel.

- What will be said at your funeral?
- Who will speak? What time of day?
- Who do you want sitting in the front row?
- What songs will play, videos shown, pictures shared?
- What memories of you and your loved ones would you like to have shared?
- Who do you want in attendance and who isn't invited?

- Who from your family is coming or who isn't coming?
- Where is your funeral?
- Open or closed casket?
- Do you want to be cremated or do you have your ashes scattered in nature?
- Do you have a memorial service?
- Do you have a party, and are people toasting and celebrating your life?
- What do you want the first day of your life on the other side to be like?
- How do you want to leave this world, where and when?
- Who is with you when you pass over to the other side?
- Do you want to be alone?
- Who do you want to speak to before you leave?
- Do you want to clear up any misunderstandings?
- What secret do you want to tell your ex-partner, wife/husband or long-lost love?

The list is endless, and hopefully you're now getting the idea that passing across the life line takes a lot of preparation in order to leave things in better shape than how you found them. This not only includes your legal will and belongings, but all your relationships. One of the key projects before leaving is for you to learn your life lessons and leave this life in better condition than when you entered it! Your inner spiritual transformation is your single greatest project and undertaking. This isn't simply estate planning as much as it is spiritual/life journey planning. Ultimately, leaving your world in better shape, with greater insight and greater capacity for love than how you came into it, is the game plan. Regardless of our individual life path directions, how we get this task accomplished (more about this in Section III) are all of our inner focus points.

Your Life/Spiritual Journey Planning—Now consider what you want the rest of your life to look like, feel like and be remembered for on the day of your funeral and passing to the other side. Visualize your funeral, the location, day, and what is said about your spiritual legacy. Who speaks at your eulogy? Does your ex-partner come? Do your estranged children come? Do your business partners come? Is there any love in the air? Do you like the atmosphere surrounding your passing? Please don't discount or dismiss the power of these considerations; they are incredible sources of information about your current path and where you want to be when you pass to the other side.

Remember from Chapter 1 that the ghosts of Christmas past came to visit Scrooge to awaken him from his self-centered, greed-driven, and meaningless material life. Now is the opportunity to take a complete inventory of how you are feeling about love, forgiveness, self-acceptance, service and generosity. How do you want your present life crisis/challenge to play out? Your decision can transform you and all the people in your life. Ask yourself the question: *"what would love do"* in your current relationship, business deal, parenting, health choices and financial decisions. You know what fear would do—now what would love do? Your answer is an invaluable source of feedback on what to do next to heal your heart and the people surrounding you. It's amazing how petty resentments, relationship misunderstandings, romantic or business betrayals all seem so small when you look at the end of your movie/life.

The Biggest Myth: Fear of Failure—There are many different ways to heal, mend and change the fear of the unknown and begin to truly live your life. The absence of fearing others opinions or painful judgments instinctively breeds self-confidence, passion and direction going forward. Some people, for instance, have gone through what is called near-death experiences when they see the other side of life and their own life simultaneously. Others come face to face, through various circumstances, with their greatest unspoken fear: death. These types of profound life experiences propel people into immediate spiritual enlightenment that forever changes their life pursuit from *material wealth/acquisition to spiritual hunger.* This instantaneous cognitive/emotional shift from the pursuit of possessions and acquisitions to the pursuit of the intangibles of serving, giving and learning the endless life lessons of loving self-acceptance is remarkable. It's the intangible things in your life that always hold the most meaning, power and influence for you. The intangible elements such as love and self-acceptance are never temporary escapes from your life. Rather these inner qualities of life provide the sustaining energy and peace of your life. We all crave and desire to have in our lives the new uninterrupted positive experience of loving, emotional energy. This innate soulful desire allows us to connect on a higher more meaningful level with our romantic partner, family, business partners, colleagues and our entire world.

Lasting Success is Inside of You—The stark contrast from living in a wanting mode of existence to a life-afterlife perspective is drastic and fearless. The vanishing illusion of wealth and people's approval is replaced with a deep abiding peace. Your new focus is inner lasting comfort which leads you through the foggy painful days on your journey. The irony is that your inner lasting happiness and fulfillment comes from pursuing your destiny, which always requires courage. The fear of failure is only an illusion that our ego and society has created to try and keep people from being different. *Clearly your shifting from a fear of life/death to embracing your entire death/birth cycle is one of the biggest transformations and direction changes along your journey of life.* Accepting the idea that there are no failures along your journey— only misdirections that you correct and evolve from—is liberating from your inner critical voice ego. Your inner satisfaction of living a loving, purposeful, and motivated life is the successful reconnection to your soul. Your ego will never understand or fully cooperate with your soul's desires and outcomes. The misunderstanding is that your self-acceptance process is no longer based on the fear of being exposed, shamed and/or embarrassed. Your inner self-realization is that there isn't anything in your life to obsesses, panic or be terrified about. *Nothing!* Your intuitive perspective shift is the game of life change that you have been secretly craving, but was not sure how to accomplish. The fearful ego belief of failing has been viewed for centuries by spiritual teachers as a simple shift in perspective. The mistake that we make in our lives is one of never truly wrong actions, but rather a lack of pursuing the treasuries, riches and wealth within our hearts and soul. Avoiding your inner passions based on ego and the approval of others is what is really considered a mistake:

*"There are only two mistakes one can make along the road to truth:
not going all the way, and not starting."*
—*Buddha*

Moving Forward—Given what Buddha and many other great teachers have taught about the value of not allowing fear to impede your journey reminds me of a great story about our own spiritual path. A story from the Bible's New Testament (recounted below) reinforces the importance of your journey and the lightning bolts that the universe will use to get our attention. These lightning bolts of life are only for your spiritual/life awakening. These happenings in your life have clear motives—destiny and purpose that only seem random and out of your control. These events are for the sole purpose of correcting, healing and moving you along in your soulful development. For review purposes, the five life lessons that we discussed earlier in this book are:

- *Money/Finances-Lesson* (Values/generosity vs. greed/dishonesty/ emotional deprivation)
- *Family of Origin-Lesson* (Individuality/passion vs. enmeshed/ abused/addictions)
- *Love/Marriage-Lesson* (Self-worth/esteem vs. inferior/unworthy/ dismissed)
- *Parenting Relationships-Lesson* (Competent vs. people-pleasing/ nlovable)
- *Health Issues-Lesson* (Trusting life/self-acceptance vs. resentments/ self-hatred/entitlement)

The "Soul" Purpose of Emotional Suffering—Incredibly, these different challenges are all designed to get you going in the direction that you were intended to travel in this lifetime. These perfectly designed divine lightning bolts of enlightenment come through many channels and experiences, as we discussed earlier in the book. Many times, the degree to which you resist your internal changes, challenges, and lessons is the same degree to which your crisis will impact you. *The relationship between your emotional pain and suffering is in direct proportion to your resistance and denial of your inherent spiritual direction/awaking.* If there is any failure of sorts, it's in our resistance, fear and thinking we know better than to accept our destiny. There is no failure, loss, or waste of time when looking at your life from a higher-self intuitive perspective and purpose rather than from the material ego level.

Getting back to the classic example of how the universe works on our behalf at all times comes from the New Testament. The shorthand version of this timeless Biblical story is about the conversion of the Apostle Paul from a secular lawyer to a spiritually motivated teacher/leader. He was on the road of his life (sound familiar?), angry, resentful and resisting the power of love that was all around him. Symbolically, on the road to Damascus, God/Universe asks him what he is doing with his life? Paul didn't have a good answer—as all of us don't when confronted with the error of our purpose, thinking and behavior. Hopefully you haven't been struck more than once by the lightning power of the universe to gain your attention and passion for your journey. If you have been impacted to a severe degree like the apostle Paul was, you will never be the same. Paul was immediately transformed and forever clear about his life mission and purpose; he never questioned or waivered from his inner guidance and knowledge again. When you accept your life and a soulful connection to all things present and in the future, there is no doubt left in your heart. The transformational experience of connecting to your spiritual self and the divine within you is the ultimate auto- correction on your spiritual/life path. The fears of life are no longer relevant and only serve as a distraction to your mission and purpose.

Moving past your fears of the here and now is a night and day difference in how your story ends. Paul, like many before and after him, has seen the bigger purpose to his journey now and in the future. Seeing your own world from a loving prosperous perspective erases the distorted view of fear and failing in whatever is causing you regret and suffering today. *The resounding truth and message of this entire book is that the fear of failure is really your resistance to your life journey challenges and afterlife.* This may sound overly simple and trivial, but it is anything but that, Trust me, walking along your life/spiritual path with an attitude of acceptance is really the road less traveled. The late brilliant author and spiritual master/psychiatrist, Dr. M. Scott Peck, championed this concept in the last 30 years of the twentieth century. He introduced to mainstream culture the concept that your life lessons, challenges, spiritual values are priceless rewards for pursuing your inner journey. He wrote the timeless masterpiece, "The Road Less Traveled." Starting to view your life as series of lessons that need to be mastered is a source of motivation and courage. I love this quote by Ram Dass, also a modern-day spiritual teacher and guru who is reminding us that we are all connected in this life regardless of tension, betrayals, deception and painful heartbreaks.

> *"We're all just walking each other home."*
> —Ram Dass

The good news is you already started on your life/spiritual journey many years ago. Now you want to finish what you have come to do and accomplish in this lifetime. You don't want to allow your illusions of annihilation and terror of the black abyss to cloud your inner and outward path and judgments any longer. Buddha refers to "not starting" as resisting your afterlife and the timeless moral responsibility you have now and in your next life. In previous sections we discussed the role that emotional and mental fear-based thinking can play in derailing your journey for years at a time, and in the worst case, for several lifetimes.

The idea of having to repeat junior high or any heartbreaking part of my journey as a spiritual lesson has motivated me to be purposeful and responsible with my own thoughts, actions and decisions (at least I attempt to). You wouldn't be reading this book and other books like it if you weren't committed to reaching your own life/spiritual destiny. Just like my spiritual mentor said to me many times, "You didn't come here to lose (resistance/fearful), but to play your heart out." *The thousand-foot wall of fear of going outside your comfort zone and insistence on playing it safe are all symptoms of the fear of failing/death!* You don't want to encircle your life with the Great Wall of China, but rather with the timeless connection of your soul to the endless supply of universal love and courage. Looking at your life today, tomorrow and going forward with an afterlife perspective is emotional freedom. You don't need to know or control the outcomes of your life; rather you need to be mindful of your purpose. The ageless myth of failing is one of the biggest ego misnomers and paradoxes in life today, and of course the subject of this entire book. Your spiritual path can involve turbulent personal times but that doesn't mean you're going in the wrong direction. It only means everything is time-limited, including your current struggle, life and learning phase.

"We have to live with the choices we make. You can make a spiritual choice,
one that takes into account the physical, emotional,
and spiritual consequences. A
spiritual choice is not made by your ego or out of fear...
A spiritual choice is a responsible choice."
—*Jeff Van Praagh*

Your Life Has Far-Reaching Effects: Your End Game—I am very taken by the idea of "how do you want to leave your life." Retirement planners and wealth management experts are great at asking these types of questions from a material point of view. They are asking the right questions regarding how to properly manage your resources and acquisitions. But how do you want to finish your life lessons, love, empathy, serving others—what is it that you want to have accomplished inwardly that is timeless? Ask yourself this question from a life-after perspective and life/spiritual path point of view? What is the purpose that you came to this life to fulfill? How do you overcome, resolve and heal the nagging lifelong personal issues and lessons? Pondering these types of questions is what Jeff Van Praagh is explaining in the quote above. Your responsible spiritual actions will create a better world for you and the people surrounding you. Like the movie, "Pay it Forward," your loving actions are the life now and afterlife practice that changes everything.

For instance, your persistence in trying to resolve your anger and resentment about the family that you grew up in or the betrayal by your ex-husband/wife is valuable. It feels like you take five steps forward (actually do) and then something happens and you lose your perspective. Your residual fear of never changing or healing this particular relationship is frustrating beyond words. Consider the idea of stopping your fear response with the question that immediately creates clarity and wisdom for any situation or circumstance. The question to ask yourself and not anyone else is: *What would love do?* The answers are as creative as the beauty of nature and as powerful as the sun rising after a three-month winter storm.

If you wonder if the question of love works, ask the inverse question: *What would fear do?*

Hmmm, that answer is as limited as trying to change someone else and wondering why it doesn't work! Fear, anxiety and your ego will always keep putting your life, options and possibilities into smaller and smaller boxes. The answer is that love is the most powerful action that you will take along your life journey. Fear will always keep you in your frustrated emotional status. Love will change everything in ways you couldn't imagine, dream of, or thought possible. The ultimate healing of your fear factor is taking action with the force and understanding of the entire universe behind you with love as your inner guide. Love is the spiritual, self-action acceptance process in real-time.

The Courageous Question—What is one thing that you hesitate to ask yourself: "What would love do with...?" Pause and wait for the answer. The answer is already within you ready for a chance to express itself in ways that many of your friends and family will not understand. Regardless, don't avoid it (action) because that is the subject of our next chapter. You couldn't answer that particular question if you didn't have the inner resources, love, courage and understanding/insight to do it! Knowing the answer, the proper action step, and the path to take and resisting and avoiding it are more problematic than not knowing the answer. Your spiritual path, life and soulful responsibility always lead to actions that Love inspires within you. I know it's tough and scary to do the "unthinkable" which we will discuss in Chapter 8. Let's first focus on reducing our escapist, avoidant, and fear-based mind and soul numbing practices. Remember any resistance in your life is fear based and a limiting belief that never leaves you feeling or being empowered. Your untapped "bliss" is waiting for you to spend some time experiencing and engaging.

> *"Follow your bliss and the universe will open doors*
> *where there were only walls."*
> —*Joseph Campbell*

Chapter 7

The Avoidance-Addiction Factor—
Managing the Pain in Your life

In Sur Master Rumi's "Table Talk," there is this fierce and pointed message about the importance of finding your life purpose:

"The master said there is one thing in this world which must never be forgotten. If you were to forget everything else, but were not to forget this, there would be no cause to worry, while if you remembered, performed and attended to everything else, but forgot that one thing, you would in fact have done nothing whatsoever. It is as if a king (spirit/divine nature) sent you to a country to carry out one special, specific task. You go to the country and you perform a hundred other tasks, but if you have not performed the task you were sent for, it is as if you have performed nothing at all! So man has come into the world for a particular task, and that is his purpose. If he doesn't perform it, he will have done nothing."

—*Sogyal Rinpoche*
(The Tibetan Book of Living and Dying, pages 146-147)

Your Task—After reading this short but powerful admonishment for making sure we don't squander the opportunity to fulfill our life purpose, which begs the question, what is my purpose? It is a widely accepted fact in religious writings, philosophy, astrology and psychology that there is a special purpose, important meaning and valuable reason for your life! Regardless of their particular orientation, spiritual teachers/leaders throughout the centuries have repeatedly told us that we all have a specific purpose and a life task to discover, accomplish, complete and pass along to others. There is no excuse, no reason and nothing that can keep you from discovering your life mission, purpose, and task *other than you!* In spite of our own fears, self-doubts, and shameful feelings, our inner pathway is within reach at all times. It's always a matter of looking within yourself and getting past your ego into the heart and soul of your life.

Once you have looked within and feel something bigger than your own life, then the king's orders which you have been sent to do can be completed. The "king" is your intuitive nature divine self, higher-self, Holy Spirit and/or God—the part of you that is connected to your inner soul. It's not an important matter to name the king, but rather to follow those desires, passions and intuitive impulses within you. According to the above quote, these feelings and inner drives were sent to you prior to this lifetime. You are currently living to do something great in the eyes of the "divine king" who is within your heart.

What's Your Mission?—*The resounding timeless truth for your purpose is that the primary mission of our/your current life is to achieve reconnection and union with your higher enlightened self.* The task for which the king has sent you into this strange, dark turbulent country, which is symbolic of your life without spiritual enlightenment, is to realize and connect to your true being/soul. Once that connection is achieved then the first stage of the mission is completed. How that reconnection is made, relearned and discovered is part of your own individual joy, mystery, struggle and beauty of your personal divine life/spiritual path. There is no wrong way to do it (enlightenment process) or only one career path, or any particular religion, faith or church denomination. It's the own inner journey of your intuitive soul discovery that will transform both your inner and outer world. *The masters say there is ultimately one inner direction to go and that is to allow your life journey to become your spiritual journey.* Your life journey, regardless of all the losses and apparent defeats, will always lead you to discovering your spiritual-self. All the emotional roadblocks and barriers of life can be resolved and transcended as you evolve on your life/spiritual mission.

> *"All religions (your enlightenment process) are like different cars all moving in the same direction. People who don't see it have no light in their hearts—One truth, many different songs."*
> —Ajahn Chah

We Are All Headed in the Same Direction—*As all rivers lead to the ocean, so do all life paths lead to a spiritual awakening.* So eloquently stated by spiritual master, A. Chah, there is an unlimited number of ways to find, reconnect and awaken spiritually. The question isn't what path or track are you on, but rather are you awake? Like the quote states, whatever path you're on will lead to where you need to go, what you need to do, and who you need to meet. You can choose to avoid your inner task and ignore or postpone the lessons on your life curriculum. Metaphorically, dropping out of high school (avoiding your life) and going to work full time (numbing out) isn't a positive spiritual option. Your inner work is to learn, to act on, to do and become the person/soul you wanted prior to this lifetime. Full acceptance of your life and spiritual journey opens your heart, soul, and mind to unlimited options that are specially created for you. Your intentional conscious avoidance or fears of failing become ultimately your life choices. Your emotional default of fear is what the introductory quote is describing. Repeated personal choices to not follow and ignore your inner passions will eventually become an automatic behavioral pattern of avoidance and fear.

The spiritual connection within you to your higher-self becomes remote and distant because of deliberate, willful neglect. It is at your precise moment of despair that the universe will typically use one of the five life challenges discussed earlier to awaken you from your sleep-walking, slumber state or angry psychological coma. *Whatever is needed to get your inward attention will be used by your higher-self, intuitive-self, and soul to awaken your enlightened self.* Your process of awakening is part of your inner mission and purpose.

Avoiding Your Ego—As stated previously, your ego is adamantly opposed to your inner path and will create painful detours for merely selfish and foolish purposes. All the varied challenges, trials, tribulations and crises will ultimately wake up your inner heart/soul's desire for reconnection to your higher self. No matter what has happened or how far you feel from being a loving caring acceptable man/woman, father/mother, husband/wife, your inner intuitive self always wants a chance to reconnect with you! *Your ego, which represents your non-spiritual self, wants nothing to do with the power of your inner passions and divine journey/purpose: Nothing!* There is no situation, circumstance or action that can separate you from your inner self, your divine purpose and the grace of the universe (unconditional acceptance): Absolutely nothing! Many people will argue that some things in this life are beyond psychological repair, forgiveness and reconciliation—but not from a spiritual perspective! Never surrender to your ego's harsh reprimands or to your inner chronic critical judge and jury. These common personal self-doubts and personal self-haters are all pieces to your life puzzle and not the disqualification material for completing the mission which you were sent to accomplish. Your life purpose, buried within your heart/soul, is only yours to discover, act on and accomplish.

Your "Mission Impossible" Assignment to Fulfill—It's our choice and challenge to embrace, develop and connect internally with our awakened self. Free will is a gift and has to be exercised all along the road of life. Your destiny is a series of life/spiritual choices that will culminate in your inner transformation regardless of the incredibly painful detours in your life. There is no mandate or imperative that you either do or don't do your heart's desire. The universe (God/Higher-Self) doesn't demand your loyalty, love or undying commitment. Rather it's always your own decision to go soulfully inward and finish your task. The old TV show (now a movie series) "Mission Impossible" is an excellent metaphor for explaining your assigned special life mission; the secret agent (that's you) is always given direct orders via a self-destructive audio tape (past life) on what mission he/she needs to complete. The orders always came from the agent's superiors (your higher-self) who know that the agent (you) are capable of completing whatever the daunting task required. The special agent always is challenged to complete the particular task to which they were directed. The agent (you) would never do something different than the assigned task because it might be helpful or similar to the mission assignment. The task is clear, and it is their (your) mission to complete it.

For the sake of our discussion, the Mission Impossible TV show and your life calling are very similar. You either listen to your inner voice or you ignore the specific directions for your life today. For many people, doing their own mission is not doing what someone else thinks they should do. It's up to you to follow your inner calling and become who you secretly desire to be. This isn't a discussion about predestination or God's prevailing will; rather it's about the personal power of choice that you have been given to use for your betterment and spiritual growth. Choice, free will and freedom are spiritual birthrights that we all have within us regardless of our particular country, zip code or governing powers.

Your path requires all the courage, intelligence and resolve that you possess in order to succeed at your own personal transformation completion process (fulfilling your mission). The real life detours and roadblocks of self-defeating behaviors are endless and always foster psychological hopelessness for continuing on your inward journey. The power of avoidance and addiction (all types) is never to be underestimated or dismissed as trivial details in the uncovering process of becoming your highest and best self. Avoidance is a very subjective behavior specially designed by our own fears and limited ego perspective. In the prose below, Death describes the two paths in our life and how avoidance of our purpose and journey is an empty and very painful pursuit:

> *"There is the path of wisdom and the path of ignorance. They are far apart and lead to different ends. Abiding in the minds of ignorance, thinking themselves wise and learned, fools go aimlessly hither and thither like the blind led by the blind. What lies beyond life shines not to those who are childish or careless or deluded by wealth."*
> —*Tibetan Myth of the Wise Man vs. Foolish Man*
> (*The Tibetan Book of Living and Dying*—page 285)

*"It's never too late to change the programming
imprinted in childhood, carried in
our genes or derived from previous lives; the solution is mindfulness
in the present moment."*
—*Peter Shepard*

How did it Start?—These two old wise stories illustrate the themes regarding the path of ignorance verses the path of enlightenment which are discussed throughout Eastern and Western literature, including the Bible. The challenge that all people face at different points along their own individual journey is coping with the power of avoidance and addiction. Nobody wants to deliberately be a fool in their own life story/movie. How one becomes that fool, described so eloquently above, is when that the person refuses to address the issues in their personal world. Instead of making the choices of self-love that are in front of them, they do the opposite—*self-loathing*. They avoid the perceived emotional pain through mind and emotional numbing behaviors. These avoidant behaviors start as early as five years old and develop into bigger personal problems and patterns with age and adult responsibilities. Personality disorders, which are pervasive maladaptive behaviors, have their beginnings in the men/women as early as 3 to 5 years old. These avoidant behaviors can become fixed personality styles/patterns and impairments to all social, personal, family and romantic relationships. Avoidance can become an emotional cancer (consuming of your conscious energy, thinking and living) if left unexamined, unresolved, and untreated.

What I am referring to here is that addictions start with the unconscious need to not feel overwhelmed or fearful. Without exploring and healing these old painful beliefs, the emotional defensive need to not re-experience the overwhelming feelings and of being powerless is a steel monorail track going nowhere (expect in circles). The railroad track of avoidance and addiction is a very difficult emotional cycle to break. The repetitive actions of avoidance become the burden and consuming energy and focus of your life. Young children, teens and adults can experience a subjective catastrophic event—loss, heartbreak, betrayal, illness—that is so emotionally terrifying that they put a stop to emotionally feeling.

Many times the young girl or boy is unconsciously emotionally frozen at the age of the traumatic event/experience. What happens with emotional and psychological paralysis/freeze is the built-in resistance and diversion to ever going beyond the internalized trauma. Over time, the person will develop an elaborate behavior scheme to avoid any chance of feeling or being in those types of traumatic emotional circumstances again.

Avoidance is the Creator of All Addictions—Let me expand and elaborate on the concept of how we can build an emotional wall around our life with no openings or exits. Your mind's intent to protect and preserve you is natural and appropriate. The problem is that after a childhood crisis (such as chaotic abuse) has passed, your inner child continues to live and react as if it is still 1981 and not the present day. In order not to feel, think, or re-experience any type of these powerless emotions, scary behaviors, we build (create our inner wall) in emotional-psychological avoidance responses. Over time and into adulthood, these emotional detours automatically operate when any type of uncomfortable feeling arises. The cycle of personal addiction is now born and in full force for keeping your life developmentally stuck and frozen in the past, with no new emotional insight. It is nearly impossible to break down your inner walls of childhood protection without a higher perspective. What is always possible is to begin to interrupt your entrenched cycle of avoidance/addiction with your enlightened mindful self. It takes a third-party invention (your spiritual-self) to break into your cycle of emotional paralysis. Your ego isn't a neutral or useful third-party to any lasting change or spiritual insights.

> *"Everyone is gifted, but most people never*
> *open their package!"*
> —Dr. Farrah Gray

Taking off Your "Spiritual Blinders in Life"—The cycle of addiction and avoidance has no tolerance or patience for you to open, uncover and discover your gifts and abilities (your mission). Your self-serving ego has no interest in this at all and will create masterful emotional blocks on your inward path. I want to illustrate how avoidance is a common reaction and standard operating procedure for people (no one is exempt) along their life/

spiritual path. Let's accept that we all avoid things at times to a greater or lesser degree. The ultimate cure for any avoidance or addictive behavior is to replace them with approach behaviors. It's a personal blind spot and somewhat arrogant to think *"I don't have any areas in my life that I avoid."* Everyone has some aspect of their inner life that is not completely in conscious view/feeling for safety reasons. The primary problem, concern, and issue with any type of avoidant and addictive behavior are that it keeps us from new personal insights or discovering our inner gifts and purpose.

Avoidance blinds us from clearly seeing our own life journey and the pitfalls that are along the road of life. The box/present within our heart and soul is always waiting to be opened and used. *It can't be opened if you're avoiding the pain and reoccurring personal/spiritual issues of your life.* Your gifts in this life are all part of your learning and growing process. You have all the gifts and talents necessary to manage, address and overcome any trauma along your journey. This isn't to minimize anyone's struggle and suffering, but quite the opposite. Dealing with your avoidance is a very empowering and life-changing action to access other parts of your destiny.

Your Undiscovered Personal Treasures—Avoidance/addictive behaviors are like standing outside your own house and wondering why you can't unwrap the presents in your own living room; it's because you're "removed." Avoidance always distances you from what you want, who you desire to become and what you secretly hope and crave. The gifts within you are always available if accessed by you. It's impossible to know your gifts if they are left unwrapped and unopened. You know how it feels to give a gift, and the person doesn't open it but rather sets its aside. What's worse is that they reject your gift even though you know that they truly want it. It's an emotionally awful feeling, and it's very insensitive of the recipient to reject your present. The same is true when the universe gives you gifts and you reject them outright or refuse to open and use them! The spirit (your gift giver) inside of you is repressed by the denial and avoidance of your gifts, passions, and purposes.

In my psychological practice over the years, I have found that clients who protest that they have no avoidant behaviors are usually in some type of major emotional denial. The particular issue or personal challenge that is repressed inside of them many times is connected to extremely sensitive issues such as sexual orientation, sexual abuse, self-loathing and/or a personal shame-based secret (alcoholism, gambling, sexual deviance). Regardless, no one is without some degree of denial and avoidance that can be reduced and healed. Our ego is extremely judgmental of us when we begin to uncover, reveal, and heal our inner wounds and hurts. The ego knows that its grip and control is completely lost when you begin to discover the life within you. The two stories below illustrate the power of avoidance and addiction in service of not re-experiencing the trauma of terror, loss and hopelessness.

Mike's Story—Avoidance of His Life: On the surface Mike's story is very compelling and seems obvious that he would have some ongoing residual denial, terror and avoidance/addictive behaviors. His experience is similar to people who have experienced a tremendous personal loss that remains frozen on their personal path. Mike is a 44-year old young man, smart, soft-spoken, recently divorced for the third time, and not knowing how to emotionally move beyond his teenage crisis. When Mike was 16 years old, he came home on a Friday night after a high school party to find that his father had hung himself f in their family garage. When Mike used the automatic garage door opener, he found his deceased father's body hanging there. Mike's father (Stan) had struggled with making and losing millions of dollars on shaky real estate investments. Stan had now recently lost several properties to foreclosure and was facing bankruptcy. Stan always joked that he was worth more dead than alive. Unfortunately, Mike never believed his father would ever really be that despairing or serious about killing himself (otherwise he would have sought psychological help for his father). Mike's mother, Joanne, was a family practice medical doctor who carried the family finances during the down cycles. Mike had no idea or indication that his father was suicidal or desperate enough to take his life. The entire family was in shock about the suicide. The family never went to grief counseling or individual/family therapy to emotionally process their loss.

According to Mike, for the 10 years after his father's death, he was a "zombie," just walking through the motions of his life. Mike felt that his whole world stopped moving, and he mentally was always seeing his father's limp cold body in the garage (Mike had grabbed his father's body and tried to wake him up). Shortly afterward, he attended an Ivy League university (Princeton) back east as a freshman, but transferred to a local Los Angeles university after his freshman year. Mike left Princeton because he knew he was emotionally avoiding his father's death and thought being back in L.A. would help. He dropped out of college after his sophomore year and started working as physical fitness trainer at a local gym. After his three-year marriage to an old high-school girlfriend abruptly ended, Mike moved home at age 29 to live with his mother. His first wife got Mike to commit to a 30-day hospitalization treatment program for his marijuana addiction. Mike never stopped smoking and his marriage was not reconciled or healed. Mike has been divorced three times. All three ex-wives had the same complaint—that his marijuana addiction was the primary reason for their leaving. Mike will argue that they (the three ex-wives) just didn't understand him (denial at its finest).

Mike began to smoke large quantities of marijuana (at least four times a day) immediately after his father's death until the present day (now age 44). Prior to his father's death he rarely (three or four times) smoked. Mike calls himself a functional stoner, meaning that he is able to get out of his house every day and train his clients. One of the major problems with his self-medicating behavior (marijuana addiction) is that it has created two major depressive episodes in Mike's life—one at 23 and the other at 38 years old. Each time he had to be put into a psychiatric hospital for inpatient treatment for marijuana (cannabis)-induced depression.

Mike's three older sisters had a strained relationship with their father. Mike now acknowledges that his chronic marijuana use could be related to never dealing with the loss of his father and all the personal and family changes that transpired afterwards. Yet he still isn't willing to address his current emotional decline, numerous romantic heartbreaks/divorces and lack of passion for his life. Mike is burned-out on Mike. Mike is adamant that he isn't physically or emotionally dependent or addicted to marijuana (no-one is ever addicted while being addicted). Mike argues with me about the abundance of evidence (his emotionally avoidant lifestyle) pointing to his profound emotional dependency on marijuana as a reaction to the loss of his father.

Mike's mother remarried within three years of his father's death to a neighbor who knew his father. Shortly after his father's death, all three of his sisters moved away from Los Angeles to the East Coast. His father's parents told Mike that his father's death was an accident; it was a result of difficult marriage to his mother; and not of his fathers "own doing." All of these factors had Mike in a chronic state of emotional numbness, and now the marijuana was no longer keeping his head calm or silent. In fact, he was having recurring dreams about seeing his father's drooping face and limp body hanging in the garage. Recently, his own medical doctor told Mike that if he didn't stop smoking and abusing alcohol he would not live to his 50th birthday. In addition, his mother and stepfather recently threw him out of the family home. Mike is currently living with his new girlfriend and her 15-year-old son. Mike loves her son, but his father died from a drug overdose when he was eight years old. Mike and this boy are both "fatherless sons," regardless of their age.

Linda's Story: Addiction to Love and Red Wine—Linda is a 60-year-old woman who is going through her second divorce from a verbally abusive husband. Linda tells me the following: *"My second husband, Jeff, is meaner and more verbally abusive than my first one."* Her second husband is a very successful investment banker who owns his own company. They have been married for 12 years. Linda's first marriage lasted 24 years. She was single for only two years after her first divorce prior to marrying Jeff. Linda grew up in Pacific Palisades, a very affluent beach community in the suburbs of Los Angeles, California. Marguerite, her mother, was an immigrant from Madrid and very a passionate woman. Her father, Bradley, was a traveling salesman in the life insurance business and was on the road three out of four weeks every month during her childhood and adolescence. Linda describes herself as a rebellious teenager because of her mother's strict European parenting style. She would sneak out of her house as teenager and go to nightclubs in Hollywood and Sunset Strip. Linda also experimented with a wide range of drugs as a teen. Her drug then and now is alcohol. Marguerite believed that corporal punishment for children was the only way they learned manners and responsibility. Linda openly admits that her mother would have emotional melt-downs and then become physically abusive to her and her two younger siblings. Linda ran away from home at age 18 and lived in New York City for several years until her met her first husband, Ray. She was a bartender and freelance artist prior to being married in her early twenties.

Linda came to see me because she wanted to heal and stop her people-pleasing tendencies. She doesn't believe she has a drinking problem regardless of her numerous monthly drinking blackouts. Linda felt that her drinking was caused by her husband's "meanness," but it was now under control. She does report that her two adult children think she drinks too much and should stop. Linda isn't receptive or open to discussing her possible addiction or abuse of alcohol. She is currently dating a new man who she met at a wine-tasting event in Napa Valley, California's wine country. Linda doesn't believe that there is a direct emotional connection between her mother's abusive behavior, the abusive men she picks, chronic drinking and always wanting a man in her life. However, Linda is open to considering that her drinking does cloud her emotional judgment at times and contributes to her depressed feelings and despair.

Psychology of Denial: No More Detours—

> *"Until you have felt your own pain, you*
> *Cannot feel the pain of others."*
> —*Gary Zukav*

In the quote above, Gary Zukav, a modern-day spiritual teacher and author (see bibliography for his outstanding books), sums up the reason to go beyond our denial, avoidance and addictive behaviors to move into our potential and unlimited possibilities.

Mike and Linda have both began to dig below the surface of their repetitive addictive behaviors that were becoming more and more self-defeating and problematic. Each of them acknowledged that their childhoods were severely painful and are a big source of their sadness. On the surface, they seemed to have very different stories, yet they were both profoundly impacted by their unresolved life lessons from their childhood-teenage years. The idea of re-experiencing their losses from their teen years seemed too painful and impossible to heal. The idea of re-experiencing the emotional terror of complete powerlessness was to be avoided at all costs. Yet the average psychological, emotional age of all addictive behaviors is 15 years old, according to extensive research from the Alcoholics Anonymous (AA) World Services Organization. Mike and Linda both felt that their ability to handle or cope with difficult situations was indeed at the level of a teenager—15 years old. Teenagers believe that their life is "infinite" and long-term consequences don't apply to their particular circumstances. Hence, 15 years old is the emotional age of denial, avoidance and addictive behaviors. Regardless of an adult's chronological age, they are never emotionally older than a 15-year-old teenager.

Your Avoidance & Addiction Take-Home Exam—All avoidant personalities, addictive behaviors and related emotional behaviors have to be self-diagnosed and treated. Medical, psychological and cognitive behavioral handbooks underscore the importance that the subject (you) be objective and honest in your appraisal of your conscious and unconscious behaviors. Mike and Linda answered the questions below and found them to be enlightening and many times difficult to answer either true or false. Yet they both found their emotional default was to clearly avoid, dismiss and downplay part of their present day self-medicating behaviors in service of avoiding their present and future responsibilities. Psychological research has reported for decades that typically 15-year-olds tend to have a world-view sense of invincibility, no insight into future consequences and omnipotence (they rule the world). The 15-year-old adolescent mindset considers only that living for today has little or no consequence on tomorrow or even later today. This sense of recklessness is the common developmental age (15), and emotional wiring of the avoidant-addictive personality and all their associated behaviors. Consider the following questions with either a true or false answer. Answer with the first impression or thought that comes to mind. There are no wrong answers. You don't have to be emotionally guarded or defensive about your current actions. Your goal is to move beyond any avoidant-addictive cycle you're stuck in.

Something to Consider: Mark either a (T) for true if this applies to you or (F) for false if this question doesn't apply to you. Don't edit or amend your first response:

- Do you tend to avoid potentially uncomfortable emotional encounters or situations?
- Do you crave immediate relief from an uncomfortable emotional encounter?
- Do avoid new situations (relationships) for fear of being rejected or exposed?
- Do you get absorbed in your job to the exclusion of other parts of your life?
- Do you feel uncomfortable being alone?
- Do you have music, noise, and electronics (cell phones) always around for immediate connection to you and your world?
- Do you have difficulty allowing your mind to slow down and be still?
- Do you acknowledge that you distract yourself from feeling anger, sadness or grief?
- Do you fear the idea of becoming older?
- Do you tend to resist expressing your thoughts and feelings?
- Do you love escape activities in your daily life whenever possible?
- Do you feel invincible in terms of food, drinks, drugs and smoking?
- Do you avoid feeling low or blue?
- Do you over-schedule yourself for fear of having nothing to do?
- Do you fear being lonely or alone on Friday night or weekends?
- Do you prefer animals to human connections?
- Do you prefer nonverbal (emails, texting, social media) types of communication rather than speaking or meeting in person?
- Do you seek the approval and acceptance of others continually before your share personal information?
- Do you share with anyone in your life your personal wishes, intimate desires and fears?
- Do you avoid being emotionally vulnerable for fear of criticism?

- Do you avoid any type of critical feedback from your peers/friends?
- Have you been told that you have a drinking problem or substance abuse issue?
- Have you ever been arrested for drunk driving or any related intoxication behavior?
- Do you always have to be moving or be constantly busy?
- Do you acknowledge you had a difficult childhood or some type of traumatic event in your past?
- Do you describe yourself as having low self-esteem or lacking self-worth?
- Do you feel inferior to others?
- Do you tend to exaggerate ordinary events in your life?
- Do you fear being embarrassed in new situations or relationships?
- Do you avoid new social or work activities for fear of criticism, disapproval or rejection?

Where Do All Your Dots Connect?—What question or series of questions spoke to you? Which ones described how you might avoid or have a tendency to be impulsive/addictive? This list is for you to see yourself from 10,000 feet rather than at your daily street-level perspective. Stepping back from your automatic psychological responses and looking at why, how and when they become so strong and powerful is a productive exercise. There is always a thread, connection and insight to anything you do that seems addictive/avoidant and makes you feel powerless. If you tend to be avoidant, addictive and/or fearful of rejection, loss or being dismissed it is now a great time to remove these types of reactionary roadblocks to your inner happiness and spiritual purpose.

All avoidant behaviors have their roots in some type of unresolved trauma in your past. Resolving your past emotional blocks isn't about blaming (yourself or others), but rather it's about accepting the path that your life has taken you on for your own spiritual awakening. Your life is waiting for you to step around these very old beliefs, emotional blocks and detours on your journey. The quote below outlines how much your life changes when you emotionally step away from the ego's control of your life (avoidance/addiction) to allow your inner strength (soulfulness) to engage your life.

"When you start living in accordance with the soul
*joy **overtakes** negativity,*
*abundance **overtakes** limitlessness,*
*peace **overtakes** chaos."*
—*James Van Praaugh*

Power of Addictive Avoidance: Emotional Paralysis—The questions above have several themes running throughout. What theme stood out to you with the questions that you answered "true?" Were there any questions you skipped over? For the sake of review, some of the common underlying emotional-psychological issues with avoidant/addictive behaviors are low self-esteem (emotional neglect), self-hatred (victim of abuse), and a low tolerance for frustration (feelings of loss). Do you notice in your relationships any threads of self-doubt or the fear of rejection? Do you often feel emotional impatience for any type of perceived rejection or misunderstanding? Do you notice your hesitation to engage in new personal, social, or work situations where the potential for rejection or emotional exposure is high? The automatic emotional tendency of the avoidant-addictive personality is to always be protected and make safe choices that insulate themselves from any type of perceived potential rejection or criticism. This unconscious-conscious automatic protective emotional barrier (we all have one) keeps you from experiencing your inner loving self. What happens to all of us to a greater or lesser degree is that our wounded (inner child) self-reinforces our deepest unspoken feeling of self-loathing, or in more severe cases, self-hatred.

All the activities, motivations, personal choices of the addictive or avoidant adult tend to be centered on the need to protect the highly sensitive heart and soul of the wounded man/woman. It's a fact that we are all wounded. No one is excused from the harsh realities (emotional pain and suffering) of this dark foreign land (disconnection from your intuitive self) that we all travel through along the road back to our original destination. There is no shame or rejection in being open and honest with our emotional pain and fears. Wisdom dictates that we resolve, heal, and continue developing our loving self-acceptance in spite of our deepest resistances. It's the height of narcissism, arrogance, and the scared ego to assume that you have no wounds or healing that needs to be addressed or resolved. **No one is exempt, excused or dismissed from their personal transformation journey!** We all have a journey to walk regardless of our resistances, turbulence or crisis. You wouldn't be living in your body, current life, and relationship circumstances if you and your soul didn't have specific lessons for you to master. Few people acknowledge the universal truth about our common vulnerability to and emotional struggles for self-love, self-forgiveness, and acceptance (who ultimately doesn't want that?). There is an old saying, *"We all have feet of clay,"* meaning that we are all perfectly imperfect and wounded while walking along our life/spiritual path.

No Time Limit on Healing: It's Ongoing—The avoidant/addictive man or woman believes that if they address their repressed emotional pain, rejections, losses or disappointments they will be simply die. This illusionary ego-driven irrational belief couldn't be any further from the truth or the divine life/spiritual purpose of any man or woman. Everyone can heal and awaken along the way of their own creatively designed life/spiritual journey. It doesn't matter how far away you feel from your higher-self (illusion) or the tragedies you are involved in. It's remarkable that everything works out in a brilliant unbelievable manner. No one could write or create the miraculous stories of how the universe (spirit of life within you) finds the threads of hope in your darkest and most painful moments. It's astounding how your life will come together when you have just about given up on yourself and your intuitive inner nature. *Spiritual awakening happens when you aren't even looking for it.* The avoidant-addictive personality doesn't believe or trust their life path enough to allow the process of change to be completed. The avoidant adult doesn't want to feel or allow for the uncertainties of current relationships to unfold. It feels easier to leave (die) or hide/numb-out (addiction) than wait in the balance of love vs. rejection. Ultimately, your inner emotional, psychological, and physical *healing process will require you to stop avoiding the "pink elephant" in your own metaphoric living room.* There is nothing in your life that will derail your purpose once you decide. What does slow down, impede, and detour your journey is always you and your resistance to your bigger life plan.

No More Silence—The avoidant-addictive emotional personality mindset only furthers a person's silent suffering and despair. The most effective, clinically proven and timeless spiritual truth for this type of suffering is taking direct action (lovingly inspired). Approach-direct behavior allows you to address within yourself what prevents you from feeling complete, safe and spiritually connected to your life purpose. All addictive behaviors have one primary purpose in mind—to avoid any uncomfortable feelings which might be emotional deadly and endless. The fear-based lifestyle approach of not feeling vulnerable, taking no chances, and never feeling rejected is painfully limited and lonely. *Our losses are never losses, but part of the powerful process of our own transformation.* All your life lessons ultimately require that you approach the underlying issues of your own emotional pain, unspoken fears, and self-doubts. Embracing your loving self-acceptance process is the fastest direction for removing any and all roadblocks on your life/spiritual path. Developing your inner self-acceptance (spiritual awaking) is taking direct, productive action to healing the lost wounded boy or girl within you.

The Drive Home: Your Freedom—Another way to think about the long-term damaging impact of avoidance is how your inner child feels about it. Any type of avoidance and all addictions are akin to leaving your vulnerable, adorable four-year-old little boy/girl waiting for a ride home after school. The painful image is that of a child sitting on the bench outside of school; it's dark, cold and everyone else has already gone home. You don't want to ever be that parent to your own children or to yourself. Metaphorically, you don't want to forget your responsibility to pick-up, nurture, and embrace that adorable young child within you! Your heart's imperative is *"I must go immediately and get that little boy or girl."*

Drive, run, fly past all the roadblocks and hug that scared, frighten, neglected perplexed little boy or girl. Remember that he/she has been waiting all of your life for you to come to the rescue. That child has appeared to you in so many different situations and personal circumstances, always hoping to get your undivided attention. It's worth the emotional (metaphorical) drive regardless of the neighborhoods (unresolved issues, Valley of Despair) of your life that you need to go through. Take the fastest, most direct route to your heart and soul. Ask yourself, like Linda and Mike had to: "Why don't I go get my child? What am I scared of? What will happen if I look him in the eyes and apologize for my absence? What will I do when I connect to him again?" The questions are endless, and all the answers are the same: take direct loving action. Remember that you always know what that next step requires. Don't focus on the long staircase, just on the very next step. For both Mike and Linda, the next step meant getting physically sober so they could begin to feel their emotions and repressed unresolved pasts. The scared lost child within them had been screaming for their attention for years with a series of emotional meltdowns and tantrums. Neither Linda nor Mike ever considered that their extreme emotional reactions to things were in part motivated by their wounded inner child.

"Our lives improve only when we take chances and the first and most difficult risk we can take is to be honest with ourselves."
—W. Anderson

When we are scared, frightened, panicked, anxious or procrastinating, we will find creative and ingenious ways to stay removed from our inner spiritual self-awareness. Our activities, work, leisure hours, drugs of choice are all purposeful in keeping us away from our higher empowered self. Like the quote says, "honest with ourselves" is the first step to stopping your self-defeating cycle of avoidance/addiction. Your personal history is what you are avoiding in the present. *Don't allow your history to define your life!* What is happening today isn't your childhood or what Linda and Mike went through as young teens. The avoidance and addictions are only replays of the past, every single day, 30 years later. We all act, avoid and at times hide from ourselves (inner child) because we lose contact with our inner true loving self. We feel like an orphan within ourselves with no one caring or loving us. Direct action within yourself (loving self-acceptance) will always heal, empower, and move you forward. Only you know what the next step to take is.

No More Repeats of History—Now you can *consider the idea that you are no longer defined by your history*; this is a staggering game-changing concept. Removing and peeling back the layers and layers of denial, anger, and embedded defensive behavior is the foundation and pavement for your life path. Part of the solution to your current crisis will always include taking approach behavior actions and exploring all your present day options. What would you feel like for a few minutes if you let go of all your resentments, avoidance, emotional vices and addictive behaviors? What would you do differently? Who would you call? Who would you tell? Who would you be without your denial? What would you feel inside of your heart, your body and your mind? How would your addictive drug usage change?

Undoubtedly, the power and courage to move beyond your losses, heartbreaks, and self-destructive choices is your royal highway to fulfilling your inner purpose/mission and life lessons. Linda and Mike both had to approach their painful teenage years. There wasn't enough alcohol or marijuana that could silence the inner fear/despair that was always on the periphery of their minds in calm moments. They both had to accept that nothing had been lost, only disconnected from within. Their up-and-down life/spiritual paths got them to where they needed to be today. Their act of self-forgiveness is considered by spiritual masters as the greatest single act of love. Self-acceptance of your heartbreaking circumstances always opens the doors of your heart and life to this moment and wipes out the power of your past. All addictions and avoidant personality styles lose their purpose and need in your life when the painful source is revealed, healed and understood. You no longer need to numb-out from your current life experiences or avoid your past emotional disappointments. All our behaviors are purposeful, even the self-destructive ones. Approaching yourself with loving self-acceptance, exposing and healing your inner demons displaces all self-defeating behaviors, beliefs and emotional malaise.

"You have been told about the survival of the fittest and the victory of the strongest, yet little is said about the glory of the most loving. When you choose the action love sponsors, then you will do more than survive, you will do more than win. You will experience the full glory of who you really are!"
—*Neale Donald Walsch*

Approaching Your Next Step—One of the first steps with any avoidant-addictive behavior starts with self-acceptance. Many times the biggest barrier to removing any type of avoidant and addictive behaviors is the need to finally accept and forgive yourself for your perceived losses or mistakes. The greatest loss (your negative ego inner voice) tells you that your life is beyond the reach and recovery of meaningful life purpose. The emotional horror that you somehow "screwed up" your entire life isn't true. Never forget that your ego (non-spiritual side) is a drama queen implying that everything in your life is lost, ruined and beyond repair. What is more accurate is that you might be completely sidetracked and stalled out in your life, family, career, health and finances. The displacements of your old outdated avoidant-addictive styles of ignoring yourself are now unnecessary. Regardless of what happened, what you did or didn't do is no longer relevant. What is relevant is approaching the tasks, issues and people (yourself) necessary to take the next step.

Many times the next step is about allowing yourself to accept what seems unacceptable. The last chapter of this roadblock section is about forgiveness. The topic of forgiveness is always as emotionally, psychologically and physically charged as any topic we have discussed on the road of your life. No one is neutral about the concept of forgiveness and how it works in relationships, past and present. In the quote above, Neale Donald Walsch is discussing that we all win. There is the spiritual secret that this entire school-of-life education is all about you becoming the highest and greatest version of yourself. *Your life isn't about winning, but rather becoming!* Your life was never about winning and making sure no one passes you up. Becoming never implies crushing or stepping on your romantic partner, others or business colleagues. Your path isn't about all the material things—as we have previously discussed throughout the book.

Becoming requires approaching your secrets, your shadow self, and developing full self-acceptance. The greatest barrier that all addictions, avoidances perform is keeping you detached from fully living in the present moment without the fear of being too vulnerable. Allowing this ultimate act of forgiveness requires that we let go of our perceived failings, tragedies, heartbreaks, financial losses, differences, resentments, anger, and status symbols of success. Becoming who you desire to be and being in a calm emotionally balanced place starts with forgiveness. In the beginning of this chapter, the short story about the king sending you into a distant, dark land for only one purpose should always be someplace in your mind and part of your ultimate destination. Finding our ultimate purpose involves loving ourselves in spite of how we got to this present moment in time.

Love Always Prevails—Your journey might have been extremely painful to the casual outside observer, but where you needed to be at this point and place in your life is perfect. In order to launch your life forward with emotional/mental clarity, passion and never-ending purpose requires a certain degree of personal understanding of your own forgiveness. The next doorway to your emancipation from avoidance-addictive self-loathing behaviors leads to finding your purpose and goes through the Valley of Healing. Consider that Linda's and Mike's ultimate challenge was self-forgiveness for their parent's behaviors and their powerful reactions to those behaviors. They both had to personally accept that they weren't responsible for their parent's choices and emotional pain. Mike struggled with letting it all go (sadness) to make room for his present day life. Linda had to stop blaming herself for the fact that her mother wasn't able to manage her own life.

In the next chapter let's explore what you secretly hold onto that is wrong about you. What is your own personal grudge against yourself, against life, against God and against your loved ones? You have decided to not avoid, get stoned or drunk in order to feel the full force of your life. Your priority is connecting to those lost parts of yourself. It's unnecessary to try to avoid your life; it is now no longer an option.

"Action expresses priorities."
—Mahatma Gandhi

Your life is a personal priority, and self-forgiveness is part of your process. No matter what you stop avoiding within you, stopping self-medicating behavior (any addiction) is always an excellent step forward on your life-long spiritual journey. Consider the following quote as a road sign along the highway of your spiritual journey. There will always be signs, wonders and direct hints of what to do, who to see and where to go. Your responsibility is to take your next step without pause. Your inward being/ soul is always urging you to move forward. It isn't the size or magnitude of your action, but rather the action you take based on a premise of love and self-acceptance.

> *"Sometimes the smallest step in the right direction ends up being the biggest step of your life. Tip toe if you must but take the step."*
> —*Lao Tzu*

Chapter 8

Your Self-Forgiveness and Unforgivable Factor—The End of Your Road

*"Forgive yourself! And then Forgive yourself again
and again, and keep doing it until you believe it."*
—Sue Fitzmaurice

*"We are here to accept ourselves and others with love and compassion. If we
could learn this one thing, we would feel more content and
enjoy our time on earth."*
—James Van Praaugh

Your **Big Step into Your Awaking**—These two quotes above are an excellent introduction to what many scholars, psychologists, spiritual masters and religious leaders over the centuries consider the single biggest action you will ever take or do in your life: *Self-Forgiveness!* Forget about forgiving others, your parents, ex-husband/wife or that hated abusive monster-person in your past. It's all about YOU doing the impossible—forgiving and accepting yourself! The ongoing task of forgiving requires that you look at your life from a completely different perspective, one with genuine nonjudgmental concern and compassion for the person who needs it most, and that would be you! Yes, you need to experience the fresh spring breeze of self-acceptance, self-love, understanding and empathy for you and within you. It goes without saying, but let me say it anyway: ***The degree to which you forgive yourself will be the same as that which enables you to forgive others in your past/present life.*** There is a direct correlation between forgiving yourself and others. Simply put, you can't give what you don't have (forgiveness). There is absolutely no way or any remote possibility of changing your life or making any significant lasting changes in it without walking down the road of self-forgiveness and self-acceptance. This is the crossroad on your path, road, and journey where many intelligent men/women say "no-way, I am not doing it." The adamant resistance to any type of reconciliation, forgiveness, and pardoning is always at that individual's own peril. The secret to life: It is within your heart to do what common sense wisdom (ego) considers impossible and completely unnecessary. In the last chapter, death is depicted as mindless and clueless, which is our non-spiritual approach to love, forgiveness and self-acceptance. Following your ego is your own personalized form of spiritual death/denial. Forgiveness is the cure to all the metaphorical dead parts within your heart, your life and your relationships. Living your life to its fullest spiritual potential with lasting inner peace, acceptance and joy are all by-products of your ability to be forgiving of yourself and of your loved ones.

Living Forward and Letting it Go—There is a direct correlation between love, acceptance/forgiveness and happiness, and accessing your divine intuitive nature and developing your life purpose—they are all related. Forgiveness is an automatic school-of-life course requirement in order to fully experience your next chapter of living at this point in your journey. *Without developing an open attitude of forgivenes toward yourself and others, there is no chance of ever achieving any degree of lasting inner peace and comfort. None!* Let's refer to your self-forgiveness process on this part of your trip as the true starting point for the second half of your life. The idea that you are entering into uncharted territory and moving toward the practice of personal and spiritual understanding via your roadway of forgiveness is courageous. This is a brand new highway for you to discover. It's an absolute deal breaker for your emotional growth and spiritual transformation to resist your personal experience of forgiveness. Your inner heart and soul are craving the relief and new energy that comes from letting go of all your past resentments and betrayals. Without the spirit of forgiveness and compassion, transcending your own old capacity for giving and receiving, love is greatly limited. Holding onto your resentments and lists of wrongs only increases your suffering with no possibility of a new resolution. All your detours, romantic relationships, career crisis, different paths, challenges and heartbreaks have led you to experiencing your untapped inner power of love in a new way. The ultimate master key to unlocking all your potential starts with allowing yourself to become more accepting, compassionate and insightful of your past mistakes, impulsive choices and "crazy" moments. Men and women struggle with accepting that they weren't at their best when they chose self-defeating actions (who is ever at their best when they've acted out?). Your life/spiritual journey is all about realizing that your life isn't beyond the reach or compassion of the universe. Everything can be resolved from a higher perspective than on the level it occurred.

Closing Doors and New Openings—Self-love via the direct route of forgiveness is your fast lane to transforming your life and your entire world. If you're in a hurry to heal and straighten things in your marriage, career, family, friends, then practice giving and receiving forgiveness. Your sincere heartfelt forgiveness for yourself and others immediately widens your personal acceptance, tolerance and understanding of who you were and are becoming. We have all had ridiculous moments and crazy phases of life. No one is exempt from the experience of being human and imperfect.

The "Art" of Forgiveness—Never forget that humility is the first cousin of forgiveness. Its takes an incredible amount of courage, honesty and humility to say to yourself and to any of your relationships (i.e., parents, children, romantic partners, colleagues, and siblings) something like this: *"Please excuse me. I was totally incorrect and I apologize for what I said, have done, and incorrectly assumed. Please accept my deepest apologies and regrets. I didn't mean to hurt or harm you or blow up our marriage/business. It's unacceptable, but nonetheless please accept my sincere apologies. I appreciate what you have meant to me, and I hope you have room in your heart for my sincere regrets. If you can't accept my apology, I understand because I accept* *my responsibility for hurting you, and hurting us."* These types of heartfelt apologetic statements are very powerful tools in helping you to come clean about your shame and unresolved resentments towards yourself and others.

Many people immediately scream, argue, adamantly protest and insist that they want nothing to do with this "psycho-babble" or religious jargon about forgiving themselves or others. The ego will argue that some things (actions, people) are simply unforgivable. I don't know if that is true, because we are not on the other side of this life where everything gets enlightened and evaluated. What is true universally is that forgiveness is one of the ultimate acts of love and spiritual mastery. What is important is for you to detach and forgive yourself for holding onto any long-term resentment, abuse and/betrayal. The concept of looking inwardly at your life and not holding onto your past painful life lessons because your ego was bruised is a very powerful course of action.

The Biggest Loser: Your Ego—The only reason for letting go of your resentment, blame and revenge is accepting your spiritual awaking journey: *You need every experience, disappointment and challenge to open your heart to the possibility that your ego isn't God.* Your ego is part of this life/body but not part of your destiny and soul connection to your higher-self. Putting your ego in time-out is one of the fastest ways to begin to experience the full force of your own self-acceptance and self-forgiveness. Your ego doesn't have a vote, or a voice, or an opinion that is of any use to your inner awakening and spiritual transformation. *None.* Going beyond your ego's resistance and viewing your life journey with more compassion and understanding is necessary to be able to detach from your emotional anger. Resisting your ego's natural impulse for revenge is in itself an act of forgiveness within your heart and mind. The emotional transaction of allowing yourself to step back from your broken heart, disappointments, impulsive decisions, anger (ego) or resentment are all pieces of your self-forgiveness and self-acceptance. We will discuss these action steps later is this chapter.

Your Heart Bolted Shut—*Let's settle the issue right now: everything is forgivable!* The only thing that is unforgivable is an ego-driven life that rejects the concepts of love, self-acceptance and forgiveness. As I stated previously, many people, regardless of their pain, want to hold onto the belief that some things are unforgivable, and the person or people involved should rot in hell. The unforgivable sentiment is powerful and can become a wild fire (uncontrollable anger) within the entire psyche/soul of the person who embraces it. The short-term and long-term issue is that this fire of passion tends to badly scorch both the holder and recipient involved. A famous writer, Oscar Wilde, perfectly describes what happens when love enters into a seemingly unforgivable situation. The egos get upset and the souls are relieved.

"Always forgive your enemies; nothing annoys them so much!"
—Oscar Wilde

One result of unforgivable feelings is that the raging anger becomes a lifetime personality pattern. In the worst-case scenario, there is a complete rejection of the power of love within your heart and soul that leads you to total despair and an emotional-spiritual impasse. I know this sounds very ominous, but it is the truth. We all know people whose lives have been entirely consumed with bitterness, contempt and hatred. These wounded individuals have completely lost their inner spiritual compass and are resigned to the ego's solution of revenge. Your ego isn't the source of healing or reconciling the issues of your heart/soul. Personal and relational forgiveness isn't an elective course option, but rather a life course requirement for moving forward on your own spiritual path. Forgiveness isn't an option in your life. It's part of your journey. Seeking revenge is like drinking poison and wondering why the other person isn't suffering while you are dying. Revenge (the ego's ultimate weapon-deception) burns all the parties involved—no one is healed or helped. Revenge is always acted upon in the complete absence of your intuitive self and sense of divine love.

The person (victim/you) who adamantly clings to the emotional position that they will never forgive or forget the horrible things that their father did or ex-partner did by running away from the family is going in the wrong direction. The list of wrongs can go on for several lifetimes with no spiritual relief or healing ever achieved or experienced.

The possibility for any type of loving healing action is impossible when we decide that our situation is unforgivable. *When you say NO to self-love and self-acceptance, your resistance turns into a mind, soul and heart-numbing approach to your life.* Don't panic if all of these concepts of forgiveness seem daunting and beyond your emotional capacity for change. I will explain further the actual process of forgiveness, detachment, and moving into your future without that 500-pound ball and chain of rage/resentment dragging behind you.

Healing Yourself: Three Phases—Resisting, fighting or ignoring your inner voice of wisdom can lead to many generations of rage and psychological/spiritual distress and misery. The discussion of the value for disconnecting, detaching and forgiving could very easily be its own book with volumes and volumes of timeless wisdom. For the purposes of our discussion, let's break down the forgiveness process into three introductory sections. *The stages are You, Them and Freedom.* Let's examine each of the three following quotes separately and look within for the needed action, truth and pearl of wisdom that each writer is presenting to you. It can take years and years of moments of emotional clarity and divine insight to fully see the merit of your own self-forgiving actions. This is right now one of those moments in your life. You wouldn't be reading this book and anticipating taking life changing actions if you weren't ready to reopen your heart. Whatever you do or think about this topic, consider your soulful and inner peace when choosing to let it all go.

Phase 1: I Really Don't Like You or Me

Everything that irritates us about others can lead us to an
understanding of ourselves"
—Carl Jung

This quote by Dr. Carl Jung is one of his fundamental psychological themes throughout his writings about our personal triggers, resentments and grudges with others. Dr. Jung's interpretation that our irritations with others provide information about our own personality issues is brilliant and 100% accurate! The most irritating issue, behavior or attitude that bugs us in others, all starts within you/us. The person in the mirror is usually the most difficult to see or to understand, and that person is you! The person looking back at you can't see the back of his own head. They can feel it, touch it, but never see it. The only way to see the back of your head is to hold up a separate mirror, or change the position of how you're looking at yourself.

The analogy is that what you see in the other isn't the primary relationship issue; it's your unresolved issue being reflected back to you. The truth is that your emotional triggers, relationship challenges and personality trait blind spots need to be seen by you. Judging and forming negative opinions of your mirror image in others is a relentless cycle of frustration. Hating others, resenting them, gossiping negatively about them always leaves the holder of the issue in a weakened and compromised emotional and psychological state. The negative energy that is generated within you about your own unresolved issues in others is a painful process in your daily life. No one is winning in your world when you dislike yourself! Disliking others always starts with you disliking yourself and that same unpleasant quality you both possess.

How Emotional Rigidity is Formed—For some reason (explained later), we tend to have 20/20 vision of the certain personality flaw or character deficiency in that particular person. Over time, the irrationality builds and the negative disowned parts (unresolved issues) of us begin to become a relationship style (barrier) in all areas of our world. This distorted emotional style is then projected onto those "types of people" without our conscious awareness. The barrier (distorted relationship) becomes our fixed perspective about what we are and how people in our world should be! Over time, our emotional and personality barrier/distortion becomes an automatic reaction within us. Our own unresolved issues are glaring in those around us—the ultimate blind spot in us.

Our own wall of isolation continues to be built within us with no clear insight. Understanding the irritations as valuable information about us allows us to discredit or dismiss our negative basis toward that person. *All forms of discrimination come from our fundamental root of blind projection onto others.* Dr. Jung believed that if a person/client was unaware of their psychological blind spots and struggles, he would encourage them to think about what bothers them in others to discover their own personal unresolved issues/problems. This sounds easy, but it's like seeing the back of the head. You can touch it and rub it, but you can't see it without a mirror or assistance. *Your blind spot can always be exposed and resolved with your active self-acceptance.*

Accept Your Personal Triggers—Take a moment to think of what person is the most irritating, annoying, hurtful or problematic to you? What do they do that is so troubling for you? What issue, trait or behavior disturbs you about them? What recent situation or event upsets you about them? Could you be struggling with the same or similar issue? Do you find that they are doing, saying or acting in ways that you resent? What scares you about accepting that your blind spot might be your own unresolved feelings about your partner, children, business, health, and yourself? Dr. Jung, Eastern philosophies and spiritual traditions subscribe to the notion that your blind spot is your own problems, issues or fears projected onto others. **The irritation isn't about the other person, but rather *your own unhealed emotional reaction within you about yourself.* Any type of** strong emotional reaction to someone's behavior, actions or attitude is an unhealed, unexplored issue within you—it's not about them. This is a very self-revealing, vulnerable and positive perspective to take and explore. People who emotionally trigger you are a wealth of untapped personal information about you and your current healing process. Don't avoid people who bother you, but accept that it is a means to understand what is going on within you. The information you gain about yourself from understanding others is one of the greatest emotional and psychological freedoms you can experience along your life/spiritual journey.

The "Jerk" Factor—Suppressing your loving forgiving insights might seem necessary to feel safe and justified during an argument or disagreement— but it's ultimately the wrong choice. Long-term avoidance of any degree of self-forgiveness and self-acceptance only reinforces your continual unhappiness, self-loathing and despair. The life path of self-acceptance always requires forgiving and accepting your past and present choices, decisions and old/new beliefs. Anyone in your life, at the store, at work, etc., who triggers a strong emotional response within you isn't just a jerk or an asshole; they are a deep well of untapped information about you. This no-jerk factor and "it's my problem" are issues as I write this chapter. No one is blaming or finger- pointing here. We are all growing, changing and transforming on our spiritual journey.

If you find that you vigorously hate someone, take another look at yourself and consider what is possibly off balance in your thinking about yourself? These people are simply reminders of your necessary ongoing healing process. Try to see the value of the problem person and challenging personalities in your immediate relationship circle; this is another spiritual mastery step. These strange irritating people, family members, neighbors, business colleagues, ex-husbands/wives, and parents are holders of priceless information about what issue you need to focus on for your continued evolution and healing in your life going forward. The greatest problem person in your life is one of your greatest spiritual gifts for your awaking and spiritual transformation: *What do they reveal about you?* Don't allow yourself permission to resent, dislike or hate someone because they upset you. Ultimately, your personality school-of-life challenges are always going to be revealed to you in the people surrounding your life.

Phase II: Losing Your Grip

"Forgiveness begins when you want the best for those people who have hurt you....despite the pain that they have caused you."
—*Bill Philipps*

Letting Go of Your Disappointment—This quote by Bill Philipps is about seeing the gift of heartbreak" within the context of a close personal, intimate or business relationship. It's important to remember that all your feelings of anger aren't about anger; rather they are your unresolved issues of deep personal disappointment. In my clinical practice over the last 30+ years, disappointment is one of the most dismissed, misunderstood and trivialized emotional experiences. I hear men/women of all ages say to themselves, *"Get over it, don't be a baby, get some backbone, disappointment is part of life."* This avoidant and bitter ego-driven sentiment is one of the primary reasons people are carrying their wounds, resentments/grudges and disappointments with them down their road of life and into their next life. These well-meaning people never consider the possibility that their romantic betrayals, losses, heartbreaks, and life- changing disappointments are all perfectly designed for their personal inward transformation. When we dismiss our life lessons, it is a complete rejection of the universe's genius in creating special circumstances to get your soulful attention. Resistance and denial of your inner feelings, thoughts, and intuitions cloud your ability to consider another perspective.

Accepting that these people (who is it for you?) are important players in your transformation process via your family, close friends, children, parents, your romantic partner, your business partner and yourself is critical. All these different people have made valuable contributions to your life journey up to this point. This perspective isn't from an ego self-serving or superficial material level but from a spiritual perspective that all things work together for your greater good. Attempting to see the value in your relationship struggles is a huge spiritual step forward. I know this is a complete game-changing spiritual shift—to go from resentment to self-forgiveness, compassion, understanding and experiencing love in action.

> *"We treat love and hate and the other emotions like they are all*
> *on the same level, but they aren't. Hate, fear, lust, greed, jealousy—all that*
> *comes from the ego. Only Love comes from the soul."*
> —*Ram Dass*

Love is Your Soul Passion—It is impossible to experience a sense of love, personal freedom and spiritual insights when you resist your own process of self-forgiveness. Your ego creates all the negative emotions within you that narrows and isolates your life from love and intimate relationships. Resentments, grudges, passive-aggressive vengeful behaviors (non-loving actions/beliefs) are absolutely incompatible to your life evolving forward with any degree of peace or happiness. Finding the inner courage to drop it, let it go and forget the issue with that particular person is one of life's greatest miracles. Who is that person in your life today? We all have one, me included. Can you imagine in your mind's eye reconciling yourself with this person and the circumstances surrounding your pain? How does it feel to let go of the anger, pain, negative energy and self-blame with that person and circumstances? How good does that feel? Remember that *allowing someone in your heart to no longer be held accountable for your struggles, pain and disappointments is an act of God within you.* Forgiveness is always a gracious act of God/Spirit coming through your life. If you wonder if God/Spirit exists, take the step and extend love and forgive your enemy. The experience of forgiving is timeless and connects you/us immediately to the greater universe. Forgiveness is an act of gratitude that transcends you and others with love!

The deliberate action of love (forgiving) is beyond this physical material-driven world and is your divine personhood emerging in your life. It is your higher (God within) self-taking action that will positively affect your present and future. The following is a universal spiritual truth that has nothing to do with what club or religious group you belong to: *There is nothing that can't be healed, resolved and detached from once you decide to stop being a victim of your own limitations and negative ego beliefs.* I know that this is a huge life statement, but I would never say it if I didn't personally know it to be a spiritual truth and a worthwhile experience. What stops your life flow and movement forward on your journey is that of allowing your past to become a fixture that will not allow new information to enter your heart and mind.

Removing Your Old Perfect Fixtures—First, part of this fixture phase/idea is realizing that most of our personality conflicts, resentments towards others, and prejudices all have to do with our fixed opinions on how our particular world should work (past, present and future). This rigid life approach applies to us and all the different people in our sphere of influence and living. Second, the biggest problem with our own fixed view is that it is usually in direct contradiction to the greater life plan for us and others. Third, over time, our fixed external and internal emotional state negatively impacts our entire life (physically, mentally, relationally, etc.) and the people in our life. *The development of fixed beliefs, opinions and attitudes does more damage to our life journey than any other single act or behavior.* Why? It's our staunch resistance to accept how the universe works in spite of our need to control the uncontrollable (other people). There is no way in this life, nor is it necessary that any of us know exactly why or how everything should be, could be, or must be. Fixed, rigid, and inflexible opinions are the foundation for the ego's building material for rejecting the process of your own self-forgiveness and self-love.

Change is an obvious element in the everlasting movement of life that tends to be ignored and forgotten. We want to create permanence when our life journey is all about managing our own constant impermanence/change. *The timeless struggle between imaginary permanence and impermanence is one of the core paradoxes in life.* Our divine connection is timeless, constant, and everything is changing within and around us. We simply don't need all that information about the process of the universe during this lifetime to fulfill our mission and purpose. The fixed personality has decided how their world should work, including everyone else's around them. This attitude decides who should be forgiven and who isn't worthy of forgiveness. Many times these personality types who are rigid, obsessive, and know it all are labeled as control freaks by their close friends and family.

Rigidity and the Power of Change—Another significant problem with the fixed perspective is that the universe and nature are in an ongoing and dynamic process of change: nothing is fixed or rigid. We have decided in the Western culture that we can predict forever; this is in direct contradiction to how the bigger world works. There is no forever, except your soul. Impermanence is a given life condition, as is the sun rising and setting each day. Change is going to happen regardless of what we think or want. *Change is a given human school-of-life-process.* Everything is changing every minute of your life. Our life is a process of continuous self-discoveries. Nothing is static in our life. ***Accepting the idea of impermanence is the spiritual air we breathe for our soul.*** Acceptance of your invaluable life changes allows your heart and soul to experience your limitless potential. Resisting change is what helps create a fixed, anxious, angry personality. The fixed life approach has no room for differences, self-forgiveness, change, or the natural evolution of things. Our deepest wounds are a result of how we continue to relive, day after day, how our ex-partner should have treated us or how our parents could have done a better job parenting. Our fixed personality beliefs, emotional wounds, rigid spiritual perspective and inner critical voice are the cement barriers in the middle of our life path. The fixed controlling belief system of the past, present, and future stalls you from moving beyond any and all of your painful life circumstances. Resistance and a lack of self-forgiveness to the on-going changes in your relationships, self-acceptance development, and spiritual insights is a dead-end street with no outlet or relief from the fear of living.

Important People—The true art of inner healing (forgiving self and others) is beginning to see the hidden value of the wounds that important people have caused in your life. Important people, from a spiritual perspective, not an ego perspective, tend to be the ones who have stirred up all of your fears, opened up wounds, and created huge emotional disappointments. Each of these people in your life are like a two- headed coin. One side is a magnet to your past with no new information—just anger, resentment, and blame. The other side draws you towards letting go of your past and being open minded to change in the present moment. There is an automatic response to one side of the coin or to the other when you see, hear or feel that particular trigger (old issue). *Removing the magnetic pull to your habitual thinking about the wrongs someone has done in your life is transformational at its deepest level.* You are starting to dismantle your old outdated structure of resentments, old beliefs, and old perspectives about you and your world. This action (forgiveness) to no longer being a victim to your past (no fixed opinions) and the people in it is your key to lasting happiness and peace of mind.

The key to the door of your inner peace starts with releasing old emotional attachments to resentments and being open to your bigger spiritual life perspective. We all want lasting inner peace and a deeper sense of security. Forgiveness is the door through which these natural human desires can be attained and experienced. It's no longer an option to live without inner peace. You can't bring your old suitcase of resentment or revenge into your new house. Your new perspective has no closet space for any type of non-forgiveness any longer. The biggest change to effect is leaving your old suitcase behind containing your ego's non-loving, fixed revengeful opinions.

Phase III: What Are You Holding Onto?

"Forgiveness opens the way to your Freedom"
—Jeff Van Praagh

Let's look at some very common themes of fixed thinking, resentment, an unforgiving attitude and living with one foot in the past and one foot in the future. Neither of these approaches (past and future) is for your highest and best good. Psychologically speaking, holding onto deep-seated old resentments and disappointments causes these to continually reappear in your life as your greatest source of emotional pain and wounding. Consider some of the different types of relationships that developed unforgiving, fixed, angry, unresolved personality issues: Parent child relationships, love/romance, no self-acceptance/shame, lack of your own individuality/fear, betrayal/disappointment, and physical health challenges. As you know now, these are the five common lightning rods for your self-awakening journey. We have all struggled with them at different points and times along our path. Often our handling of those situations feels like a complete disaster/failure and seemingly worse with our involvement. The long-term reality is that the failure, if there is one, is actually a lack of spiritual insight into the inherent value of these major disappointments on your life journey.

No More Running—All of these factors usually grab our full attention when our suffering (feelings of failing) exceeds our avoidance, denial, or resistance. Suffering ultimately will push you to reexamine your fixed anger, grudges, and your declarations of unforgivable deeds done to you. The correlation between emotional trauma/suffering and pleasure is a direct relationship: *When your tolerance for suffering and pain rises above your comfort level, that is when change (self-forgiveness) is in the air.*

The inner dynamic of change might have taken what seems like years upon years, but it does eventually get your full attention. It is only when we have exceeded our own high tolerance for suffering, self-abuse, and emotional pain that we consider other productive options for relief. It's at these precise moments that compulsive, addictive and/or self-defeating behaviors no longer work for the purpose of numbing our heart. Avoidance and resentment are no longer valid reasons for our emotional isolation/resistance to change and to healing. The learned practice of suppressing, tolerating, and avoiding our own imperative for change is amazing. We all know people who will spend a lifetime running from their shadow only to run right into at the next crisis. Let's look at some of the common pitfalls that impede our self-forgiveness and self-acceptance movement along our life path.

Peeling Away the Layers of Your Pain and Your Disappointment

"The worst thing is watching someone drown and not being able to convince them that they can save themselves by just standing up."
—Wayne Dyer

Your Process of Peeling Away Disappointment—You don't want to drown in your own misery, anger, or bitterness—right! Standing up in your life is stopping your own emotional suffering and detaching from your tired old rehearsed stories. No more "re-runs" of your painful story of resentment, betrayal, rejection, and blame. It's very important when exploring your inner raw nerves, sensitive issues and long-term struggles that you recognize that your healing isn't accomplished in a straight line or a one-time event. In fact, you will find that your healing is an ongoing process that peels layer upon layer off your heart. Your healing process isn't a destination, but rather an on-going journey into your spiritual awaking—never finished. You might think that you have resolved your anger toward your ex-partner, only to re-experience that old feeling of betrayal again when you see him.

The truth is that when you have resolved previous levels of resentment and the old familiar pain there is another new layer of healing. Self-forgiveness, self-acceptance and any act of loving forgiveness is not limited to a linear process. Reconciling with yourself is an abstract process that isn't bound to a one-time experience or special occasion. It's the fourth dimension of human experience that isn't bound by time, person or place. Rather, it's your healing, happening at this moment regardless of what has happened in the past. Your healing is a fluid process of connecting you to your spiritual path with new insights and compassion.

Game of Life Questions—The following lists of five common forks in your road are some jumping off points for your own self-exploration. Before we go any further, consider the following questions for clarity purposes:

- Who is the someone in your life past/present that seems to be an ongoing source of suffering for you?
- Who is one of the sources of your greatest wound?
- Who upsets you the most in your life?
- Consider each of the five following areas of personal transformation and growth for your next chapter in your life.
- What area (fearful) in your life are you holding onto that is holding you back from your destiny in this life?
- Who and what is it?
- Why are you holding onto to it so tightly?

Don't allow your ego or pride to gloss over this section and tell you everything is fine. We all have some tender sensitive spots of emotional healing that need to be addressed that are buried inside of our heart and soul. No one is exempt from the journey of self-realization all of its different relationship experiences. The awareness to allow yourself to feel and acknowledge your self-imposed life roadblocks is a very freeing experience—the net gain being inner peace and contentment.

Letting Go: The Big 5 Lighting Rods on Your Self-Forgiving Journey

#1—Your Parent-Child Relationship, Past, Present and Future: The misunderstandings that can be passed down from generation to generation are troubling. Resentment within a family can be passed along to the next generation the same way as your genetic DNA. Physical characteristics and emotional traits are all handed down throughout the emotional generational relationships and family behaviors. *What would you want to stop passing on?* Remember you can't let go of what you don't know you're holding onto—or admit to holding! Many adults, and myself included, had painfully turbulent childhoods with narcissistic (self-absorbed) parents. Taking an emotional step back from your aging or deceased parents is necessary to see the bigger picture of what role they played in assisting in your spiritual development.

The ego's insistence that all those wrongs from your early years can be righted by confronting or mistreating your parents now is incorrect and self-destructive. Any vengeful type of punitive thinking is illusive, damaging and never heals the situation or our inner pain. The deep emotional wounding from your childhood has to be exposed by you and released by you. No one can do it for you: No one. Your parents, dead or alive, don't have the means or ability to heal your pain—they just don't. *They might have been actively involved in your wounding, but ultimately it's your responsibility to heal yourself.* Your parents aren't the source or cause of your current issues; your choice to keep the past alive is your biggest challenge/problem. Reliving the past is a very strong psychological addiction to avoid dealing with your responsibility in the present moment. Your parents have their own spiritual issues to address within themselves, and it is not your place to correct or punish them.

Ending the Family War—No More Blaming. This isn't about what's fair or not, but rather your eternal soul/spirit being perfected through the fires of love. *Remember the first woman you ever loved was your mother, and the first man you loved was your father!* This unique relationship sets your parents apart from all the other relationships in your story. It's so disturbing to speak with a 27-year-old or a 70-year-old person who is still blaming their parents for their painful adult choices and disappointments. Blaming your parents for your current day suffering and emotional challenges is a short-sighted approach to the hardships of your long-term journey. Blame only reinforces your own personal sense of powerlessness and victimhood with whatever parent/issue that you're holding onto.

What parent carries the most resentment for you? Ladies/daughters—what did your father do or not do for you as a young girl growing-up? Maybe your father had an abusive personality and scared the whole family? Men/sons—what demands did your father place on you that could never be met or achieved? Did you suffer from an abusive parent/child relationship? We are all sons and daughters regardless of our age, education or wealth. No one is neutral about his problem parent. What action within you would help you to let go of your problem parent in your heart/soul?" I have had clients who resented their father for dying when they were 10 years old. I have had many clients who resented their mother for not divorcing their jerk father growing up. What is it (issue/parent) for you that need to move out of your life today? Do you want to stop your personal and spiritual drowning by forgiving your father/mother? What would it feel like to be at peace with your parents? Being at peace with your parents is a very positive choice and a decision that will heal you and all your relationships going forward.

#2—The Power of Divorce-Romantic Breakups: Anger, resentment and disappointment are three very strong emotional forces of the ego. My professional and personal experience is that divorce and/or romantic breakups are all very powerful life- altering wake-up calls. Going through a romantic separation/divorce pulls up within you every unresolved unconscious issue, wound and emotional disappointment. Going through a divorce, regardless of the years together, is like sticking your hand into a raging campfire and wondering why it hurts so badly. How we emotionally, psychologically and spiritually process our heartbreaks and losses is as important as the relationship was. Taking a nonjudgmental look inward about our needs, wants, desires, dreams and intuitive longings always has a productive outcome.

Men and Women and their Reaction. For instance, I have many adult men in my practice who want and desire a loving, caring, intimate relationship with a partner. Rather than taking an emotional pause and time out to reflect, they go from one relationship to another without ever exploring the recurring deeper themes of their own heartbreak. They go through romantic partners, marriages and intimate relationships at laser speed in order not to feel or experience their own unresolved emotional loss. I have many women who are on the opposite side of the spectrum of relationships and dating. They go into their emotional cave, never to be seen again. They not only never date or become romantically involved again, they never let go of their anger connected to their ex-partner. These women seem emotionally frozen in time with bitterness and resentment toward their ex-partner and all prior relationship disappointments. Neither approach (running away or hiding) nor avoiding the inner healing of the heart is functional, positive, or curative. When there is *no new spiritual insight*, it automatically guarantees repetitive outcomes of heartbreak, despair, and hopelessness. The pathway of developing a deeper, more meaningful relationship with you, the universe and a partner starts with not replaying all the previous disappointments. *Love is easy. Relationships are difficult to process and understand.*

The soul/emotional work of growing in any type of significant relationship is finding your inner voice. Your voice/intuition is the key to knowing, understanding and loving yourself and your (new) partner. By ignoring your inner voice, ideas, suggestions, and feelings will always lead to the marriage/romantic relationship going off the road of life. Your inner voice is the door opening to what you truly desire in order to feel loved and cared for. The emotional and spiritual components (desires) of your life can't ever be properly addressed (your purpose) until you sit down and listen to your inner voice and heartfelt needs. Your intuition guides you toward your own self-acceptance/forgiveness. A key to your self-acceptance/forgiving process is realizing *there is no failure in divorce/ breakups—only spiritual life lessons.*

Placing your spirit, heart and emotional feet in cement shoes starts with your ego's best friend for life: *blame.* Blaming your ex for your heartbreak, relationship ending, betrayal are all excellent excuses for avoiding yourself. You are 100% responsible for your 50% of the relationship and your role in it. There are no secrets, no surprises in an intimate relationship. None! Being disappointed is a very different issue from blaming or seeking revenge toward your ex-lover. The emotional experience of disappointment is the underlying cause for anger, resentment, and heartbreak in all types of love relationships. ***Metaphorical sleepwalking in marriages and romantic/ dating relationships is common, but surprises aren't.*** Denial, avoidance and emotional distance are issues that cause the bond between you and your ex to erode over time, which isn't a surprise. Being angry only stalls your healing process and moving your journey forward.

What do you resent about and hold against your ex-partner, lover and/ or significant other? Be aware that your resentment could take you all the way back to first love relationship with your mother or father. Viewing your love life in the present requires you to lose your old story line about not being good enough or lovable. Self-forgiveness is the biggest step toward developing the next chapter of love in your life. Don't allow false limitations such as age, looks, money or fear of intimacy hold you back from becoming the person and partner you desire.

#3—Separating from Your Family: This is the process of handling, coping and understanding family resentment about you becoming your "self." Many times, one of the strongest deterrents to letting go of the past, old grudges and vengeance is a lack of personal acceptance for whom and what you're becoming. One of the challenges to separating is that of no longer seeking approval by being or trying to be a good boy/girl. Trying to be someone else for love, acceptance and emotional security reasons never works and leaves you empty, spiritually lost and psychologically dependent. The problem is that your developing spiritual self requires you to go inside and answer all the questions about yourself with an attitude of loving self-accepting understanding. Co-dependence, approval-seeking and people-pleasing behaviors are all your own rejections of who you are and can become. This type of erasing yourself behaviors to please others leaves you in a very despairing and emotionally empty relationship. ***The***

single greatest act of love in your adult life will always be your self-forgiveness and self-acceptance!

All the issues of personal shame, romantic disappointments, self-loathing, people-pleasing, fears of rejection/abandonment, self-doubt (lack of inner connection) are healed within you by accepting your own good enough policy. Perfectionism breeds a fixed, rigid, cold, loveless, scared personality within you. Being perfect is a guaranteed formula for creating a life full of self-loathing and envy. *Your life isn't about perfection, but rather about embracing the process of self-love and fulfilling your destiny.* Failing and perfectionism are ego issues that work against your development of spiritual insights, self-loving concepts and compassionate concerns.

Many times families have a horrible time accepting any difference within a member, and view a son/daughter's spiritual awakening as a betrayal of the acceptable family mythology. Sexual orientation is one the hottest issues that many adult children face when reconciling with who they are and aren't. *The question within any family system isn't a moral question, but rather a sameness issue,* which simply means: why can't we all be the same? The obvious answer is that we aren't all the same because we all have an individual destiny, spiritual awakening journey, and personal life lessons to learn. No one in your family is the same as you, and the same applies to the inverse. The pressure to be the same is called the family prejudice dynamic. There is nothing in your life that you need to avoid in order to keep operating within the illusion of sameness. Personal authenticity is an invaluable feature of your own individual spiritual awakening.

Whatever family member rejected you is no longer the issue today. It's your issue to not continue the self-devaluation shaming process any longer. Tolerating your family's disapproval, disappointment and lack of understanding about what and who you are is critical for moving your journey forward. Getting comfortable with not following the family's outline for your life is absolutely necessary for developing your own identity. Accepting that you can't change anyone in your past or present or their attitudes toward you is an important step for detaching from your own anger. You can only change your personal perspective on being open and receptive to your own journey. The rest of your family has their own individual journey to fulfill. You must focus on your path regardless of what your life journey reveals and where it takes you.

#4—Your Career and Money: Self-Worth-Greed-Deprivation: The Buddhist teachings discuss that there are eight worldly predicaments that all men/women will process, struggle with and hopefully resolve during their life journey. The four pairs are presented as direct opposites: *pleasure-pain, gain-loss, fame-disgrace and praise-blame.* These opposing struggles are each on the same spectrum in opposition to each other in your personal, professional, social, intimate beliefs and relationships. For the purpose of our discussion, the dynamic of gain-loss is all about the internal seduction and craving for material possessions and wealth, as well as the socio-economic positions we have or don't have in life. Competition—cutthroat, ruthless actions in service of acquiring wealth, power and position is a characteristic where the ego is gaining and your spirit is losing. Stepping on people isn't a loving philosophy in your life. Any discussion of the gain-loss factor regardless, of where we live in the world, is controlled by the need, desire, abundance or lack of money. *Money isn't neutral or an easy issue to understand when your identity and self-worth have been defined by it.* The emotional power of money for many people becomes their alter ego when they are wealthy and their devil when they are bankrupt. Neither end of this particular spectrum is good or productive for our life journey. The struggle between gain-loss is a challenge that requires spiritual insight to avoid the pitfalls of greed and the loss of inner happiness for not being generous (selfish).

Illusion of Lasting Happiness—Money can be many different metaphors for how you feel about yourself, others, power, control, competition and spiritual values (i.e., generosity, charity, service). Your career, acquisition of wealth and all the things that go along with the outward appearance of success are ruthless taskmaster. *The inner critic or taskmaster within you chronically pushes you forward because nothing is ever good enough.* This relentless sense of emptiness is based on the fear of losing everything. The lie or temporary illusion of position, power and wealth is that it will ultimately deliver lasting happiness. There might be a short reprieve from the fear of loss or emotional deprivation with the abundance of money and or/new positions of power. The problem with resolving the challenge of loss vs. gain is that it requires foresight into your spiritual destiny, purpose and death. When you no longer examine your lifeline from a gain or loss of money controlling view to one of gaining wisdom, everything becomes much more meaningful. Spiritual insight allows you, via your wealth, to embrace your death and next life. When visionary genius and incredibly successful Steven Jobs, founder of Apple Computers, was diagnosed with cancer, he said the following about freedom from the power of money, pursuit of wealth and worldly power that he had experienced:

"Remembering that I'll be dead soon is the most important tool I've ever encountered to help me make the big choices in life. Because almost everything—all external expectations, all pride, all fear of embarrassment or failure—these things just fall away in the face of death, leaving only what is truly important. Remembering that you are going to die is the best way I know to avoid the trap of thinking you have something to lose. You are already naked. There is no reason not to follow your heart."

Unfortunately, the pursuit of happiness from a material level will always lead the pursuer into the Valley of Despair and hopelessness. When Steven Jobs looked at his impending death, it was the pivotal transformational moment that changed his entire spiritual perspective and view of this life. As we saw in Chapter 3, the secret to lasting happiness is always found within you, not outside of you. No amount of wealth, competitive victories, worldly achievements or corporate power positions will ever satisfy the deep longing within your soul for something more! The problem is the ego and the Western world culture believes that money can create happiness along with the virtues of love, peace and self-acceptance. Money can be of service to these true life- changing spiritual qualities, but it cannot be a substitute or filler for these priceless inner divine qualities. The belief in wealth and a material perspective comes from an earthly system that is run and controlled by the power of fear. Fear never rewards its followers with peace, but rather it fosters the illusion of someday attaining it or losing all of it. The world's religious writings and other spiritual sources all discuss the illusion and deception of wealth as a phony spiritual decoy/substitute.

The God you seek isn't in your bank account or retirement fund; it's inside of your heart/soul. Money can't buy the inner power of love and lasting happiness. Money isn't evil: it's all about your relationship to it.

No Losses only Spiritual Gains. The fear of losing your wealth, position and/or possessions is a very emotionally consuming occupation. The nonstop inner fear of loss is driven and fueled by your sense of emotional deprivation. The true lasting achievements in life are never at the expense or devaluation of others. Competition at the expense of others isn't a spiritual practice but rather an ego game designed for abusing yourself and others. Many times the feelings of greed become a person's primary operating moral compass. The transitory empowerment that comes from owning, controlling, and directing money and/or people is very seductive. Money, in all its different forms, is energy. It is either flowing towards you or away from you. The destruction of many a man's soul while pursuing worldly possessions instead of investing in people, love and service has been well documented throughout human history. The pitfalls and blessings of wealth and social status have been elaborated on as challenges that certain souls either resolve or become consumed with. Money, wealth, material possessions, private jets and all the joys of life have a glass ceiling for insight and your soul's development. Remember the story about Scrooge in Section I of this book and his awakening from a money perspective to a spiritual perspective. The analogy is timeless for our spiritual evolution and divine intuitive connection.

What is Lasting? The painfully powerful experience of losing your fortune, career, position, social status is a very difficult life lesson that has driven many to committing suicide—the ultimate act of despair and hopelessness. The horror and fear of not having enough in the world is real and can only be solved by a perspective in something higher than our immediate material life. *What are you willing to lose in order to gain your inner peace?* What are you grateful for? How many different ways are you prosperous in life? What are you withholding from the people in your life, professionally, socially, romantically, lovingly? Your life is much more important and bigger than your income or wealth. It's all about your ability to have compassion for yourself and others.

#5—Your Body (A Container): A Love/Hate Intimate/Nurturing/Physical Relationship

#5—Your Body (A Container): A Love/Hate Intimate/Nurturing/ Physical Relationship—Our physical body is with us from the day we are incarnated until we leave for the other side. *Your body encapsulates your greatest asset, gift and possession: your soul!* Appreciating the facility that houses your emotional and spiritual heart is incredibly important. Your physical health and well-being enables you to experience your true essence: spiritual and physical living. Self-acceptance of our physical appearance, body shape, size, coloring, hair, weight, height and DNA gifts is part of every person's journey. The rejection of our physical body via abuse through eating disorders, illegal drugs, psychosomatic disorders, unresolved emotional resentments and neglect on any level is a serious life-altering course. Rejecting or punishing our body is the beginning of a long road of personal physical, emotional and spiritual suffering. Your body isn't the enemy or a distant friend, but rather an intimate part of your current life journey. Physical challenges, disease, and cancer are some of the body's tools that get our attention and many times lead to our spiritual awakening.

> *"In the blink of an eye, your life can change due to disease. Your goals, dreams, priorities are forced to take different turns. You are grateful for the little things and worry less about the big things."*
> —*Nicholas Sparks*

You aren't Your Body. One of the challenges of shifting your life journey perspective is realizing that you aren't your body. Your body can serve as an excellent alarm clock to awaken you to what's wrong within your emotional and spiritual life. The shock of your body failing you, aging and breaking down is a valuable source of information about you and for your use. What is your body telling you today? Where is the physical pain in your body? What does your pain tell you about your self-acceptance process? Your life is more than your appearance and physical giftedness; rather, all your physical attributes are part of your overall spiritual development. Many people along their path assume their body is the sum total of their purpose and destiny: *not true.* You are a soul with a physical shell/body covering it. Your physical body, regardless of its shape or size, helps you to properly function and learn on your life path. *Your life isn't your body, but rather a housing unit for the soul/spirit within you.*

We came to this life via a human birth in order to have a series of learning experiences accomplished while in our bodies. We can choose to learn and experience an incredible life while living on this planet. The body is like a car's dashboard warning system. When something is off or out of balance emotionally, psychologically or spiritually, your body will develop certain aliments based on the particular crisis. Metaphysical understanding is that our body, emotions and spirit are all interconnected and balanced together: no separation. There is an energy balance within you that can either benefit your life or derail it. Physical symptoms, the onset of sudden disease, chronic health concerns have their healing and answer on a spiritual self-acceptance level. For instance, the pathology of eating/food disorders is always connected to some degree of self-rejection, self-punishment and/or unresolved anger. How we relate to food literally and emotionally is a great barometer for how we nurture, love and accept ourselves. The term "comfort food" or "emotional eating" is just one example of the countless invisible connections between your body, your soul and your emotional state.

What is your Body saying? Your body's ability to fight off disease and illness is greatly compromised when emotional issues are avoided and suppressed—those feelings have to go somewhere! *The avoidance, suppression and energy necessary to keep you away from your feelings are enormous energy outputs for your entire body.* The long-term effect of these types of avoidant-resistant choices of revenge, self-loathing or blame can be the body's critical breakdown points. Our bodies are designed to handle our physical functioning, not our emotional dysfunction or spiritual resentments. Many times our serious physical-life threatening problems have their roots in our unexplored, buried or avoided emotional, psychological and spiritual concerns.

> *"The significant problems we have cannot be solved at the same level of thinking with which we created them."*
> —*Albert Einstein*

This quote by Albert Einstein is a reminder that many of our physical challenges, problems and concerns need to be resolved from a metaphysical level rather than on the same level they were created (ego). What are you holding onto, not accepting or are angry about currently? Who are you angry at in your life? Where do you feel your feelings of worry, anxiety, and fear in your body? What would you feel like if you didn't use your body as a defense mechanism against your emotions? Many times after a big emotional crisis (death of loved one, divorce, retirement, money loss), your body, within an 18- to 36-month period, might develop a serious disease. The reason is that physical issues along with the emotional and spiritual components have a big influence on your crisis. This mind/body discussion isn't to blame you for every illness, disease or physical problem you have. Rather, it is to awaken you to the possibility that your body might be trying to get your attention about other areas in your life. Lastly, your body is a vehicle to assist you on your journey along your spiritual path, not the other way around. Your body and soul are deeply connected, and your awareness of this dynamic is valuable.

Action Steps—Walking the Extra Mile in Your Own Shoes!—

"Forgiveness is the most powerful thing you can do for yourself on your spiritual path. If you can't learn to forgive, you can forget about getting to higher levels of awareness."
—Louise Haye

We have covered a lot of issues that are all related to your continuing journey of insight and increased happiness/love. One of the goals of this book is to remind you that there are so many different ways, paths, and circumstances that are all creatively designed out of what appears to be utter chaos for your greater good. *Your personal story has the divine threads of grace, compassion and love woven all through it with your name on it.* No one is exempt from getting emotionally blasted along the journey of life. It will come through marriage, family, career, health and your children, but it's coming nonetheless. These extremely painful and oftentimes unbelievable experiences are all part of your successful failure life process. Accepting that your soul, ego and self-understanding needed to be awakened/traumatized by one of the Big-Five lightning rods is emotional freedom. Coming to terms with your unspoken soulful desire for your transformation, regardless of the ways or means you experienced to get there, is true self-realization. The overwhelming feelings of disappointment, despair and loss seem unbearable to experience, but you do. Many times the automatic default for feeling defeated and a failure is wanting to give up and sit down on your path. The emotional pull of quitting or escaping or taking a break for a season or two is tempting. The rut of self-pity is seductive and very appealing until it becomes your worldview— then you're a slave to your past.

> *"Be grateful for what is right now.*
> *The grass is never greener on the other side.*
> *What you have now is perfect for your souls learning and journey."*
> *—Bill Philipps*

The incredible emotional, psychological and mental resistance to changing and accepting your life journey is your ego trying to control the uncontrollable (the universe). Remember, the ego is only concerned with its ability to control and keep you on a limited program of emotional/spiritual well-being. *Your self-acceptance and forgiveness for yourself and the key players in your story are invaluable.* Experiencing and allowing the incredible process of your new heart unfolding is accomplished in many ways. One of the most powerful steps is your attitude shift from resentment and anger at yourself and others to understanding, accepting, forgiving and allowing the energy of your life to continue to move you forward. When you resist your Valley of Despair and where your life ended up, you are similar to the caterpillar resisting the opportunity of becoming a butterfly. The caterpillar has no idea that its transformation will be so beautiful and freeing. We don't know the final outcome of our own journey or all that it holds for us. What we do know is that holding onto our old wounded-bitter-blaming story of all the wrongs that have come to us is a dead-end spiritual street. One of the ways to move your life forward on all levels is through the doorway of forgiveness.

You Can Do This—There are things that have happened to you that are unexplainable on this side of life. Expecting to understand or know how your life ultimately turns out is the ego's attempt to hold you back. Taking action steps to forgive all the players in your life story, including yourself, is something that words can't describe. The inner experience of freedom, enlightenment, inner fulfillment and the power of love is something you have to experience. ***You can't think yourself through forgiveness, you have to feel all of it within your heart and soul.*** This is one of the major forks in the road of your transformation. There is a small voice within all of us that says, *"Don't quit, keep going, and forgive them."* Moving your life out of the Valley of Despair, past the graveyard of your old life, and letting go of your old story is a process that is a prerequisite for the next chapter in your life. In order to access it fully, consider the following ideas.

First Type of Forgiveness Action: Forgiving "Them"—My professional, spiritual and personal experience is that there are two extremely powerful types of forgiveness. One is when you detach and forgive and you allow that person to have another chance to be in your life. This is a very powerful act of self-love and universal love. *The ego can't let go of its wounds or wrongs, but your soul can.* A spiritually motivated approach to loving, accepting yourself, your partner/friend/children or whomever you forgive does something to both of you. Even if the other person tells you to go die and rot in hell, it doesn't matter. You have freed yourself from the shame and lower energy of despair from your past. You will always ascend to a higher level of insight, wisdom and life/spiritual perspective with any act of genuine forgiveness. When you release the issue, grudge and/or emotional darkness for everyone's greater good, something miraculous happens.

Second Type of Forgiveness Action: Forgiving "Yourself"—This very important second type is when you detach and forgive, but move on in your life without that partner/person (living or deceased). The circumstances surrounding the relationship no longer serve your highest and best self, your good will, and your life/spiritual journey at this time. This includes all types of abusive, controlling, manipulative and suppressive relationships that are counterproductive to your transformation and destiny. Knowing when to stop the insanity and blaming is part of your forgiveness process. Use these two types of forgiveness wisely in all your relationships, including your own spiritual identity development. You might have to forgive some situations or people 10,000 times—and then one day it's all done.

> *"Success is not final, failure is not fatal; it is the*
> *courage to continue that counts."*
> —*Winston Churchill*

Forgiveness is the courage to continue along your life/spiritual path. Let's go to the next chapter of your life. What would that chapter look like?

Section III

Your Transformation Process—Ascending Your New Limits

"You are not on a journey to God.
You are on a journey With God."
—Steve Maraboli

"The spiritual journey is individual, highly personal. It can't be organized or regulated. It isn't true that everyone should follow one path. Listen to your own truth."
—Ram Dass

"The soul always knows what to do to heal itself.
The challenge is to silence the mind."
—Lao Tzu

Chapter 9

Accepting Your Life and All of its Relationship Lessons—View from 10,000 feet

> *"The goal of the human experience is to transform ourselves from beings who long to attain power in the physical world to beings who are empowered from within."*
> —Caroline Myss

> *"Sometimes the only available form of transportation is a leap of faith"*
> —Barry Weichman

How "It" is All Coming Together for You—Looking and wondering about your present-day circumstances and not fully comprehending how "it" has happened is appropriate and understandable. The "it" is all the seemingly random events, relationships, lovers, family members, deaths, health challenges, financial hardships, breakups, disappointments in your life which have all led you to this place of entering a new vista along your life/spiritual journey. *Nothing in your life is random, lost, failed, or wasted.* Your inner focus on the emotional, psychological, spiritual and literal place that you're standing in needs your complete attention. No longer will emotional inattention—sleepwalking, avoidance, denial, shame, blame, fear and self-loathing serve you in disconnecting or disappearing again.

You're different now. You can't pretend that you're not aware of your higher-self anymore. Everything is different, starting from the inside (soulfulness) going outward (daily living). You have rediscovered your own spiritual connection, bond, and soulfulness. This inner discovery is a complete game changer, one that is never going to stop developing. Your entire view of your life, career, love, family, money, God and you has evolved to a new place of insight. You know intuitively that everything in your life is different, even if the extenuating circumstances aren't completely resolved or settled. Your ego isn't happy or pleased with all the new changes and actions within and around you.

In her quote above, Caroline Myss is reminding us that it is important to not try to figure out our entire story prematurely—rather make the priority our inner journey of awareness. Understanding all the whys and why-nots isn't necessary for your continued awaking and spiritual transformation. It's a complete waste of your time and a deliberate detour from your journey when you attempt to understand how all it works together—no one in this current life knows all the answers. Accepting the endless stream of miracles in your life while living in the moment is a positive balancing and grounding experience. Your best moments of your life will always be in this moment of time. It's never five years down the road or ten years back. The best way to get to your next level of deeper awareness and spiritual awakening might require a leap, step, or crawl of faith forward. Regardless of your previous moments and how you got here, you are here! Yup, you're here, and now is the time to readjust your inner compass of spiritual understanding for the next level of personal awareness. Blaming, arguing, or resisting how you got here only slows up your process of inner peace and soulful understanding. We spent the last section of this book illustrating and discussing the merits of releasing some of the most insidious ego-driven emotions that are merely psychological and spiritual roadblocks in your life, not dead ends.

Accepting Your Awakening Process—For instance, yes it "sucks" that your ex-marriage partner took your life savings, lied to you, and married your best friend. Yes, it is heartbreaking and disappointing that your business partner embezzled the company profits and you're now unemployed. It's unexplainable that your child died or your life partner was killed (no amount of words can describe the loss of a loved one—see epilogue). The saga of your life up to this point is endless for your own awakening. Many people resist these powerful wake-up calls and prefer to go back to sleep: *don't do it.* They decide via the ego that it's God's they are suffering, and they reject their inner divine self in the process. It's no one's fault! You are looking at your life through the eyes of your extremely limited ego perspective. You're no longer sleepwalking through your life in your relationships, or along your spiritual journey. All the old ego roadblocks have absolutely no respect for education, wealth, status, race, social position or heritage, but yet we felt stuck.

We all struggle with inner challenges of self-doubt, and yet *we all seem to feel that we are the only ones doing it.* The truth is we are all going back home to where we all started this journey (paradise). How our particular lesson plan and school-of-life courses unfold is very specific for our highest and best good. Your school-of-life's homework assignments are for your specific divine purpose. As much as we would like someone else to step into our current transformation process and finish it for us, it can't be completed by anyone else. You didn't come to this current incarnation to run and hide while blaming and ignoring your destiny, mission or spiritual purpose! The quote below is a reminder of your courageous hero's journey into the heart and soul of your life. Your life is much more than making your physical and material life work succeed. Your current life circumstances are the direct pathway to your awakening.

> *"Like heros in a mythic journey, we are meant to struggle to make*
> *the right choices. Our divine potential calls us*
> *to rise above the Self's basic needs*
> *for survival in the physical world."*
> —*Carolyn Myss*

Your ability to continue your self-accepting process is ongoing in spite of the moments of doubt, silent fears, personal struggles and nagging regrets that you experience along the way. Your life is never defined by any one event, but by rather the colorful tapestry of your entire journey.

We ended the last chapter with Sir Winston Churchill reminding us that neither success nor failure is permanent. *The only lasting relationship that is constant is your spiritual connection to yourself and your higher power/universe.* It's an emotional comfort and a motivator to further develop the hidden treasure inside of you —your soul! The pearl of great price is finding the unlimited inner happiness within you and discovering where your journey's treasures will take you. You came to this life for specific personal and soulful reasons. Your inner awareness and intuitive understanding of your life will always shed new insight on the outer circumstances for your next step.

> *"Everyone you meet is fighting a battle (including yourself)*
> *you know nothing about. Be kind. Always Be kind!"*
> *—Philo (Philosopher, 20-50 BC)*

Can't Stop Now—Relationship Changes—Going forward is your utmost priority while discovering the deeper knowledge (your mission assignment) of your bigger plans, goals, and purposes. In order to not repeat some of your more painful life lessons, you need to ask yourself honest questions about your emotional and behavioral relationship patterns. Absolutely everything in this life is about relationships and our connection to all the various types of them: social, career, family, love, child, parent, self and Spirit/God. Relationships are the glue providing personal information about the process by which we live our daily life. Your relationship difficulties are part and parcel to your life/spiritual journey. Without any relationship feedback, it is impossible to have any idea of where and how our life is moving and changing. The most valuable lifelong relationship you will ever have is with yourself and with your divine inner self. All of the various types of relationships in your daily life and those emotional connections and bonds that come from them flow from this primary spiritual union within you. Consider the following questions as a way of providing new insights into opening up new spiritual relationship doors in the next months and years. All these questions are designed to help you to assess your long-term wishes, purpose and life mission/passion.

Personal Relationship Questions:

- What relationship (past or present) do you consider your most profound lighting rod experience for emotional pain, disappointment and transformation?

- What is the recurring relationship issue that seems insurmountable and chronic in your life today?

- What relationship, experience, or situation seems impossible to heal, resolve and find peace with?

- What relationship feels like a complete failure in your life, even though there isn't such a thing as a failure?

- What regret, mistake, or choice still haunts you with regard to your intimate relationship history?

- What action, event, and/or relationship would you consider to be an absolute miracle in your life?

- What issue, concern, and/or problem would you like to see resolved and healed in your immediate future?

- What do you secretly want to do and with whom?

- Do you believe that you have currently learned your important life lessons from your painful experiences?

- How has your recent journey changed your perspective on your life, your death and your afterlife?

- What still angers you about your particular life experience, situation, or childhood?

- Where and how do you feel cheated, ripped-off or that you were dealt a raw deal by life/universe?

- What is your primary emotional or psychological resistance to in your life (we all have one)?

- Who do you want at your bedside when you pass onto the other side?

- Do they know (loved ones, friend, and ex) you want them with you at the moment of your passing?

- What do you currently consider to be your toughest obstacle going forward on your spiritual path/journey?

Your Relationship/Spiritual Path—Take a moment and consider all your answers to the questions above. We all have come from a painful place that is mixed with so many variables, and it has led us to this point of spiritual self-realization and inner awakening. How your awakening happened is secondary to whether it truly woke you up. For many parents, their teenage children at critical steps of development have suddenly "blown up" the entire family. For many divorced adults, the challenge is reconciling themselves with a painful and mind-boggling breakup with a partner after perhaps 27 years of sharing and building a life together. For others, this moment comes out of our family-of-origin's childhood trauma issues with siblings, needy parents, and/or angry relatives. Your personalized wake-up call could be your career that has completely dropped into a black hole with little prospect or idea of how to move forward. You have lost your job, have no money and can barely support yourself. You could be estranged from your siblings or children, and there appears to be no opportunity for a new dialogue. The options are endless for your pathway to enlightenment and meaning.

The frustrating and seemingly hopeless circumstances are as varied as the people reading this book. There isn't any one issue, circumstance, relationship that isn't amenable to the power of love and your intention for healing. None! Everything in your relationship world is an opportunity for healing. The most important question is: *Are you open to healing your relationship world in the next chapter of your journey?* Let's not forget or dismiss who you want at your passing as a window into your heart and soul's desires. Many times the people who have caused us the most pain are also the ones we don't want out of our life. We will discuss this concept later in the chapter.

> *"Inner Peace is the result of retraining your mind to process and*
> *Accept your life as it is*
> *Rather than as you think it should be!"*
> —*Dr. Ellen Albertson*

All Your Life Paths Lead to "Rome"—Everyone has a powerful individual story miraculously converging into their own personal life/

spiritual awakening. How we all get to "Rome," the metaphorical place of enlightenment, is as creative as the men/women walking into the next chapter of their life. The challenge is accepting how you got here without carrying any further emotional, psychological, or shameful residue. Your challenge going forward on the road/path of your life is accepting your role in your relationship disappointments. One of the gifts of your recent journey is translating your old beliefs from failure to successful failure without wasting any further energy on needless personal judgment or self-loathing. Your ego will *always* judge, abuse, and dismiss you with shame regardless of the outcome. Your soul/spirit will embrace your life lessons as gifts, finding the pearls within the seemingly disastrous circumstances of your relationship world. The powerful combination of self-love, self-acceptance, and self-forgiveness will allow you to begin to nurture your soul and gain new spiritual insights from your life lessons. Your ego will always demand perfection and revenge for the process of your painful personal growth. It will leave you stranded in the desert of life with no hope of getting back on your spiritual/life path. *The good news is that your story starts in the desert of hopelessness and takes you to your river of life.*

> *"Failure is not falling down but refusing to get back up!"*
> —*Chinese Proverb*

The Next Chapter in Your Acceptance Process

Let's be Abundantly Clear and Direct—You're on a journey to your own spiritual awakening! How you come to your personal awaking and/or spiritual transformation is the subject and matter of our discussion. Your life's goals, purpose, and mission are all coming into much better focus from a higher more meaningful and enriching perspective. Acknowledging that you have lived through the fires of your heart for the purposes of refining, creating and directing your awakening is priceless. When you're feeling moody, hopeless or overwhelmed, never forget that ***you can buy just about anything in life except insight and love!*** Your newly enlightened inner spiritual compass is your own trust fund of infinite wealth and lasting security. *Who isn't searching for personal wealth and lasting security?* As we have discussed throughout this book, few ever think to look inside the soul for the true spiritual inheritance and permanent soulful security. It's a paradox that while living in an impermanent world, we want to change that process to a permanent world fraught with frustration and despair. This dynamic of trying to control the uncontrollable is a chronic source of unhappiness, desperation, and fear of life/death. The quote below is worth repeating, memorizing and becoming part of your thinking today:

"You can buy just about anything in life except insight and love!"

The Gift of Impermanence—After all of your personal events, you now know that your journey has a profound purpose and meaning. You can call it anything you want to, but you have an updated inner compass that doesn't follow the old-school ego rules of greed, control, fame, and position. You accept the universal truth that everything, including your life, is always in a state of change—impermanence. One of the most significant changes in your life is that your ego has been replaced in the control center of your life by your heart and soul. Your new inward hero's journey is unfolding before you through your perfectly imperfect successfully designed trials and tribulations. Your newly enlightened life road map demands that you consider some different geographical relationship information for continuing along your road.

Everyone in Your Life has Value for You—One of the keys to your next chapter along the road is to recognize the value of all the different people involved in your life plan. As is often the case, the spiritual element, value and purpose that certain people have in your life is irrelevant to them (clueless). Many people don't have any concern or regard for the intuitive divine nature within you or themselves. What matters are the spiritual life lessons that you learn and accept through these relationships. Focusing on difficult people is looking in the wrong direction by not accepting or resisting the inherent lesson/gift that their presence in your life brings. As you begin to awaken and accept that your world is transitory, impermanence allows you to begin to feel freedom from the pulls, illusions, fears and limitations of our relationships. All the pieces, events and relationships in your life have led you to this point. You want to keep going forward, but how? Let's start with your relationship arena.

Understanding your important relationships allows you to have better insight into what you are becoming and where you might have more growing and learning. Never forget or dismiss that our entire life is all about relationships. Everything in this lifetime is focused around relationships. Secondly, all relationships change (impermanence). ***The classroom setting of your life is in the world of your relationships.*** Let's reexamine your story line of love, intimacy, and emotional connections.

What Do You Leave Behind or Bring— Ego, Friends, Family and Partner?

Changing and Updating Your Relationship Pattern—many times the first thing people worry about when progressing down their newly awakened spiritual path is dragging everyone they know with them on their path. This approach never works and everyone (yourself included) usually ends up with a lot of hurt feelings and resentment. It is never a good idea to attempt to bring all your friends, family and partners along. Why? Well, this is where things get really interesting. Many of the greatest life lessons you have experienced are through people who have no idea or concept of the spiritual element. Frankly, spirituality isn't relevant or important to these people along the route of your life—nor is it for you. The universe has no problem or prejudice in using an atheist, a donkey or, if necessary, your husband or ex-wife to get your attention and understanding about your inward and outward journey.

The problem is that we tend to want to bring everyone along our path even when their purpose and usefulness in and to our life has passed. *The idea that every relationship has an expiration date is scary and unnerving to all of us (impermanence).* This idea of time-limited relationships isn't intended to advocate divorce or reckless romantic encounters, or it designed to take advantage of the loved ones in your life. Further, this doesn't imply that you should avoid your responsibilities to the people and relationships where you have bonds and commitments. Rather, it's taking an inventory of where you're going and how your self-acceptance process is developing within the context of your relationship world: social, family, business, love, health and parenting.

For instance, who are "you" in romantic, social, or work relationships? Several important questions need to be asked at this point on your trip. How is your passion, destiny, and life mission playing out in your present-day intimate relationship? What relationships push you forward with confidence? What relationships do you allow to hold you back in fear? What part of your inner feelings do you withhold in your close emotional connections? Who do you feel safe with in your life right now? What relationships trigger your old issues?

Your Life Is All About Relationships—Let's discuss your movement forward to the next chapter in your life within the context of your relationships. *Everything in your life is about relationships*—everything including your relationship to yourself, to your higher power, to your inner child, to your family of origin, to your work colleagues, to your friends, to your wife/husband, to your lover, to your environment, to your body, and most importantly, to your inner-self/soul/God within you! There is nothing in your life that isn't relationship-based or related. We all try to make or control the timetable of how our relationships should be. It is a common tendency to define which ones should be short-term, long-term, and/or forever. A very important step in our spiritual journey is accepting that we can't control the length and duration of the relationship and how the other person will act, how long they will stay, or when they will move on from our life. We can choose when we want to begin or end a relationship, but usually it's the learning component" (life lesson) that is the best indicator of our relationship timetable. We will get into more detail about how all relationships in this life, including your own, is time-limited.

Nothing is forever except your soul connection within you. Allowing your relationships to be in the present and learning from them in the moment is priceless. Trying to hold onto or force a relationship is where many of our most painful personal, spiritual, and emotional challenges occur. Our life journey is an ongoing composite of so many different types of relationships on every level of life: visible and invisible. This fact may sound elementary and, at the same time, very profound. How we attempt to control others and ourselves in our relationship world is of vital importance for you to understand and accept.

Take a deep breath, emotionally stand back, and look at your relationships—all of them. Start with the most important one: you with you! Doing this helps to create some emotional distance and wider perspective of how your life has and is evolving with all the different types of connections, relationships, and bonds. The timing of transformational relationships is something that is always very interesting. Let's discuss some of the key relationships in your life and how they will factor into your future going forward. The following quote illustrates the magnitude of how relationships are the most powerful force, tool, and instrument that God, Spirit, and/or the universe uses to shape and teach us. Your entire life has been impacted by relationships that have taught you about the core life lessons that you needed to learn. Your future will always be a combination of many different types of emotional, spiritual and, intimate/love relationships. The pressing question is which ones come with you now, and which ones need to be released? The second question is how do you want your relationship world to look, be like, and feel as you go forward?

New Relationships and Your Future

"When you are in the final days of your life, what will you want?
Will you hug that college degree in the walnut frame?
Will you ask to be carried to the garage so you can sit in your car?
Will you find comfort in rereading your financial statement? Of course not!
What will matter then will be people.
If relationships will matter most then, shouldn't they matter now?"
—*Max Lucado*

Relationship Style—It's Your Inner Connection! Max is pointing out the very powerful reminder that your entire spiritual/life journey will always involve, include and be about the relationships in your life. There is nothing in this current school-of-life that isn't relationship-based, orientated, driven and experienced. It's stunning to consider that your entire spiritual awaking is ever-expanding of your inner and outer relationship circle. We are all wired for inner emotional, spiritual, physical, and mental relationship bonds. It's in your DNA programming to desire, crave and naturally move toward relationship/emotional bonds. Yes, there is a small minority of people who don't bond or connect to people or themselves (less than 2% of the population), but that is for a separate discussion. Our focus is your relationship factor. The question is: "What relationships do I keep and which ones do I let go of?" Hmmm, this is where the answers can become very challenging.

For the sake of our discussion, let's create a spectrum of relationship types. At one end is the *always leaving person* who views relationships as disposable, using them for a while and then moving on (fear of abandonment—leaving first). These people are always leaving relationships and never staying to do the soulful work of love, self-acceptance and developing compassion, forgiveness and intimacy. At the opposite end of the spectrum is the *never leaving person* who views all relationships as permanent and forever unchangeable (dependent personality—needs people to function). These people become possessive and controlling when the natural progression of your life cycle changes your inner and outer relationship landscape. The emotional connection becomes very possessive, controlling and demanding of your alliance and soul commitment to them first and foremost. The rest of us are someplace in-between these two types of relationship styles.

Disposable/Disengaged/Avoidance
vs.
Your Relationship Balance
vs.
Possessive/Controlling/Enmeshed/Demanding

What about Me? The most important relationship you're going to have going forward is with yourself and your inner soul higher-self. The relationship spectrum is a framework for viewing, valuing, understanding and accepting your style. The degree to which you develop, foster and nurture your inner self/spirit/soul will be the same degree that your relationship world will reflect that same self-acceptance and self-love. It's all related and connected, involving a delicate balance between your inner-relationship (divine nature/you) and your outer-relationships (family/lover/you). Look at this balance and think about where your important relationships have been on this spectrum. What do your relationships reveal of your inner feelings about yourself, your family, your partner, your career, colleagues, etc.? You will eventually notice that there is a pattern to the types of relationships that you have and desire.

Many times we vacillate between the two extremes, hoping to find our own inner-self balance and voice. This grid/spectrum isn't a value judgment on what types of emotional, mental, physical and spiritual connections you make or have. Rather, it is an overview to see the delicate balance between your two extremes. It is a very courageous task to look at your style of intimacy, communication, and emotional transparency. What people, lovers, colleagues, family members fit into your relationship graph?

"You will keep attracting the same people and situations in your life until you finally release and forgive your past. Think of forgiveness as a key to the door of new possibilities."
—*Bill Phillps*

What's My Biggest Relationship Challenge? No one wants to keep running on the relationship treadmill, never going anywhere and always feeling exhausted afterward. Addressing your personality flaw, shame (remember you are flawless), self-doubt (resisting self-acceptance), anger management (powerlessness), fear of intimacy (ego control) or anything else that has been a relationship hindrance, means that you are open to change now. Expanding your inner feelings and spiritual perspective about yourself will automatically change your entire relationship world. Let me say it another way—*you will not recognize yourself when you start to evolve from the inside (soulfulness) and allow your true loving nature to direct your relationships.* Approaching any type of relationship from a place of self-acceptance, love and empathy/concern takes away all the illusions, fears and pretense of your ego.

You can approach your relationship world from a calm place of inner self-love, rather than trying to fill in your inner blank spots without any insight. Lastly, all relationships are purposeful. Some relationships are more impactful than others on your spiritual awakening process. Never dismiss a frustrating relationship as useless, meaningless or a waste of your time because they all matter.

When you look at the overview of your relationship story, history and patterns, you will discover a wealth of valuable personal information about yourself. Digging below the surface of your relationship wounds, you will find keys to use for your new direction. As we previously discussed in Section II of the book, each of these particular styles influence, empower, or disempower your self-acceptance progress and spiritual transformation. Next, we are going to discuss how the wounds and life lessons actually play-out in your day-to-day life with your spouse, significant other, family, colleagues, superiors, authority figures, children, and social connections. It is critical that you explore each of the five self-acceptance impairments, relationship hindrances and soul/spirit roadblocks discussed below for the next step in your life/spiritual chapter.

It's a foundational corner piece of understanding and accepting your spiritual and life journey to realize that relationship challenges are part and parcel to your ever- increasing wisdom and insight. *There is absolutely nothing about yourself, your world, and your soul that isn't impacted and shaped by your relationship choices.* Your relationships are the school-of-life classroom material that allows you to discover and learn about your soul's mission. Your full participation, focus on, and completion of these assignments are the course requirements for your life/spiritual journey. At this point in your process, you don't want to redo or retake these relationship courses over again—right? No one wants to retake or go through the most difficult years of school ever again. The same analogy holds true for your life lesson's curriculum. Consider the following brief working descriptions for some of the different types of relationships and how they currently relate, interfere or empower your inner soul and outer (physical/ego) relationship world.

Five "Self-Acceptance" Relationship Challenges

Shame-Based Relationships—This relationship style is where you never feel "good" enough. Your secret unspoken wish is that your partner can make you feel good enough and lovable. It's a relentless cycle of frustration and despair that makes you feel vulnerable (emotionally unsafe). You privately set up your relationships to hide your unspoken fears of being discovered as a phony, or a fraud. Becoming comfortable, open and transparent is not possible because of your self-loathing for being secretly flawed. *All you truly want is to be loved, but don't believe that you are lovable.* This erroneous negative self-perception drives and controls your entire friendship/relationship adult life. There is nothing you do or choose that isn't a reaction to or influenced by your shame factor. If your partner or people love you, then something must be wrong with them! You believe and know (erroneous belief) that you are damaged goods. Within all your relationships, you're constantly seeking, to a greater or lesser degree, to be approved of and accepted. The lack of self-acceptance and feeling unlovable is a relentless cycle of isolation, fear and despair of having your personal flaws discovered and exposed. Fear of being disliked, having people upset with you, or making a mistake is emotionally crippling and psychologically devastating. You must have everyone's approval or your anxiety becomes extremely high. You lose sleep, lose money, lose jobs, and ruin your friendships with the need to hide your shame. Shame-based relationships are always held together by secrets, anger, and disdain for both parties.

Co-Dependent Relationships—You are an expert at rescuing wounded birds, regardless of their circumstances. The recurring problem is that over time, you ultimately resent the person you're trying to save and rescue. Resenting the person that you saved has a guarantee outcome with any/ all co-dependent relationships (unfortunately no exemptions). The other person doesn't have the tools or resources to heal your inner wounded child—it's your sole responsibility. Your relationship approach is to be the solution and the nurturer in your emotional world to avoid ever being or feeling rejected or vulnerable. You aren't able to truly feel loved or accepted, or emotionally safe and vulnerable with anyone (yourself included). You need to be the fixer so that you possibly avoid feeling dismissed or rejected. The only way you feel like you can get love and attention is to be the perfect savior. Over time you begin to resent your partner and feel used, betrayed and taken advantage of when you want them to fix and save you. These types of relationships aren't equitable, mutual or emotionally balanced between giving and receiving.

You feel like a victim for allowing your relationships always to be at your own personal, emotional and spiritual peril/expense. You don't allow yourself to express your wants and needs to create an equitable relationship or partnership. The operative method is that you don't believe or trust that your partner can or will meet your emotional concerns, wants and desires. You will begin to resent and dislike your partner, friends, and colleagues because you have allowed yourself to be a doormat in hopes of being loved. The endless search for love, acceptance and spiritual understanding is your source of ongoing disappointment, frustration, and bitterness. *Your search for self-acceptance and love always starts within you and not with your partners' opinion.* This dynamic is very difficult to address without the spiritual perspective of your soulful purposeful journey and necessary life lessons via disappointment.

Addictive Relationships—This type of emotional bond is geared toward instant "chemistry" and the immediate inseparable emotional fusion that happens. The two adults immediately merge emotionally into one lump of mash potatoes. There is a loss of the "individual," loss of the independent soul and separate mindfulness. There is a total blending of the two individuals to become one complete soul (but you already are complete). This type of emotional bond never works out well. The emotional, physical, and spiritual fusion is in hopes of compensating for the loss of the love object deep within you. The emptiness is a spiritual issue that can't and won't ever be resolved by another person. Your search for your life meaning is within you and not in the person lying next to you in bed. The search for the perfect relationship in order to feel completely fulfilled is fleeting and impossible to maintain over the long term. The perfect relationship starts with your own self-acceptance process. The instant relationship for both people becomes a glued-at-the-hip type of connection. You're familiar with this—it's the first date that lasts three full days and then living together within one week of meeting. It's speed-dating on steroids. Neither person can get enough of the other. The energy in the relationship is emotionally intense, powerful, and reckless, and often sexually supercharged. As quickly as the two fall in love, they can just as quickly fall out of love, and then do it all over again in the morning with someone else.

The relationship is a drug that both people crave and resent simultaneously. Love isn't the problem, but rather the emotional wounds that overshadow the persons' unresolved, unfinished life lessons. The relationship isn't sustainable over time because the highs can't be maintained or tolerated for too long of a time. The natural lows are viewed as bad and a sign that this is the end of the love affair. The potential for a long-term romantic love relationship tends to be ignored because of the impulsive and addictive nature of these intense emotions. Many times the prolific use of drugs of all types and alcohol is the external fuel for a wildfire within the relationship for each person. Neither person wants to lose or give-up the "rush" of emotion that this relationship can generate. Ultimately, the emotional intoxication wears off, and the couple leaves one another to find another addictive partner. Emotional and spiritual sobrieties aren't considerations or important values in these encounters. Any type of addictive behavior, relationship or fusing is an escape from your uncomfortable feelings and difficult life circumstances. The emotional drug of love is ego-driven and invariably ends up as a painful encounter for both parties. The avoidant/addictive relationship tends to be a cover-up for something else in your life. The underlying question is: *What are you hiding from within you and in your relationships?*

Abusive Relationships—These types of relationships can range from horrible domestic violence to cold emotional isolation and verbal torture. *No type of abuse is acceptable in any circumstance, situation or* *relationship—never!* The question that has to be asked is what is your tolerance level for abuse (self-loathing/shame) vs. your love tolerance level, and the ability to express and accept love (self-acceptance, esteem).

Consider this a new source of valuable information for developing a clearer sense of self-worth/value and for your life/spiritual purpose. Ideally, you want your abuse tolerance to be very low and your self-acceptance/ love scale to be very high (your open-heartedness to life). The glaring discrepancy between abusive relationships and self-accepting loving relationships might not seem that outrageous or obvious to you. Clearly, you have survived by being strong and ignoring the abusive patterns for years, but something isn't working anymore. That something is your denial of your abused heart/soul. Now, your heart/soul wants to change your relationship story. It's not random or accidental that you are considering changing your relationship cycle from abusive/fearful to safety/loving. Your spiritual life journey has brought you to this point via perceived relationship failures to heal the wounded little boy or girl within you. Ignoring or continuing in abusive situations, relationships, marriages and/ or business relationships is no longer a viable option. Your inner voice of wisdom (soul/spirit) and intuition is calling for you to take new action.

Why did this Happen to Me? Abused men and women suffer their primary soulful wound in childhood and continue the abusive cycle/pattern to a greater or lesser degree in all their current relationships. Developing a high tolerance for any type of abuse has its roots in your early childhood years (0 to 8 years old). Pursuing the topic of why is another way to avoid, postpone and delay your inner healing and spiritual awaking. The reasons, circumstances, and responsible parties involved aren't as important as your present-day action of love, acceptance and self-forgiveness. Be extremely careful with the discussion of why, because it can quickly turn into a blame game or a cycle of self-loathing. Neither position is productive or helpful for your greater good.

Becoming more aware of your tolerance for feeling awful, allowing yourself to be abused and being abused in the past far exceeded your level of self-acceptance and love. It's imperative that you switch your abuse tolerance scale around so your spirituality and soul (intuitive nature) have a chance to be expressed in the context of a loving, caring intimate safe relationship. I know this sounds easy on paper but it is a lifelong process that is now being addressed within you. Compassion, understanding and self-love are some of the tools necessary for addressing your old style of low self-respect and diminished personal value. *It's never too early in your life to learn, practice and take new action that empowers you.* This discussion isn't about becoming an ego-driven person but quite the contrary. Your inherent self-worth, value and life purpose are some of the healing elements for stopping the cycle of abuse in your life and in generations to follow. Abusive relationships aren't limited to the bedroom or the family room of your life. This negative abused self-view tends to be your primary inner picture of yourself! The pattern of low self-worth, self-doubt and lack of self-respect tends to be an old rerun issue in your relationship world that can and will change.

The recent national sexual abuse case at Penn State University (background: assistant football coach molested teenage boys in the men's football locker room on campus during summer camp) and others like it raised public awareness that neither young boys nor girls are immune to this disastrous behavior by adults. This discussion of abuse raises the repressed emotional issues surrounding early childhood abuse (sexual, physical, emotional, neglect and abandonment) for the victims. The sexual abuse experience at any age is difficult to emotionally process. One of the major hurdles to healing an abused inner child is the personalization of it being the victim's fault. This typical response of blame for many victims is heavily impacted with shame, guilt and embarrassment. Unfortunately, sexual abuse is very common and greatly dismissed, ignored and repressed by both the perpetrators and victims. Any type of sexual assault, rape, exploitation, extortion of your physical body and emotions will ultimately require the victim to address this emotionally charged and vastly disturbing issue.

Changing Your Cycle—our discussion up to this point is a step toward in seeing the healing of your present-day abuse relationship cycle. The psychological, mental health community has long viewed any type of unresolved childhood abuse, regardless of its severity, as automatically predisposing the young boy or girl to a shame-driven self-concept/image. Healing the distortion of your self-acceptance belief system is the doorway to ultimate physical, emotional and spiritual freedom from your traumatic history. You and your higher self/soul want to and will co-create a new relationship story going forward on your spiritual/life journey. *All your important relationships don't have to be at your own personal expense in order for you to feel loved and accepted.* The irony of your spiritual journey is that you are already loved, accepted, and healed. We are the ones who won't believe or allow this intuitive divine experience to happen within us. In the next few chapters, we will explore how to transcend these inner wounds to your heart and soul.

Loving Supportive Relationships—Yes, these relationships do exist, and they start with how you see and view yourself. We all struggle at times to a greater or lesser degree with the above-mentioned relationship barriers, emotional blocks, and romantic disappointments. The ongoing process of our collective inward journey and enlightened understanding allows us to feel "good enough" during this incarnation. Going beyond, rising above, transcending your ego, and embracing the limitless power of love within your spirit and your soul are all possible today. A peaceful fulfilling relationship of any type with yourself and others is always attainable and within reach. Throughout the ages, spiritual masters have all taught that transcending your ego/body's impulses, wants, and desires are the pathway to your lasting enlightenment. Your inner wounds are no longer controlling how you're reacting to feeling ignored, blamed, dismissed, and disrespected. Your ego isn't choosing your response now. Your soul/ heart has taken over. Your approach to yourself, intimate partner, children, family, colleagues, clients, social circle is in a responsive mode rather than in an angry ego-reactive mode to perceived hurts and blaming. As you begin to listen, develop, and connect to your inner guide/soul/spirit, you will experience the ultimate liberation in your life.

Following the demands of our ego will lead to a very disappointing, despairing, and hopeless life experience. The man or woman that begins to see their relationships through the eyes of divine love will always have deep, fulfilling relationships and secure emotional connections. Your new relationship focus is from a loving and giving perspective for you and your intimate partner. Your deeper and higher understanding of your life and theirs (all others) opens doors of emotional connection that previously would have never been seen or considered from an ego/self-absorbed mindset.

Continuing to process your emerging sense of self and spiritual purpose fosters loving acceptance of your entire journey. You can't give what you don't have within your heart. Now, you can give your endless source of loving life energy to yourself and the people in your world. You will accept the natural ups and downs of all the different types of relationships and how these shape your self-acceptance, self-forgiveness, and compassion for yourself and others. Your ability to accept yourself and others is the tangible ingredient that builds a loving bond with all the people in your world. You and your romantic/marriage partner can experience the transcending power of divine unconditional positive regard/love regardless of how long you have been married. This applies to all the men/women who have had breakups, divorces and romantic disappointments. The first step is developing this loving bond within you and your soul/higher-self. Your new level of relationship insight begins to free you from the powerful inner and outer relationship obstacles described above. You will begin to view and experience parts of your life that at one time seemed distant and beyond your reach. Your new-found source of loving energy creates relationship opportunities that you never saw or conceived previously. Your new inner vision for the greater good of you and others opens up unlimited relationship potential and new meaningful connections.

Relationship Lesson 101: Soul Mates

"Soul mates aren't just discovered. There is no formula to "finding" those who enrich your life. They are already a part of you, so stop looking. Open your heart and your paths will cross as they are meant to."
—Bill Phillips

Recurring Love Relationship Patterns—There is plenty of material in this chapter about your relationship style, your concerns, and how you will want to evolve moving forward. It's very challenging and emotionally sobering to take full responsibility for your entire relationship circle. It's also very freeing and empowering to go within your divine heart and find your untapped loving potential. Consider the following questions for a better understanding of relationship style:

- Which of the relationship styles above best describes your past relationship themes?
- What personal or relationship issue, pattern or outcome from Bill's quote keeps reappearing in your life?
- Who in your life has been one of the biggest sources of emotional pain and suffering?
- How did you help create, consciously or unconsciously, the dynamic with them for your own benefit and change?
- Can you accept their value, purpose and divine involvement in your journey up to this point?

We discussed at length the value of self-forgiveness, and now this is where the "rubber hits the road" with your frustrating relationships. What are you going to do differently going forward so that you don't keep repeating these painful and frustrating relationship choices? What message, lesson, or healing do you feel that the universe, via your relationships, is trying to help you master and move toward? The answers are usually very close to the surface of your understanding and emotional acceptance.

"A soulmate usually only comes once in your life to shake things up,
show you true love, and stand up to you in ways no one else ever has.
They adore you yet challenge you to your fullest potential. A soulmate
relationship isn't only peaches and cream, it's roses with thorns."
—*Carolyn Myss*

Turbulence With Your Soul Mates—Everyone has a relationship that, currently or in the recent past, feels like their soul mate connection. Regardless of the outcome or status of that particular bond, your soul mate ties can be your greatest source of comfort and misery. Like the quote by Carolyn Myss, your soul mate can be a thorn in your heart and a blessing in your spiritual transformation. The myth that having a soul mate is akin to lovers holding hands in a grassy meadow with rainbows, butterflies and dancing unicorns is wrong and clearly overstated! The popular social idea that soul mates are blissful and effortless relationships is incorrect and terribly misleading. Your soul mate is anyone who helps you to touch your divine connection to God. Soul mates are the people who aren't only your present-day and ex-lovers or family members, but people from past lives. They are your greatest spiritual teachers of love through conflict and discomfort in this life. Soul mates are typically the individuals who are iron-on-iron or a "pain" in your life. These relationships are challenging and very transformational for both parties involved. Who is that in your life today? The magic with all your soul mates is probably that you have all been together in previous lifetime's, working together for each other's highest and best good. You all agreed on the other side prior to coming to this life at this particular time to help heal and awaken your soul's purpose. Look around at your relationship landscape and make a note of who emotionally charges or deflates you. There is more spiritual significance to these connections than just "awesome" or a royal pain in your side.

Who's Going With Me—Start Here!—

"When you see the way in which we get trapped in the sense of separateness
and identification with body and personality,
how do you awaken out of the illusion
that you're separate? The doorway out of that is
the heart. Your heart is the door to
the unlimited Universe and Source of Love."
—Ram Dass

Many times, looking down your road of life seems bleak and causes a deep longing in your heart. Don't worry! That feeling of emptiness, loneliness, and separateness is so important to factor into your new chapter. These feelings are signs, gifts, and tools to move you toward feeling, being, and knowing that you are complete, and knowing and accepting that you are loved as you are regardless of any particular day or relationship loss. The empty place inside of us is a reminder that maybe something has left our life, and something new and grander for our life is evolving—i.e., spiritual awareness. The death/birth cycle is never-ending and always getting rid of the old and making room for the new. The open space in your heart for new or old loves, passions, and creativity has to be cultivated. Unfortunately, in our current school-of-life, the difficult process of peacefully detaching from past relationship styles and resentments and allowing them to go is critical as we prepare for new and different relationships. This cycle of renewal and rebirth all comes through the doorway of our heart. Opening your heart to your relationship world will always involve courage, patience, and insight that everything does work out. Your goal is to be open from within for your expansion and new loving connections.

> *"Like heroes in a mythic journey, we are meant to struggle*
> *to make the right choices. Our divine potential calls us to rise above the Self's*
> *basic needs for survival in the physical world."*
> —Caroline Myss

This quote by Caroline Myss is important because it encapsulates the on-going journey of your spiritual awaking via love, self-acceptance and soulful courage. Realizing that you aren't alone and are not empty or disconnected from yourself or the people you love is a big step toward creating your next new chapter. Your spiritual ability to choose love over blame or resentment will always prove to be in the best interest of your soul and all the people in your life. Let's now look at how to further implement, access and feel your spiritual "heart from a new higher place of unlimited power: *self-love!*

Chapter 10

Power of Loving Self-Acceptance and Forgiveness—Your Personal Rebooting and Retooling

B elow is an open love letter to you from our Higher Power, your divine nature. Read it several times. We all need to reconsider the depth and breadth of this very compelling truth about our journey of processing loving, caring and intimate relationship(s). The inner power, courage and purpose of our personal forgiving, acceptance experience isn't always clean, smooth and without disappointments. Rather, the path of our journey into the heart of our loving soul is a very special road. The power of self-acceptance/love can't be measured in a linear fashion or counted, it's an experience within. Enjoy and accept your experience of love as a positive lesson regardless of your wishes and desires. No one is exempt from the ups and downs of love, life and the process of transformation of the heart.

"Dear Human:

You've got it all wrong. You didn't come here to master unconditional love. That is where you came from and where you'll return. You came here to learn Personal love…Love through the grace of stumbling demonstrated through the beauty of messing up often…You didn't come here to be perfect…You already are…You came here to be gorgeously human, flawed and fabulous…then to rise again into remembering."

—*Courtney A. Walsh*
(*Author*—*Dear Human; A Manifesto of Love*)

Death/Rebirth Cycle: "It's a Wonderful Life"—This letter absolutely describes the messy perfectly imperfect journey of love and all its variations during our life/spiritual travels. There is nothing about the experience of love with our intimate partner(s), family, children, friends, and siblings that isn't emotionally charged with all types of energy, to say the least. Our heart and soul's expression gets wrapped up in all sorts of personal issues of feeling unloved, rejected, scared and not truly understood. The letter is a reminder to not give up on love or the deep passions and desires within you. Your world desperately needs your personalized expression of love, which is why you are living today. Our egos get exhausted from the highs and lows of our spiritual pursuit of living with a theme of love. Our ego isn't remotely equipped or desirous to be selfless, sacrificial and generously giving of itself. The consummation of your life is ultimately defined by your ability and receptivity to love and overcoming your ego. All of life's purposes, relationships and endeavors have the foundation of love—for you, others and your higher-self, spirit, divine intuitive nature and God.

It's this chronic cognitive struggle between your ego and your higher-self that makes you question your value and purpose in all your relationships. Your life is similar to a movie with many moving parts, plenty of characters, and themes seamlessly woven together throughout the love story of your life. It's always interesting to note how certain events happen and certain situations evolve for the purpose of showing you the power of your life-spiritual journey. *You don't know how love, self-acceptance, and your passion can shape the next several chapters of your journey.* What we do know is that the power of love will shape your future even when it feels and looks like quite the opposite is happening. Love never fails or leads a soul away from the source of life. Love always awakens the soul to its calm and powerful energy. Relationships are the operating system of our current understanding of all the different types of love and experiences of love. Lastly, the following quote is about finding and connecting to your inner self, spirit and intuitive self. This new connection is the life you have always pursued and desired. Avoiding your spiritual connection is a form of death while still living.

> *"The real question isn't whether life exists after death.*
> *The real question is whether you are alive before Death?"*
> —*Oho*

Your Life Movie: We Are All in One—Let's take a look at how your life impacts everything in and around you, including your immortal soul and human ego. The timeless classic holiday movie, "It's a Wonderful Life," starring Jimmy Stewart and Donna Reed is based on how George Bailey's (Jimmy Stewart) world, community, family, business, friends and children would suffer and not exist if he had never lived or suddenly died. What follows is a brief summary of this classic story because it encompasses all the pressures of our modern-day life: work, lack of money, family, fear, isolation, despair and the power of love vs. greed.

George is confronted with paying off a debt to save the family business and town. He is so distraught from his perceived lack of money and no tangible resources that he is going to jump off the town bridge into an icy December river far below. In a moment of anger, George says to his loving and concerned wife (Donna Reed), *"I am worth more dead than alive,"* and he storms out of the house contemplating an end to his life! George feels worthless and emotionally confused and considers that the best solution to his adult crisis is to end his life. As George is walking to the bridge, he hears a man screaming for help, and he immediately leaps into the river to rescue the distressed man, Clarence, who happens to be his guardian angel (remember we all have an angel). This angel, who looks more like a drunken 80-year old Irish grandpa, persuades George to go have a drink with him and discuss their "problems."

It's interesting to note that the pivotal point in George's emotional melt-down shifts when he focuses on serving another by saving Clarence (an act of love) and taking his focus off of himself (ego). The message of serving others immediately changes George's perception from self-pity to saving this old grey-haired overweight angel. Serving and helping others always changes and improves the lives of both the giver and the receiver. In this case, George and Clarence both benefit from his act of graciousness. This is where the movie's story becomes so compelling.

George and Clarence go to the local bar where George had been (in another life) a regular. Everything has changed. George is now a stranger in his former hometown. It's as if George has never lived, and he is just visiting his life without ever having lived it. The movie shows how different the town, people, jobs, relationships, his wife (unmarried, with no children and scared of life) would be without his life force and loving energy. The entire town is without hope and living in fear without George's passionate life and dedication to help the less fortunate. George sees, feels and experiences what he thought was his meaningless life without realizing the love that he brought to this world was gone. Everything is different, much harder and severe. George is stunned when he realizes in his personal "aha!" moment that his life is much more than money and the family business, and really is about his expression of love. On Christmas Eve night, George has the soul awakening that his life does matter regardless of the material circumstances of his life.

The many different messages of this 1947 movie are universal and timeless. The movie reveals how much your (everyone's) life matters and the impact that you have on everyone with whom you come into contact. It's impossible on this side of life to know the full extent or degree of how your journey impacts people. Your life can't be minimized or dismissed regardless of your feelings of failure. The shock, despair, and regret that George Bailey feels as he runs out of the bar to recapture his lost life and his wife, children and everything important to him is painful to watch. You don't know if George's impulsive suicidal decision can be reversed or changed. Did George die or is he having a dream? The story ends well because George runs home on that dark snowy night when he realizes that he wasn't alone in the world after all (nor are you). When he left the house hours earlier, despondent, his wife had called everyone that knew George to come to his aid. The response is overwhelmingly positive. The influence that all his unnoticed good deeds and loving relationships have had on the town brings everyone to help solve his crisis to a degree far beyond the imagination. George was given the greatest gift of his life—insight into the endless impact of love.

> *"All progress takes place outside the comfort zone."*
> *—Michael John Bobak*

The Moral of Your Own Movie— *It's a Wonderful Life* has many messages, but one of the most powerful is that at dark times, we all think that our life doesn't matter, dismissing what impact it has on others. We erroneously conclude that our life really is unimportant and no one cares about us (wrong assumption). These are very powerful and negative short-sighted assumptions made by our ego. Unfortunately, your ego will never comprehend your ongoing discovery of self-love. Our divine heart (intuitive nature) cares and wants the best for us even when we choose otherwise. We like to think that we know about the positive or negative impact we have on people, our world and ourselves but we sincerely don't and simply can't. These natural emotional and spiritual blind spots remind us that we don't fully know when or how love can influence and change our world: George Bailey is that example.

These natural human misunderstandings of our true divine nature are the gasoline on a raging fire within our heart/soul. We either feed the fire of our soul with divine love/acceptance or with our ego's priorities (me-first-always, and what about "me" themes). *Our spiritual diet, meaning our emotional, psychological food (self-acceptance) decides who and what we will become.* George Bailey was having a really bad moment and gave in to his fear, losing contact with his heart and soul. The power of love always has mysterious ways of reaching us and awaking us in our most desperate moments—and in our greatest hour of needing wisdom, perspective and insight—love always prevails. George Bailey was sent an angel named Clarence who was disguised as an old Irish man. Who's your angel?). In the still moments of our hearts, we all secretly know what is and is not working in ourselves and our relationships. Clarence was sent to show George the error of his skewed fear-based thinking. It's our avoidance to giving love and being open and receptive to our life of self-forgiveness that becomes problematic. George woke up in a very dramatic way to his destiny, and he would never be the same as a result of it. *Never to go back to sleepwalking.* What has happened in your life to awaken you from the depths of your despair? What recent event changed the direction of your path? Who's your angel for your self-realization awakening?

Your "George Bailey"Awakening Experience— If you're still reading this book (thank you by the way) you will know what I am talking about concerning your own personal spiritual awakening. It's very important to be keenly aware that there is no wrong way to be awakened and to gain spiritual insight and enlightenment. None! *Whatever it has taken—near-death experiences, catastrophic health issues, or economic and romantic losses in your life—you are on a journey to someplace important.* Your soul and higher powers will keep working to get your inner attention, which is all for your greater good. It's your primary life journey task (mission) to reestablish your divine connection to your destiny and purpose. It's your own personal spiritual/life path full of lessons and challenges that is your responsibility to follow.

No one (literally *no one*) has the right or privilege to tell you that they know better than you about your own soulful journey. If there is a common mistake people make on their spiritual path (awaking), it is stalling out on their inward journey: actively avoiding (engaging in addictive behaviors for instance) and resisting the interpersonal process of changing from an ego-driven life to a spiritually driven life. The spiritual qualities of being more self-accepting, forgiving and compassionate are all part and parcel to your evolution. The "rut" and resistance to your soulful awakening is handing off your spiritual destiny and responsibility to someone else to manage for you (never works). Religion is specifically designed to tell you what to do: spirituality requires that you take complete responsibility for developing your intuitive nature from your heart. This the ultimate fork in the road for any life or spiritual journey: taking personal responsibility for your destiny! The next biggest challenge is no longer living in denial of your specific life-changing events and pretending that the hidden messages aren't especially for you. George Bailey couldn't run fast enough to get away from his terror and despair. In fact, it almost killed him.

"Sometimes our lives have to be completely shaken up, changed,
and rearranged to relocate us to the place we're meant to be."
—Dr. Wayne Dyer

Many Different Paths—We will experience upsetting events that rearrange everything in our life. Don't fall into the ego's spiritual superiority club that there is only one way, one correct method, or only one life (spiritual) path to follow. Your path is special and doesn't need anyone's permission or approval. You're going where you need to, how you need to and with whom you need in your life at this precise moment. Like Wayne Dyer says above, the universe is rearranging your circumstances to get you to a place of awakening. Your responsibility is to stay (conscious) on your life-spiritual path regardless of what is happening around you. Love is a universally understood concept, word and action that everyone's spiritual map takes them to experience.

"Love is Life. And if you miss love, you miss life."
—Leo Buscaglia

There are as many different expressions of love and spirituality as there are soul's roaming this earth. Whatever teaching, spiritual guru, church doctrine, religious group, spiritual orientation, prayer, and twelve-step program and/or meditation method brings you inner peace and concern for other souls is wonderful. The issue isn't about whose path is right or better, but rather staying on your path to learn your lessons of love through all your relationships. Spiritual masters and scholars over the years have all encouraged us to find our inner voice, to awake to our passion, and to follow it. The only wrong decision is to resist your life path awakening and try to quit, killing yourself and/or torturing your own soul with painful decisions (the list is endless). Your path isn't someone else's and doesn't need to be anyone else's—its own your spiritual journey!

Dark Night of Your Soul—

"Life always presents challenges. The challenges are tools that the soul can use as stepping stones to enlightenment."
—James Van Praagh

What event, situation, near-death experience, health scare, accident, or heartbreak was the end of the road for how you lived your previous life (without spiritual insight)? The quote above by James Van Praagh summarizes how all your personal challenges and soulful tribulations have pushed you inwardly. I know we have discussed this awakening, self-realization spiritual theme throughout the book and how it is happening within you. George Bailey had what many mental health professionals would call a "nervous breakdown." From a self-psychological point of view and a spiritual vantage point, George experienced the *"dark night of his soul."* It's the ultimate death-rebirth process that completely changes your entire world, spiritually, relationally and personally. Nothing in your life is left unchanged or untouched by this emotionally and spiritually harrowing experience. These experiences may take years to develop. but can in a single minute can break down your old ego-driven nature.

Your Soul's Purpose—You don't have to be religious for this transformation to happen because *your soul has no regard for formalities, only your inner awakening and spiritual connection.* In fact, the term "mid-life crisis" is the secular term for your dark night soul transformational process. On the other side of your "Valley of Despair" journey, how do you now live your life differently? How do you express the new insights, deeper appreciation for yourself and others? How do you redo, or better said, reboot your life journey going forward with your new awareness of self-acceptance, gratitude, forgiveness and passion for love.

Here it's important to address both men and women separately—for application purposes. I know as we spiritually evolve, gender becomes less and less of an issue. The actions of love are only what matter. In my clinical psychological practice, sometimes men and women need to hear about some of the particular challenges that are inherent with their gender. The question both genders ask is: How to lovingly express their deepest wishes, concerns, and lifetime dreams.

"The planet does not need more successful people.
The planet desperately needs
more peacemakers, healers, restorers, storytellers and lovers of all kinds."
—Dalai Lama

Men and Acts of Love—This quote by the Dalai Lama is the heart and soul of every man's and every woman's transition from the material perspective to that of a spiritual perspective. There is no greater need, calling or service than that of being a loving soul with your own personal expression. At the risk of sounding repetitive, your entire life-spiritual journey is about love. Men, myself included, have had this perception of becoming a marshmallow with no drive or direction when considering our life and spiritual direction. The reality is quite the opposite. The more that men tap into their endless source of love and its individual expression, the more our entire world immediately changes. Every man, regardless of creed, education, nationality, disability or natural ability, has all the innate skills to access their passion and love. You will not be questioned on the other side because you allowed a business deal to fall through because it wasn't fair to the other people involved. You will not be judged or dismissed from Heaven because you quit being a high-powered lawyer and became a first-grade teacher specializing in reading. Your life journey is about you and love. Making decisions from a loving perspective is putting gold bricks into your spiritual retirement account.

Your Measuring Stick of Success—The only measuring stick or report card for your entire life that counts is how did you use, expand and invest "love" into the people surrounding your life. This is in addition to the thousands of souls you came across and touched in your lifetime! Men (myself included) struggle with the novel concept that their life is all about relationships not material possessions, wealth, or accomplishments. It isn't all about that other ego "stuff" of fame, position, money, possessions, physical prowess, power, sex and control. It's not your retirement account or how many trips you took, but rather what you did with the love in your heart? Did you share your resources with your family, those less fortunate and not capable of returning the favor? Or, did you withhold your energy/source of love because you were scared you'd get kicked in the teeth again? Through the many messy loving relationships, bonds and emotional connections, it's your soul's purpose for you to experience your own power of giving love. The giving of your inner reservoir of love becomes the fabric and substance of your path. *Your entire life on the other side will be viewed through the eyes of love and what you did with that precious gift.* Your "dark night of the soul" experiences will continue happening on an escalating level until you finally accept yourself and your gift of giving love and fulfilling your life mission. Breaking through your ego's wall of denial and ignorance about the matters of love verses worldly self-important values is critical. The resistance to acting lovingly and letting go of the old-guy rules for survival is one of your defining moments. Genuine masculinity is based on and motivated by your divine love, not your ego. Let love define you—not money, status or worldly success.

> *"Stay in touch with who you are. Remember*
> *that you are not your body, but a soul*
> *traveling with a body on a journey to joy/love. Remember that*
> *your soul is an everlasting part of God."*
> —*Neale Donald Walsch*

Women and Love—Thinking in terms of acting from love for many women is often a natural conflict. On the one hand, the ability to nurture, support and give is like breathing. The other hand, it feels like a prison sentence of being dismissed and not valued. Regardless of our gender, we are all wired for love and its collateral relationships. *My professional and personal experience is that women hold themselves back from their unlimited source and spiritual expression of love.* There isn't a boy, teenage male or adult man alive who doesn't need the loving touch of the female expression of God/Spirit—every guy needs it and wants it! The feminine expression of love in relationships, conflicts, business dealings, and family fights is like shelter to a stranger on a cold winter night. The feminine energy of loving resolution, understanding, compassion, and empathy is the healing energy to any problem—personal, professional or global. *Equality of men* *and women starts with the expression of love and forgiveness.* **There is no wrong way to feel love, but there are a million ways to hide it.** As a women hearing from a man (me) who is encouraging you to pursue, express and break out of your old roles of being scared, repressed and discouraged for doing your innate spiritual expression, how does it feel? I know this sounds strange and almost unbelievable, but it is not! Consider the female mythology of love, connection and resolution versus the male model of overpower and conquest. Many times a woman's compassionate nonreactive perspective and expression of love have the power to change her partner and the world around her.

A major universal shift toward the feminine loving energy began with the 2008 money crash on Wall Street. The old male-dominated system of greed, exploitation and dishonesty had officially expired. Now it's women's time and place to bring loving values to the workplace, professional careers and conflicts, and to the world at large. For women who can step out of the old role of acting like a man in a man's world rather than being women motivated by the power of love—everything changes. *Women need women to be loving of each other, and not critical of the sisterhood for breaking through the male glass ceiling of a loveless ego-driven world.*

Consider the following paradigm shifts for both men and women. For centuries men have been defined by what they did outside the home. Women were only defined by what they did in the home. Now the roles are becoming more balanced and natural. Men need to come home and be that loving energy in relationships. Women need to go out in the world and bring their loving energy and compassion to Wall Street. Love/Spirit always seeks to balance the unbalance in all relationships. *This is now the biggest balancing act the world has ever seen or witnessed!*

Game of Life: Time for a Switch—It's a Good One

Women's Love Changes the World—Winston Churchill said that if women were in charge of the world, neither World War I nor II would have ever occurred. The misunderstandings and emotional resentments could have been peacefully resolved through dialogue, not violence. Instead, anger, no communication, and revenge prevailed: the end result was millions of lost lives. Richard Nixon admitted prior to his death in 1994 that if his wife, Patricia Nixon, had known about his plan for spying on his presidential opponent, she would have talked him out of it. Instead, the former president followed the male model of "power vs. love" with a life-changing lapse of judgment concerning the democratic challenger, George McGovern (culminating in an illegal break-in at the democratic party headquarters and the resulting "Watergate" scandal). Within two years of that mistake, Richard Nixon became the first and only president in the modern era (since 1900) to resign while in office. The examples are endless of how a woman's perspective on resolving an ego problem can shift relationships, business issues, and entire world.

In 2008, the collapse of the money markets, bank controls and old institutional rules of greed broke down and led to a universal structural power shift. The result was that the old model for operating in the world was no longer functional. This dramatic shift allowed for the injection of feminine energy, love and understanding, into the financial industry and corporate western world. Now, our male-oriented society is leaning toward allowing the feminine values of love to become the new tools of life and how business is done.

Men's Love Changes the Family—One thing that every gang member has in common, regardless of affiliation, violence, or neighborhood—is that they are all truly "fatherless sons," looking for their father figure. Women can't be a replacement for the missing father. *Men can change the family by loving their estranged children and investing their energy into people not things.* Every son and daughter craves their fathers' attention, love and interest. If you don't believe me, ask an angry teenager, or a 20-something young man about his father. The answer is more revealing than the person speaking will ever know. Even if you don't have children, there are men and women around your life that need your male support, understanding and loving energy. *Love always trumps biology; be a father figure to the men and women surrounding your life.* These people are there for a reason. The ego has it all wrong. Men think that it's the money, the job, the big house and the beautiful wife/lover that is the real sign of success and the measure of a man—*wrong!*

The true mark of your male journey is the measurement of maximizing your loving potential in all relationships. Men have given up their greatest role—being a loving man, father, partner, boss, uncle, brother, and friend. There is so much misunderstanding about men and what it means to be a man. Acting from your soul/divine nature, love becomes the new inner compass for all your business, family, health and personal/intimate decisions. Love is the inner pathway for men that will take them into the world, not the other way around (away from it). Making any decision based on the theme of love always yields the greatest results, regardless of the current circumstances.

"Whether one believes in a religion or not, and whether one believes in rebirth or not, there isn't anyone who doesn't appreciate kindness, love and compassion."
—*Dalai Lama*

"We can't push away the world. We have to enter into Life fully in order to become free."
—*Ram Dass*

Open Up Your Doors of Your Heart—The powerful experience of giving, receiving and feeling loved is the transcendent nature of our entire human experience. The two quotes above underscore the importance of acting toward others lovingly. A benefit from acting lovingly toward others is the inner peace that comes with it. Recall the experience of feeling loved by your favorite childhood pet, your infant children pulling your nose, and your lifelong partner kissing you on your wedding day. These are the gorgeous, heart-filling human experiences from which we are changed. We didn't come to this time and place to withhold, blame, resent and avoid being vulnerable. We came here to learn how to forgive and ask someone for forgiveness: this is how love becomes an action.

Many times people will seek the highs of feeling loved. This tends to be the ego trying to steal the show and avoiding your life lesson plan. The problem with love coming from the ego is like having your self-acceptance coming from a jealous person: not a good outcome. The ego's acts of love are always self-serving and always have hidden strings attached. Your self-acceptance and soulful loving relationships start within you and come from within you, not from someone else. Love is a piece of God, Divine (whatever name you're comfortable with) within your heart and soul. The piece of the universe that we all have within us has to be expressed in your own particular way and style. It is your spiritual DNA's drive to express the piece of the universe that wants to come from you. There are a lot of phony lookalikes for self-expression, and your ego is deeply invested in being part of your connection to your life. If you allow it, the natural power of love within you can influence your entire relationship arena and romantic life.

The Endless Work of Love—Over the centuries, spiritual masters and teachers view the ego and your body as a costume covering up the divine soul within you. You aren't your body (looks, shape, race or skin color) or the things that your ego craves (fame, wealth, power and position). You are a living soul having a loving human experience. *Love is a force that is always working to awaken you, connecting you (conscious mind) and your soul back together.* Your new inner awareness immediately challenges your ego's control and stops the blame game in your head about the fairness of your life. Experiencing all the ups and downs of love is a roller coaster ride with incredible highs and lows that has no limit for your insight. All these loving personal life experiences can cause us to behave, react, or respond in ways that are empowering and also in ways that are disempowering. As one of the quotations in this book points out, love is messy, and that is our learning laboratory/classroom in this life. As I have repeatedly pointed out, your life will always be measured on the other side by your own standard and capacity to be loving and receptive of it.

> *"Love is never lost, it is only forgotten."*
> —*Wayne Dyer*

We are all wired, designed and pulled toward the magnet of love. Deep within in each of us is an unlimited source (collective unconscious) of endless love, understanding and compassion. The challenge is to get our ego and mind out of the way of our soul's divine journey and mission. One of the most creative ways our soul/spirit communicates with us is in the context of loving relationships. These "karmic" relationships started before we came here and will continue long after we leave our bodies behind.

In the last chapter and throughout this book, we discussed at length the various emotional, mental, psychological and spiritual roadblocks that we all encounter. The "Dear Human" letter at the beginning of the chapter is addressed to all of us who have felt like a failure, a complete fool, a victim of love and all the other disappointments that come as a result of relationship expectations not being met or understood by you or your partner. *We all crave the same basic things in any relationship: love, acceptance, and forgiveness.* How these variables of our heart and soul play out on our journey is the true magic and mystery of your life. How do our long-term love relationships that end in a painful divorce with physical restraining orders against each other serve any positive purpose? How does a cold loveless marriage create a positive outcome for our capacity for love and intimacy? The endless questions surrounding how love and intimacy work are as varied as the people asking them. All the questions and answers point toward your inner awakening to your higher purposes and ability to transcend your current challenges. How do I get my life moving toward the direction and destiny that I want? The answers are explained below, and in the last two remaining chapters of this book. This isn't a self-help journey, but rather your spiritual walk uncovering the hidden treasures and latent gifts buried inside your heart: *your experience of God.*

Rebooting Your Life: The Law of Your Karma (Good & Bad)—To a greater or lesser degree, everyone worries that their past behaviors, wrong decisions and hurtful actions will come up from the past into the present and thus ruin the present. It takes a lot to knock, detour or alter your new life off the spiritual highway. Your best approach to resolving past mistakes is to make amends with yourself and the people involved. Spiritual masters have taught that forgiveness and connecting to your soul/love within you allows for a lot of cleansing/healing of your past transgressions, mistakes and anger. Seeking forgiveness, self-acceptance, and self-awareness is critical to resolving, wiping out your past errors, and making room for the new chapter. *Many times, karma from past lives can help create "spiritual growth" opportunities in this current life.* What you choose to do currently with a relationship is the most important determinant in your spiritual awakening and journey. For instance, things can happen in your marriage/intimate relationship that seem absolutely unexplainable. The unexplainable usually occurs because that person, event, or painful emotional lesson has its roots in another lifetime. When I first learned about this dynamic (past and present karma), it was very unsettling and scary: how does it work, and what can be done to amend it.

Your Karma Factor—Since then (the last few years), I learned that we have a lot more control and choice in how we handle our life lessons, relationships and destiny. Karma isn't some invisible third-party force punishing you. Your experiences and learning today can be directed in a positive direction by your own spiritual insight and understanding. Much of the time men and women will fight the urge to forgive someone or accept their apologies. This could be a karma issue or not. It's the resistance to change and not acting in love with ego-driven motives that create major life challenges (negative karma). The immediate solution to creating instant positive karma is taking loving actions toward yourself and others. This concept of acting lovingly (positive karma) is considered the Golden Rule in how to treat yourself and others in life. It is the practice of the Golden Rule that off-sets, heals, and frees you to pursue your destiny unencumbered by past shame, guilt and negative karmic debt (old ego patterns). The Golden Rule was defined over 2,000 years ago by Jesus, and many teachers before and after:

> *"Do unto others as you would have them do unto you."*
> —*Jesus (Matthew 7:12)*

This ethical guideline stated by Jesus for past, present, and future behavior is the answer to your karmic debt remedy and questions. The Golden Rule is basically your inner loving compass for any and all decisions. All the different versions and forms of this guiding, insightful moral principle have one concept in common for all cultures, spiritual paths, and genders: *The Golden Rule asks that people treat others in a manner in which they themselves would like to be treated.* This includes Hinduism, Buddhism, Taoism, Judaism, Christianity, Zoroastrianism and the rest of the world's major religions. According to many religious and ethical scholars, the Golden Rule can be found in some form in almost every ethical tradition and teaching. Why? Before we answer that question, let's briefly define good and bad karma.

Good Karma—This is creating, giving, and taking positive loving action with the intention of doing something that is beneficial to the person or people involved. Good deeds are the actions, words, and feelings that empower, influence, serve and motivate others. Anything done with the motivation of love is always creating positive karma. The Golden Rule" is universally considered the working definition of any type of good/positive Karma in your life.

Bad Karma—This is the ego actions that cause present and future suffering for you and the people involved. Deliberately choosing to seek revenge, wanting to get even for a perceived wrong, speaking/acting in a manner that is aggressive and harmful to you and the intended person is considered negative/bad karma. It's the treating and acting toward people with the intention of punishing and repressing their life that is discouraged. Other negative actions such as cheating, stealing, embezzlement and exploitation of others are choices that create a present life of pain and suffering. A person's present-day choices have enormous impact on how their life/ spiritual journey is and will be. There is no mystery about negative karma. It is simply ego-driven and non-loving choices.

Why Meditate and Karma? Let's now answer the question of why the Golden Rule is universally considered the definition of good karma. When a man/woman begins to connect, develop and allow their intuitive nature to be expressed with feelings, actions of love, it becomes a guideline. Thinking of, serving, giving, and considering others as you would like to be considered is one of the primary aspects of your spiritual expression (good actions/karma). Meditation is the ability to silence, slow down one's mind and step away from the body's ego impulse. Meditation is to become more aware of your mind and intuitive feelings/thoughts. It slows down your breathing, mind, and heart. When someone connects to their inner spirit and soul by meditating, there is a transcendent nature to the experience and expansion of one's life and perspective. The ability to quiet your mind and thoughts and focus your energy inward allows you to concentration on the higher aspect of life. This is a powerful process that is beyond expression.

Practicing silence allows for your inner spiritual nature to see how to treat, resolve and be a peacemaker in your immediate world. It is the Golden Rule in action. The power of meditation is in developing the ability to *respond* to your life and not *react* in old ego-driven manners or mean-spirited ways. The more a person meditates (there is no wrong way to be silent with yourself and God), the more they create positive experiences in their life and relationships. Meditation takes the practitioner out of the elementary life lessons to deeper, more profound life experiences and lessons of the power of love and your soul. According to the spiritual masters of all traditions, meditation is the fast lane to accessing your deeper more creative self/spirit. Meditation isn't prayer. Meditation is sitting, kneeling, walking and/or anything that focuses your mind on your higher-self. Meditation is listening. It's the listening part that is the lifetime challenge.

> *"When you are with someone you love very much, you can talk and its pleasant, but the reality is not in the conversation.*
> *It is simply in being together.*
> *Meditation is the highest form of prayer. In it, you are so close to God that you don't need to say a thing. It's just great to be together."*
> —*Swami Chetananda*

Your Inner Peaceful Self—I love this quote by Swami Chetananda. It is the best working definition of how to meditate. It's sitting and being in the presence of Spirit, Universal Force, God, Your Higher-Self and all the different names for the universal energy within you and all around us. Your inner loving experience is the beginning of the next chapter in your life. It's nearly impossible to be caught up in the worries of the moment when you have experienced the inner peaceful power of this calm. It's why all the gurus, stories and spiritual teachings direct us to go inward to stop, watch, and listen to our creator within our hearts. Meditation provides an immediate connection to your higher-self, spirit, and the bigger selfless perspective for any problem or issue facing you. I am not an expert on the subject, but rather a practitioner of this unlimited source of comfort and untapped fountain of spiritual awareness. If you want to meditate right now, put this book down. Close your eyes. Breathe deeply, and allow something to happen.

It's important for you to know that if I can meditate, anyone reading this book can—*anyone!* Seriously, if I can silent my racing anxious hyperactive mind, you can also. I knew that I needed to sit still for 10 minutes a day and allow my heart and mind to slow way down. Now many years later, my daily goal is to stay still within my heart regardless of the emotional storms going on around or within me. Meditating has allowed me to find my own spiritual self-realization and inner divine connection. My personal experience of God through meditating and listening to my divine intuitive nature has completely transformed my life, my heart and allowed my soul to direct me going forward. I never realized the inner compass of love that I had at my disposal simply by sitting still. *The gifts of the universe are always free: meditating is one of the best gifts.*

You and Your Conversation of Love With God—

"God is talking to you every minute of every hour of every day. You are
never alone, or without help or guidance, counsel,
or advice. You need but purely
and earnestly ask a question and God will answer
you directly and immediately."
—*Neale Donald Welsch*

Wow and wow again! I have read this quote and Neales' numerous books over the years and I am always awestruck by the power of the conversation with God concept. It's a complete life-changing concept to believe, experience, and know that God is speaking to you all the time! Meditation, the Golden Rule, your karma, heartbreaking events, incredibly difficult challenges are all designed for you to awaken and hear what's always been and will always be—your divine connection! It's the new opening in your heart and mind that allows your inner spirit to literally have a voice, dialogue, exchange and conversation with your heart and soul. Maximizing your spiritual talents, using your gifts to their fullest, and becoming the man or woman that you saw on the other side before this incarnation all starts with your conversation and/or meditation with the universe. It's really that easy to speak with the universe. Sometimes (always) in life the simplest things are the very things that will revolutionize your entire world. The ongoing dialogue experience with God and your intuitive-self is one of those that will change you beyond any wish or hope.

Stepping away from everything you once knew and into something your intuitive self has known for eternity is your spiritual journey. Regardless of where you find yourself today (literally and figuratively), your life is unfolding in positive loving ways you couldn't have imagined. It's your life taking off on another level and perspective that isn't governed by the material laws of this culture, world, or your particular class system. It's you ascending to your inner heaven while still living your day-to-day life. *Tapping into your highest and best version of yourself has no regard for your past or your present emotional difficulties.* Let's now go to the last two chapters of this book to further explain and elaborate on the importance of developing your inner hearing for that still and quiet voice within you. This inner calm, peace, and unlimited source of wisdom and power are your roadmap going forward in this life and many more lives to follow. Once you start to connect regularly to the piece of the universe within you, everything changes. You can't pretend that you don't know better or that a certain old ego action or attitude is appropriate. You now have inner access to your greatest resource, which is your greatest life lesson experience: your soul's connection to God.

Never Without God After Your Experience—The quote below so beautifully explains that we are never the same after making that conscious soulful connection to God. It's your meditating, talking to God, listening to God, and being with God that is the primary learning purpose at this point in your life. Allow yourself to step into the next chapter of your life from within, and then allow it to direct you along your spiritual/life path. The peeling away, removing of the ego's illusion of separateness between you, yourself and others, is one of the most important experiences of your entire life! Every cell, conscious and unconscious thought, moment and feeling is changed through your conversation with God. Now, go say hello to an old friend—someone who has been waiting your entire life to be reintroduced.

"If you look around, you can find a face of God in each thing, because
He is not hidden in a church, in a mosque, or
a synagogue, but everywhere. As
there is no one who lives after seeing him,
there is also no one dying after seeing him.
Who finds him stays forever with him."
—*Shams Tabrizi*

Chapter 11

Your Inward-Bound Action Plan—Continuing Your Journey with Passion and Purpose

"Banish the imagery hope that happiness will come from worldly fulfillment.
Prosperity isn't enough, gracious living isn't enough.
You want to be eternally happy?
Seize the God within you and realize that the Self is Divinity"
—Paramahansa Yogananda

This opening statement by Paramahansa is a universal truth that is the secret within the secret: *You are what you seek!* The question of a lifetime is: What are you secretly seeking? We are the ones who struggle with the idea that all of our life's treasures are within us, not outside of us. The fear of never getting or not becoming what we seek clouds and hinders our inner awareness. The next biggest secret is that we all secretly seek, want, desire and long for love—not fame and fortune. Our ego, and Maya (the delusion of this material world) tell us that all our happiness is in our possessions and status not in our being. It's in finding our own self-accepting love that we find our divinity along with all our gifts that are waiting for our awaking. The entire universe (love) and all its potentials, mysteries and particulars are contained within our own soul/spirit. The complete evolving process of your soul's journey is accessing your *divine nature* while still living within your body and within your relationship circumstances. Now it's your journey's destiny to continue to ascend in the manner you want and truly desire. Whether your life is currently filled with nagging personal issues, money concerns, family drama, tragedies, deaths and health scares, remember they are all pointing you toward rediscovering the loving divine spiritual soul housed inside your body.

You no longer have to be a prisoner to your body, or the five senses governing your physical life. You're now able to reconnect with your sixth sense, which is infinite, not limited to this time, this place, or your self-imposed limitations. We all have a sixth sense of intuition, insight and soulfulness. Your intuition, sixth sense, (use any term you like), and spiritual awareness connection are all from the same inner source: *your soul*. Your divinity is soulful living from the enlightened perspective that the illusion (Maya) of this physical life can be overcome. There is something behind the veil of your ego and conscious mind, your super-conscious (divine nature) mind: *your divinity*. Your soul, divine nature, spirit are all words for describing the indescribable. The best way to experience God within is to look at the threads of all your miracles and connections that somehow all come together to form your life/spiritual journey. Nothing is random, including you reading this book and books similar books this. There is a life momentum pulling, tugging and pushing you to go inward to rediscover your natural birthright gifts: *your divine connection*! Your life is no longer defined, measured or controlled by the external events, or circumstances of the world.

"Sometimes one feels discouraged, thinking it is too late to find God. It is never too late. The Bhagavad Gita teaches that
if one realizes that this world is
false and only Spirit is real, though it be in the
last moment before death, he will
enter a better world after his earth-exit."
—Paramahansa Yogananda

The Gift of the Burning Bush—There is a story in the Old Testament (Exodus 3:1-4:17) about Moses and his experiencing the presence of God in a burning bush. Moses was about to give up on his life, calling, passion, purpose and his family, and the people of Israel, and then something happened. It's at that precise moment of his breaking that the bush (his life) catches fire and God speaks to him. The bush never burns-up or is consumed with the fire, but rather is the vehicle designed to get Moses' attention. How did the universe get your attention? The conversation with God forever changes how Moses viewed his life and relationship to the Divine. Moses was given his life mission and purpose through what seems like a random event.

Your Own Burning Bush—The metaphor still applies thousands of years later to you and me. When the hopeless moments in your life make you feel as if it's over and you're on a dead end street of despair and repeated frustrations, be open to another possibility. You can look deeper for the presence of the Divine Spirit or God, your Higher Power and/or your intuitive nature for your divine intervention—your own burning bush. Everyone will have a burning bush that will forever change their sense of feeling separate, isolated from God and directionless. Your relationship crisis and death/rebirth process are all pieces of that exact moment when you see the divine inside of your suffering. None of your feelings of despair or thoughts of godlessness are from your soul awareness or the unlimited fund of knowledge of divine wisdom (super consciousness). They are your ego holding you back from your potential and purpose.

You're forever changed by allowing, accepting and experiencing the endless power of the Divine within you and all around you. *Moses was never the same after experiencing the presence of God, nor will you be once you personally experience the Divine!* It's the experience of God that changed Moses—not his knowledge, education, religion, temple/church organization or theories. It's the direct experience of Spirit, God, and universal force that forever changed Moses' world and his perspective of how his life will work. The same residual effects of your time looking inward always create these types of long-term benefits and dramatic changes. The benefits of inner peace, calmness, hope, confidence in the divine, and a loving view of life come only from looking inward. How are these not the qualities we all crave and want in life? *Exactly!* these qualities are your souls expression, not your ego. Your ego will never appreciate or fully understand the inner intuitive tug within you to love and be of service to people.

Now you can go forward after finding the gift of the divine within your burning bush. Your new awareness is priceless and is always timely and perfectly perfect. What is your experience of the burning bush? How were you shaken from your prior life of sleepwalking? The key is continuing our life lessons education that has been expanded with our deeper awareness of the unlimited capacity of self-love and self-acceptance. Your inner healing (letting go of your resentments) of all the wrongs is expedited by accessing your divine nature through meditation. Your school-of-life learning curve doesn't seem as steep or relentless now that you have a fuller appreciation of your intuitive/divine nature. Now you are no longer in the 2nd grade of life, but rather in the laboratory of the world of adult relationships with the backdrop of your realized God-consciousness to guide you.

Everything is now increasingly more important for the next life/chapter going forward. Throughout this book, one example after another is cited, given and explained that once you enter into "the presence" you're never the same. You are becoming keenly aware of the hidden gift of your burning bush and the fire that has torched your life. The circumstances (burning bush, death/birth process) surrounding your most recent birth/death experience are all designed to create a deeper, more meaningful spiritual destiny for you. The residual personal lessons and the resolution of your disappointment (self-forgiveness) are some of the gifts from your higher-self to you. Your loving self-acceptance process is constantly readjusting your view of how things should have gone to how it actually is now. It's surprising to finally realize that all your inner desires, cravings, dreams, and hopes all come from your soul.

"Stay in touch with who you are. Remember that you are not your body,
but a soul traveling with a body on a journey to joy/love.
Remember that your soul is an everlasting part of God."
—*Neale Donald Walsch*

After the Fire—Seems kind of outrageous, and it's very hard to believe, comprehend, and accept that your passions and what you are craving, learning, and developing were all your own agenda items before you came to this life/incarnation—yup! It's almost impossible for a man/woman who operates primarily from their intellect to see that their strongest gift, power, and energy come from their soul/heart. Your soul energy is your personal expression of love, self-forgiveness, self-acceptance and compassion for your world, others and our global family. Your being and spirit are far beyond your intelligence, wealth, rational reasoning and academic perspective. Your complete and highest inner transformation is going beyond your body, mind, and reasoning. Remember that you are no longer a prisoner to your body or this material world. You are a spiritual being passing through for a quick visit on this planet. It's important to not get lost on your current life visit, but to recall what is the mission and purpose of your current destiny.

Your True Essence—You now know some of the answers to the various questions of your life. It's all inside of you, all of it. The answers and solutions are all within you even if the questions or problems seem unanswered or unresolvable. We all wonder what's inside of us. It's an appropriate question to ask in moments of self-doubt and shame—*will everything work out?* Your ego, critical voice, and shame factor are the absolute worse sources to consult when in need of a bigger, selfless perspective, hope and inspiration. Asking your ego for spiritual advice is like asking your worst enemy if you have any issues. The answers are inaccurate, never helpful, false, and create more despair and hopelessness. Your lower-self, uninspired-self-will doubts, mocks and dismisses all the intuitive resources within your heart and soul as useless. Your true spiritual essence, nature and divinity are about love, self-acceptance, and self-forgiveness. There is an old spiritual wise tale that one day a saint asked his shadow: What is your essence (what are you made of)? The shadow replied without pause, *"Love is my essence; it's the same essence you have, and don't forget."* Legend has it that the saint was speechless as his shadow went and sat behind him again. Don't hide from your essence and true nature.

God is always speaking to you (in all circumstances) to awaken your true essence. Your evolving spiritual journey fine-tunes your inner hearing and listening. The fires of your life have burned away a lot of the junk, illusions, ego and barriers to your heart and soul expression. Your destiny and life purposes are all coming into greater and greater focus as the fires of life work their miracles. The quote below by modern-day spiritual leader, Ram Dass, again points to the developing inner spiritual eye to see the greater purpose, greater good and your greater insight into your destiny. It all happens naturally as you open up to and accept the process of your spiritual awakening.

"...with this greater understanding comes greater compassion...an acceptance
*of **how it is**...an ability to see the divine plan*
in everything, even in your failings
and failings of others..."
—Ram Dass

Fire and Your Essence—Every question, concern and issue have their solutions within you. *It's never outside of you or in someone's control.* The answers, solutions, healing to your current circumstances start from within and go outward in your world. No one controls your destiny, regardless of how much power you have given them. No one can take responsibility for your journey, no matter how lost, powerless, clueless, helpless and depressed as you might feel or believe. You may not like what you're hearing in your heart and choose to resist and ignore your awaking. These types of rebellious-fearful ego reactions are normal and nothing to be upset about. It's completely understandable that your ego is protesting against the new order in your life. *Your ego works for your soul, not the other way around now.* This inherent earthly conflict (Maya) is common and the source of many lifetimes of issues and resolutions. The further you allow yourself to go toward your inner spirit, the further away your ego will be and feel. Your inward journey doesn't imply that you should go live in a monastery or a cave in the mountains. Rather, this new insight of self-love can be applied wherever you live and work, and to whomever you sleep next to and the children you hug. Your spiritual journey isn't about isolation, but rather inclusion. It's all about detaching from the ego-driven world we all live in, and looking inward to a new value system. Your new values are based in love, self-acceptance, self-forgiveness and the actions of your divine purpose. You don't have to or should you leave all your relationships or responsibilities for your deeper inward journey. Your current life is transforming, and many old and new pieces are coming together to form the next chapter.

The people in your life all have a similar piece of love/light that is distinctly expressed in their own creative way. Your immediate world needs your inner light/love to benefit and awaken itself from the illusion of this big daydream. There is an old saying that *"one candle can light a thousand candles and it never diminishes the flame of that candle."* The theme of giving holds true for what you can do, regardless of your ability or current circumstances. Your past heartbreaking lessons, romantic disappointments or perceived financial failures are the material (fire) that creates openings in your life for your soul to be expressed. There are no limits, lack of resources, or lack of emotional/psychological energy when it's fueled by your individual light/love passion. Your ego will aggressively litigate your private shame issues and keep you lifetimes away from your true inner expression. The ultimate internal conflict in your life is always between your ego's control and your souls destiny, purpose and love.

Intuition—Your Sixth Sense

"The things you are Passionate about are not random, they are your calling."
—*Abilene Fredrickson*

Your Psychic Channel—We all have a sixth sense, an intuitive nature that requires our patient attention, development and practice. A great analogy for fine-tuning this intuitive sixth sense is the same systematic process of becoming a distance runner. For instance, your ultimate goal for jogging or running might be to develop the physical ability/endurance to run a full marathon (26.2 miles). Initially, you would start off running two laps around the track and eventually build up the physical and emotional endurance to walk/run two miles. Developing your oxygen intake and emotional capacity directly impacts your physical ability to run an unbelievable distance—a 26.2-mile marathon. *This same type of soulful conditioning is used to begin accessing your infinite inner wisdom and insight for your life and all the people around you.* We all have the innate ability to communicate, see and know things that are beyond the material world of this present moment! Many times we dismiss these hunches as trivial or odd. All your inner feelings, hunches, and gut reactions are related to your intuitive sixth sense.

Your Inner Wisdom—Your intuition is a gift that requires your practice, respect, and listening ability. Soul consciousness, which is your intuitive and all-knowing self, is always within you. Regardless of how awful you feel about your life or the challenging circumstances surrounding you, your intuitive nature is never distant or unavailable for consulting. The super-conscious mind (spiritual awareness of the greater good) is your intuitive soul nature and/or inner voice. The super-conscious is what the field of psychology calls the "collective unconscious." It's the bottomless reservoir of wisdom, insight, solutions, ideas, and creativity that's accessible to everyone. The wisdom that is available via your intuitive/super-conscious mind is beyond human understanding. I once heard it said: *Your intuition is the thinking part of your soul/inner spirit.* It's the part of you that isn't attached to conventional wisdom and practice or to worldly limitations (sight, smell, hearing, taste or touch). Your soul is the driving energy force within your body, and your soul expresses itself through your intuition. One example of your soul's brilliance is your "creative genius" which is your intuitive nature always wanting to express itself. There is no limit to or glass ceiling for the depth and breadth of what is within you.

Your Intuitive Nature is Always Begging for Your Attention, Energy, Use—For instance, have you thought of someone and one minute later they called you? Maybe you had a hunch about a friend, and then you run into them at an airport, a thousand miles from your house. Or have you been confronted with what seems like an impossible situation and then you had an idea? The idea is outside of the prior parameters of your thinking and is sincerely a stroke of genius. You have a thought, and then your partner expresses the same thought to you. You're driving, walking or relaxing, and you think of someone and suddenly feel concerned for them. You later discover that they had some type of crisis, and you intuitively picked up on their distress. These are some of the everyday examples of using, listening, and acting on your infinite intuitive wisdom. Your intuition is always active, listening, and guiding you in ways that don't flatter your ego. It is always creating and building a deeper connection for you through your purpose and passion.

"If you go intellectually, for every little thing that you do, there are ten steps. Instead of going through these ten steps from one to ten, if you jump, that is what is intuition."
—*Sadhguru*

Listening to Yourself—When you didn't listen to your gut/intuitive nature and instead default (no judgment—we all have done it and still do at times) to your people-pleasing habits or ego, it's never a positive outcome. For whatever reason, whenever we choose our ego over our inner truth/ intuitive nature, the decision leaves us with a sense of regret. Trumping our intuitive sense for our ego never ends well—*never!* The emotional and spiritual aftertaste of ignoring our intuitive nature is never positive. It's similar to eating really bad junk food and then later regretting the impulsive choice. Our spiritual decisions are so similar to our physical life decisions. In fact, they all work the same: *It's your free will.* For instance, you said "yes" to something that your first intuitive thought was "no," but you did it anyway. Later on you're upset with yourself that you didn't listen to your inner voice. You know that event, trip or relationship wasn't right for you, and your intuition was indeed right. It turns out that ignoring your gut/intuitive hunch is a source of great frustration and personal disappointment. Your intuition was the opposite of your decision, but you just didn't want to believe and trust what you know about something or someone. Practice in learning to trust what you already intuitively know about what you know sounds silly until you act on it.

"Intuition is a very subtle, but powerful sense. It is not an outside force that compels you, but rather a small inner voice that knows."
—*James Van Praagh*

Trusting Your Own Wisdom—Learning to trust your intuition is trusting that a series of what appears to be mistakes, are really gifts disguised as disappointments. The frustration isn't in your choices, actions or decisions, but in not accepting your own wisdom and insight. Your entire spiritual path is a series of choices that you learn to trust and accept (self-acceptance) as your own inner wisdom and gifts. Ignoring your hunches, dismissing your ideas, inner thoughts, and gut feelings are all forms of self-loathing and self-rejection. It is no mistake that you know something that you can't explain, but still know is true about a particular situation. Your loving self-acceptance process includes developing your own capacity for trusting your intuitive insight and wisdom. These types of doubting events are common for all of us (myself included) and *we learn to listen by not listening*. It's always in the aftermath, that we realize what we already knew is what we now know! It takes courage to admit and acknowledge what isn't the popular decision and act on it. This intuitive learning curve is steep but worth every step, lesson, and opportunity that it creates for you. Wayne Dyer perfectly describes our innate intuitive knowledge as our own system of wisdom and self-protection on all levels of life.

"Your intuition is your soul's built-in radar system."
—*Wayne Dyer*

Practice with yourself by asking yourself questions about things and events that cause you uncomfortable feelings. The reasons are always pathways to listening and trusting your inner intuitive voice. What do you know intuitively right now but can't fully accept or act on yet? What have you acted on intuitively that was spot on correct? When have you listened to your intuitive voice to realize it might have been your ego wanting to control the situation? It takes patience, practice and silencing the noise in your head to adjust the volume of your inner voice. Learning the art of being silent (meditation) allows new information within you to be accessed and experienced.

Conscious "Spiritual" Mindfulness

*"What holds us together is FAR more important than what tears us ap*art."
—James Van Praagh

We Are All Connected—In religious and spiritual practices, all great teachers declare that the soul, intuition and your divine nature are your immortal soul within your body. Your soul is from the same spark that sustains the entire universe. Your soul expresses itself via your intuitive nature. *It has been said that a man/woman who knows their soul knows their truth!* Another truth is that your soul is a piece of the same energy that gives everything life. That "everything" is the entire universe and cosmos. This is a very complex and simple concept at the same time—we are all connected. The life force in everyone is the same life force that is in you. It's also in your ex-husband/wife, your enemy and all those other people who bother you. We are all connected from within (soulfully). The illusion of differences is clearly superficial because our souls all come from the same source and return to the same place.

The mindfulness of our soul is thought to be focused in the center of the chest, which in Hinduism is called the Atman, and in Buddhism, the pure Buddha-Mind. Christ said, *"The Kingdom of Heaven is within you."* Quakers call it the *"still small voice within."* This is the space of full awareness within you that is in harmony with the universe and thus is wisdom itself. *Inside each of us is the full spirit of God.* When you want to approach God, go inward. The meeting place is your inner place of peace. Your spiritual mindfulness is always within and available for your connection and meeting with your higher-power.

Infinite Energy Within You—Your soul is beyond this finite world and is part of the infinite and bigger force of life. You're not your body, or breath, or bones, or flesh, or mind, and especially not your ego. I am often asked: "Where is my soul?" The answer is: *Your soul is part of what is behind your breath, body, mind, and feelings.* When you go beyond the material illusion of your life and realize that you aren't your body or mind but something much bigger, that's your divine/soul awakening. Your soulful awareness is that you have always existed on a much higher energy level—your divine consciousness is what you are and have always been. You are that which is rooted in everything in the entire universe. This awakening is the self-realization" of your Divine/Soul nature. Once you awake to this fact, you will never go back to sleep or live or view your world the same. This change is sometimes called the "dark night of the soul." When your soul breaks through the illusion of your life (Maya), it is your life journey transcending into your spiritual journey. Spiritual mindfulness is being consciously aware of your inner connections (soul/intuitive nature), feelings, and thoughts while living in your physical body. Regardless of how often we forget about our connectedness to everything and everyone, it's always a refreshing feeling to remember where we all began.

> *"The Divine Beloved is always with you, in you, and around you.*
> *Know that you are not separated from Him/Her!"*
> *—Meher Baba*

Spiritual Citizenship—I got the chills when I wrote about the inner presence of God-consciousness, and I get them every time I read this section. The quote by the guru above reinforces our connection to the divine, regardless of what spiritual path we are walking or practicing. These universal truths don't require you to join or belong to any particular group or organization, but rather simply acknowledge your divine citizenship today. It's not about all the old ego stuff, wealth, position, looks, or accomplishments. Rather, it's all about your new chapter on the journey! Soul awakening and realizing that your greatest asset is the endless source of wealth/wisdom is "free."

It's your choice and destiny to either engage your inner intuitive nature or keep your distance from your spiritual heart and soul. Your newly developed intuitive insight and your soul awareness is described as your spiritual divine perspective and is now a mindful influence in your day-to-day life. Everything you want is within you. Many would describe this as a complete "game changer." *Let your game of life be forever changed by your soul awakening.* Lastly, I can't resist quoting the comedian George Carlin about the meaninglessness of our ego pursuit's verses our spiritual journey.

The end result is always the same answer: *Go within and find your pearls of great price.*

> *"Trying to be happy by accumulating possessions is*
> *like trying to satisfy your hunger by taping sandwiches all*
> *over your body and wondering why you're still hungry."*
> —George Carlin

What's My Life Purpose?

> *"If you are not true to the inner voice or the divine source within your heart,*
> *you cannot be happy.*
> *Your inner voice is your voice of truth, and it will never lead*
> *you in the wrong direction."*
> —James Van Praaugh

> *"If you can't figure out your purpose, figure out your passion.*
> *For your passion will lead you right into your purpose."*
> —Bishop T.D. Jake

You Always Have a Direction for Your Life—It's important to remember that all of our life experiences, jobs and career passions are all vehicles for coming to God and face to face with our divine inner nature! It's important to accept and realize that all your life's activities are spiritual vehicles for developing your full spiritual inner awareness. The two quotes above highlight the importance of listening to your intuitive nature, your passionate drive, your soul awareness and above all to your higher-self. *All these different aspects of "you" are all pieces of the divine within your heart.*

Given that you want to live your life going forward with your inner divine consciousness in the direction of your soul, how do you do it? This is one of the most often asked questions when someone is searching from the outside trying to find the key to unlock the door within. Your life path going forward will be about bringing your gifts out of your soul to the world around you. Spreading your personalized version of love action and its miraculous power is the end result of all our activities. Your passion, destiny, and calling are always an act of love and service to your world. Your calling isn't about fame, fortune, or social status, but rather about leaving your world a better place than how you found it. Your inner passion can and will take you far beyond your current experiences and beyond your horizon of life. There is nothing wrong with worldly or ego applause for your passion. It's the motivation of love versus "serving me" that is the issue.

Don't be judgmental or critical if your current job is trivial and meaningless. You will find the pathway for your soul's desire in many different situations and circumstances. How you express your inner passion is one of the greatest freedoms afforded us in this school-of-life laboratory. Whatever you find yourself doing on a daily basis isn't an accident. The reasons, lessons, and decisions that have brought you here are valuable to understand. There are no mistakes in the career, vocation and service you do every day, *These activities either lead you closer to your passionate expression or cause you to go find it.*

Your Current Reincarnation—*Steve's early story*: I remember at about age four playing in the backyard of my childhood home and having this thought that I came to this life to do things differently—not to be greedy, cheat or steal (past life issues), but rather to make a positive contribution to the world. I knew at age four that I wanted to do this current life differently and correct past mistakes (karma). Yes, that was my thought, and to this present moment, it has never left my conscious mind. The inner direction to be a soulful guy and complete what I came to do in this life has driven my decision to ultimately write this book. The pathway here has been a challenge, lots of stops and starts. The journey is continually getting better as I become increasingly more aware of my divinity and accepting of the school-of-life lessons that I continually learn and try to avoid retaking. You have had the same type of inner stirrings, thoughts, and impressions about your life course and passions. Your incarnation is for specific purposes that you want to achieve, heal and evolve. That inner intuitive drive is why you can't relax or forget what's inside of your heart/soul that must be expressed, developed, and shared with your world.

No Mistakes—It is no mistake that you picked this time, place, and life circumstances, this body, family, community, and partners to learn your soulful lessons. You had to be in a physical body (incarnation) in order to achieve your soulful purification (complete life lessons). You don't want to slow down, impede or hinder your spiritual progress. Your free will is a tool that can move you forward or off the pathway of your life. Your current physical life is purposefully designed to help evolve your soul's awareness to higher and higher levels of connection and loving expression. How you accomplish these new levels of awareness and peel back the layers of illusion is the beauty of your life. How to explore and find your divinity within your heart/soul is your choice.

> *"The Doctrine of Reincarnation provides the only plausible explanation for the seeming injustices in inequalities among men—all of whom are God's beloved children. The soul, all perfect and ever-perfect, is compelled by the law of evolution to incarnate repeatedly in progressively higher lives—retarded by wrong actions and desires and accelerated by spiritual endeavors—until Self-realization and God-union are attained. Having then transcended the Lord's delusion, the soul is forever freed"*
> *—Paramahansa Yogananda*

Reincarnation—For our purposes, this is one of the best working definitions of reincarnation. It's impossible and a waste of your life energy to resent, demand, or expect answers to seemingly incredible and unexplainable personal events, difficult circumstances and tragedies or loss. Our goal is to get out of our own way and allow our spiritual journey to take us to new places and deeper depths that we never even imagined or conceived. ***The ultimate purpose of your life purpose is union with God.*** How you accomplish your reunion with spirit, God, higher-power and your intuitive nature is your personal spiritual journey. The process of reconnecting to your soul/spirit is why all the prior self-acceptance and forgiveness issues have been explained in great detail. It's these personal emotional, psychological, ego, soulful wounds that create the roadblocks, that Guru Yogananda explains must be moved out of your life. One of the biggest gifts, deterrents, and challenges to living our life from our truest loving essence is romantic relationships. We are going to explore why and how to navigate this advanced school-of-life course that can be anything you want as long as you're willing to surrender to the process of your own loving transformation.

Your Soul Mate—Romantic Love & Your Spiritual Journey
The Ultimate Bond

"The real purpose of a relationship is about
two people coming together to serve
the growth and evolution of each other's soul."
—Katie Blackson

How Love Works for You—At some point on their life/spiritual path, everyone asks, seeks and wonders who their soul mate is or questions whether they will they find him or her. Another classic question is: "If I am currently married or in a significant relationship, is my partner my soul mate?" The answer to both questions is yes and yes. Soul mate relationships tend not to be the popular idea of rainbows, unicorns and sitting under a tree on a summer afternoon as we discussed earlier. Rather, these soul- connecting relationships are very powerful, complicated and a source of tremendous personal transformation for both parties involved. The notion that these idealized soul relationships are without challenges is a complete myth. Romantic intimate relationships, whether marriage or living together for years, are the proving grounds for all the personal questions and doubts that you will ever will have. Your love relationships are the jet fuel that moves your life forward with a partner.

With that said, some of the concerns and interests about soul mates are: who, what and why are they important? What if I am married to the wrong person? Will I recognize my soul partner when I meet them? Before we answer these questions, let's discuss some of the basic concepts for your continuing journey with a significant other—your soul mate.

"A soul-mate is the person who makes your soul grow the most."
—Caroline Myss

Soul Recognition—The two quotes by Katie and Caroline above are both about the power and purpose of intimate relationships and *your spiritual evolution*. Marriages, love relationships, life partners are all gifts that help us to learn, see and become aware of our life lessons. Remarriage, people getting married later in life or having a several romantic partners is a discussion and debate about finding the one, which is important and vital to your journey. Who is the "one?"

The "one" is a relationship that fosters love. It is the one that is helping, supporting and walking with your current partner along the road of life. Soul mate connections can be with a partner that you might have had in an unfinished past life or it can be simply starting a new romantic relationship. Many times, when you meet or have met a prospective partner and feel that there is something different about them, it's for a reason. Many times your soul recognizes the other soul housed in a new body from a previous life. These are very powerful life-changing encounters regardless of the duration or length of time spent together. *These souls reappear in your romantic life to further your soul realization.* How that happens is always very interesting. and sometimes the relationship can be very painful in order to grab your inner attention.

If you're currently married or in a long-term exclusive intimate relationship, you're in the "perfectly imperfect" relationship. You might want to leave your current relationship for a more spiritually oriented soul, but don't be too fast to hit the eject button. There isn't any magic or easy path with a soul mate because love relationships in this life are specifically designed to help develop your capacity and ability to be a loving, forgiving, and sensitive soul. This evolutionary process in romantic relationships has been the source of some the most painful traumatic encounters men and women have in their entire life. The primary reasons, purpose, and destiny of a romantic partner are to walk together on the shared spiritual path you both have. It's a problem when the focus of ego love overrides spiritual love.

In my professional and personal experience, soul mates can be the gasoline to your unresolved issues of self-acceptance and self-forgiveness. The emotional energy, disappointment, sexual chemistry, unmet emotional needs, raising children, divorce, remarriage, blended families, in-laws, affairs, dating and starting over romantically is all the "stuff" that soul mates bring to each other. It's a perfectly imperfect romantic movie that facilitates your inner intuitive nature to becoming keenly aware of your many life purposes. Your soul mate is sent to you for developing your intuitive nature for loving and accepting the divine spirit within you.

> *"According to Greek Mythology, humans were*
> *originally created with four arms,*
> *four legs and a head with two faces. Fearing their power,*
> *Zeus split them into two separate beings, condemning them*
> *to spend their lives in search of their other halves."*
> —Plato—The Symposium

Relationships Matter—Lastly, the loving, caring intimate relationship you crave is part of your journey during this life experience. We all want to be having another soul connect to our deepest and greatest asset, our own soul. Love relationships (regardless of sexual orientation) are one of the greatest tools for healing us and pushing us forward on our journey. Allowing your partner to show up in your life is valuable and important. Some people will have several soul mates on this current spiritual path. The reason is that all of your intimate relationships point you in the upward direction of becoming more loving, more self-accepting and more forgiving. These qualities are the substance, foundation and glue for your soul/divine expression. Divorce and breakups are very intense and tend to be the source of many awakenings because all the unresolved, avoided, and denied personal challenges are exposed for our greatest and highest good. Don't get me wrong—the power of betrayal and heartbreak isn't easily understood or recommended. Going through a divorce, heartbreak and lost love is like getting hit by lightning and wondering how will you survive.

You will always survive the romance and soul mate disappointment, but did you learn the lesson that they were sent to teach you? This is the only question you need to ask yourself with regard to your past or current romantic relationship. What is your current relationship showing you about yourself? Remember this journey is all about your awakenings and allowing them to happen. Soul mates wake us up! Consider, ponder, and reflect on the following quote as we look at the last chapter of putting your soul and life together on a daily basis. This quote by Lao Tzu is centuries old and another reminder of what, why and where you're going. Allow love to guide your steps, and the rest of your life will all come together.

"If you want to awaken all of humanity, then awaken all of yourself, if you want to eliminate suffering in the world, then eliminate all that is dark and negative in yourself. Truly, the greatest gift you have to give is that of your own self-transformation."
—Lao Tzu

Chapter 12

Crossing Your Bridge of Enlightenment--
Living Between Your Self and Your Soul

"It's a journey that has taken us from primary identification with our body, through identification with our psyche, on to an identification with our souls and ultimately identified with God and beyond."
—Ram Dass

"The true value of a human being can be found in the degree to which he has attained liberation from the self."
—Albert Einstein

Living Your Soul's Dream—How do we cross our life bridge from complete body identification to an inner abiding awareness of our soul's connection to the entire universe, each other and you? We are all souls having a human experience, not a human being with a soul. You don't have a soul. You are a soul and you have a body! Going down the highway of your life, this distinction is worth repeating as a cornerstone to your ever-expanding spiritual foundation and standard operating principles. *Your greatest purpose and life task is to achieve self-realization.* Your intuitive awakening, realization, and divine awareness is part and parcel to you fulfilling your destiny. Both scholars in the above quotes know that your inner liberation includes connecting to your soul, which transcends your ego-self. One thing is for sure—when we start to grasp, embrace and metabolize our inner timeless connection to everything and everyone, *a deeper meaning of life begins to surface within us.* Our soul recognition begins to transcend all the material (physical appearance), gender, social class, educational, economic and lifestyle differences and connects to the universal force within all of us: *love!* Love is a universal language which is always translated by the heart, not the mind. Loving actions never have to be translated—just accepted by the receiver. When you recognize the soul within people, along with the realization that we are all connected, related and bonded together, you no longer need to be judgmental or critical of differences in others. Everyone on this spiritual journey isn't separate or isolated, but rather all connected with the divine threads of love in our hearts. Your expanding soulful awareness of the vast connections allows you to no longer see the seemingly superficial material and gender differences in your relationships. We all come from the same source and return to the same source. Love is the strongest force in the universe and always prevails when applied to any circumstance.

> *"Love is the secret password to every soul."*
> —*Anthony D. Williams*

How Does Your Soulful Spirituality Work?—Throughout this book, we have been discussing the presence of God, universe, higher-power, spirit, divinity and your soul. Any discussion of God and/or spirituality can become instantly heated because everyone has his/her own personal opinion of the nature of God, heaven and of good and evil. Secondly, everyone also has their own idea about how they see and experience their world and God—this is our gift of free-will/choice. When we enter to the other side of this school-of-life we will measure our own theology and behavior with our acts of love. The measuring stick of our life will always come down to love and how we used it or avoided it, withheld it or gave it away freely. Our belief in God, or whatever names you're comfortable with, always points us toward the power of love and its limitless resources.

I recently watched Carolyn Myss (see bibliography for her books) speak on the subject of God and love. Carolyn told the story of how Teresa of Avila was examined by church investigators representing the Spanish Inquisition. They wanted to know if the visions and mystical experiences that she was having were sent by heaven or were tricks of the devil? She answered, *"All I know is that when I return to my body, I am filled with love—more love than I can describe."* The question of the ages is how can the devil make you love people and God even more? What we do know about the spiritual path and connecting to your soul/higher self is that the expressing of love in your life is contagious.

The point of Teresa of Avila's story is that her spiritual path and experiences of the Divine caused her to love more and courageously share her love. People ask me all the time about some of the features, ingredients, and elements of a loving spiritual path? If your spiritual path helped you to be or do any of the following, consider yourself going where you want to go: *Changing Your World with Love.*

Important Signs of Your Own Spiritual Awakening—

- Less judgmental of others and yourself.
- Less fearful of expressing love and forgiveness.
- More compassionate, understanding and tolerant of others.
- More insight into your soul/intuitive nature and the qualities necessary to nurture your spiritual path.
- Feeling hopeful about your life with a bigger spiritual perspective of your present moment and future possibilities.
- Applying the Golden Rule to all your relationships (personal and business).
- More accepting and forgiving of yourself first and foremost. Love always starts with your own loving acts of self-acceptance.
- Choosing to be a peace maker in your own world—rather than always being "right."
- Having and expressing gratitude for everything in your life—regardless of your current circumstances.

- Choosing your soul's inclusive opinion over your ego's greedy self-centered demands.
- Giving your soul/intuitive nature the primary position to direct and guide your life, your relationships, and your business dealings.
- Wanting and developing your own form and style of meditating and/or talking to God.
- Seeing and interpreting your daily circumstances with your spiritual eyes and not the illusion of "Maya"—ego.
- Considering the other side of life by investing in people and love for the greater good—regardless of your personal gain.
- Accepting the universal concept of impermanence vs. permanence for your self-awakening and connection to spirit in this world.
- Lastly, your soul is permanent-infinite—not your body. Enjoy your walk home.

Spiritual Signs and Wonders in Your Life—Any of these types of loving actions and lessons that lead you to care for and serve people are considered by one of my favorite mentors, Carolyn Myss, to be part of a holy/spiritual path. This is one of the gifts of this life as a result of crossing the bridge from a material life to a spiritually directed life. We will always choose (it's your responsibility) how to walk on our path with no imperative other than settling the struggle between our heart, soul and ego. Being motivated by love is always the correct path choice regardless of how others view your new life chapter. Acting with a spirit of love is as creative as the white puffy clouds in the sky—there are no right or wrong cloud formations! Neither are there any wrong or incorrect ways to discovering your soulful journey when done with proper motives. Love has always been and will always be a positive guide, and no one is ever wrong with that choice. Choosing loving actions and deeds will eventually cause your ego to become aggressive, defensive and increasingly needy for your devotion. *Ultimately, your ego will surrender control of your life to the maker of life: your divine self.*

No life/spiritual path that is motivated, directed and guided with the purpose to serve, love and support the people in your family is going to disconnect from the greater divine nature. These types of choices are having your own slice of paradise on this side of heaven. *Remember, your spirituality is your personal experience of God/Divine. Religion is following someone else's experience of God.* Everyone, including you, is intrinsically designed for their own personal experience and expression (mission) of the divine. Let's never stop, judge or hinder anyone from finding God within their heart and soul. Empowering the people in your "orbit" to discover their own spiritual self-realization is part and parcel to your life purpose. In the quote below, James Van Praagh describes perfectly the internal operating system that we all come from and need to further develop—self-acceptance.

"Life is a journey made up of many twists and turns. Each of us comes to this planet with the intent to learn about ourselves through interacting with others. Without Love and awareness of self, we cannot know how to love others."
—*James Van Praagh*

Six Blind Men and the Elephant—This is a story that is very old and timeless, and it is exactly what all of us on our spiritual path must never lose sight of or forget (myself included). When we have experienced pieces of the divine intuitive soul within our life in a certain way, that doesn't make it the only way to be spiritually connected. Our experience doesn't automatically imply that someone's different experience, belief or theological perspective is wrong, any less valuable or better. Everyone's experience of their higher-self, spiritual nature is priceless and deeply personal. How you became aware of your spiritual path in this incarnation is solely your responsibility and destiny. Your soulful expression of love and service is your spiritual footprint on the world. Implying that there is only one correct way to reach enlightenment makes as much sense as saying there is only one way to communicate. There are so many different dialects and languages in the world, and no one is wrong for speaking his own language.

Lastly, there is no perfect language, even though English-speaking people tend to think that we speak the best language. English might be the most popular language in the Western world, but never is it the right or only language for people. No one is on the wrong holy divine path when their actions are soulfully motivated by love, forgiveness and self-acceptance. Unfortunately, the human nature's ego likes to form groups that exclude others. The spiritual journey includes every soul on this planet, regardless of their personal orientation toward God. **Spirituality is always an inclusive venture, never an exclusive group.** We all belong to the same club of life: *love*. The only matter of business on your spiritual/life path is addressing your life lessons, regardless of your neighbor's acceptance or rejection of you and your beliefs. Consider also the following story for the power of difference and acceptance:

The Blind Men and The Elephant

Once upon a time, there lived six blind men in a village. One day the villagers told them, "Hey, there is an elephant in the village today." They had no idea what an elephant was, but they decided, "Even though we will not be able to see it, let us go see it, let us go and feel it anyway." All of them went to where the elephant was. Each one touched the elephant.

"Hey, the elephant is like a pillar" said the first man who touched his leg.

"Oh, no, it's a like a top" said the second man who touched the tail.

"No, it's like a thick branch of a tree" said the third man who touched the trunk.

"It's like a big hand fan" said the fourth man who touched the ear.

"It's like a huge wall" said the fifth man who touched the stomach.

"It's like a solid pipe" said the sixth man who touched the tusk.

They began to argue about the elephant and each one of them insisted that he was right. It looked like they were getting agitated. A wise man was passing by and he saw this. He stopped and asked them, "What is the matter?" They said, "We cannot agree on what the elephant is like." Each one of them said what he thought the elephant was like. The wise man calmly explained to them, **"All of you are right."** The reason every one of you is telling it differently is because each of one you touched a different part of the elephant. So, actually the elephant has all those features that you said.

"Oh!" everyone said. There was no more fighting. They felt happy that they were all correct.

—John Godfreys Saxe's verison of the famous Indian legend.
See bibliography for complete listing

Moral of This Story and Your Own Story—Everyone has their own individual experiences of their soul/intuitive nature. Its part of the universal plan that everyone has their own experience of Spirit/God, the power of love and individual perspective of their own Divinity. Your spiritual path is your own journey that some will understand, but many will not (not your problem or concern). Much like the six blind men and the one wise man, there were at least seven different perspectives on the same issue at any given moment. All seven opinions and experiences were correct about the different pieces of the elephant (God). It stands to reason that the same holds true for our own spiritual/divine experience and incarnation path. This story points out the need for all of us to be more tolerant, accepting and open to different viewpoints of God and life other than our own. Being accepting and open minded about differences allows us to live in harmony with others. The ego/Maya loves to create divisions, barriers and arbitrary differences about spirituality so people focus on that rather than the universal soulful bond we all share.

Acceptance Process—This peaceful acceptance of others is known as the Syadvada, Anekantvad, or the *Theory of Acceptance*. Unfortunately, human history is full of religious wars that were fought over the simple differences of why, what and who's experience of God is the right one. We could spend the next 1,000 years lamenting the human error in pursuing the correct interpretation of God rather than the power, presence and personal experience of God/Spirit. Let's agree that one of our major human follies is trying to know God rather than having a personal transforming experience of the Divine. Experience always trumps knowledge on your spiritual path.

Fortunately, all of our experiences of God are correct and part of the bigger picture of the universe. No one on this side of life has comprehended the whole scope of the Divine—*no one!* Your spiritual journey will always be some form of expanding and accepting your capacity to express love. *It's not about who is on the right team. We are all on the same team going to the same place, since we are all connected!* Developing humility about your insights allows for greater wisdom and a greater ability to experience the presence and power of your own divine nature. Who do you need to accept in your circle of relationships? Who rubs you the wrong way? What group of people, religious group and/or race do you have a negative opinion about?

Judgment Stops/Stalls Your Life—The reason for the story above and the strong spiritual warning for tolerance is the power and deadly nature of being judgmental. Ironically, one of the greatest tragedies of spirituality is how it tends to breed intolerance and judgment of others. On a personal level, being critical, vindictive, and punitive toward others is the ego's greatest victory to stalling and hindering your spiritual progress. When you're critical, resentful, vengeful and verbally judgmental, your soul, spirit and intuitive nature are put on mute. It's not possible to be concerned, loving, caring, and accepting of yourself or others when you're verbally assassinating your friends, lover or parents. One immediate result of enlightenment is that a judgmental attitude no longer has a room or a place in your life. Your ego is highly invested in creating isolation, separation, and fragmentation of yourself, your spiritual nature and your divine relationship to others. Any type of ego-driven criticism is like pouring gasoline instead of water on your plants and wondering why they are all dying. Judgmental action is a reflection of our own lack of self-acceptance and understanding of our soul interconnectedness to everyone.

Feeling secretly shameful always feeds into all the ingredients of being judgmental of your own brother/sister. It's starts on a personal level and spreads to your entire world from that critical fearful perspective.

Choosing to reserve judgment, allowing another person's story to be told and understood allows for the connection of souls. The ego always creates ways to separate people for fear of losing control of them. Love makes emotional room for differences which enlarge our ability to actively see and accept others. The quote below illustrates the divisive nature of judgmental and negative gossiping about others. No one benefits, and it creates unnecessary suffering and emotional pain for you. All world religions have teachings advising against the pitfalls of being judgmental and aggressive toward others.

> *"Spiritual path isn't straight line to enlightenment.*
> *There are a lot of back and forth, negotiations, if you will*
> *between the ego and soul...*
> *Your heart closes in on judgment and can only be reopened by*
> *being loving toward yourself and others."*
> —Ram Dass

What Would Gandhi Do? This question may sound corny, but please hear me out. Mahatma Gandhi advocated for change by being peaceful, loving and committed to the greater good of man. He saw the soul of the men involved the six prior assassination attempts on his life. Gandhi used the power of peace/non-violence while liberating India from England— without declaring war! I have found myself asking the question *"What would Gandhi do?"* when I feel the hair on my neck standing up and my blood beginning to boil. Gandhi was a modern saint who resisted the temptation to fight fire with fire, but rather to choose peace. The Gandhi question reminds me to find the fastest way to get out of my old ego reaction and choose a loving response. The model of love and peacefulness that Gandhi used with impossible situations works, and it changed India and the world. The same can hold true for you and me, if we choose it. You can't be defensive and verbally aggressive and peaceful and non-reactive at the same time! Oil and water don't mix, and neither does fear and love!

You have either an ego reaction or a soulful divine response to any challenge. The divine response automatically furthers the greater good of you and the persons with whom you are dealing. The ego reaction only furthers the breach and disconnection between you and your intuitive nature. Fear (ego) never breeds courage, but rather a despair that perpetuates painful damaging relationships and self-defeating actions. I highly recommend that you have a "pocket mantra" ready to use when your buttons are getting pushed—reminding you to ask, *"What would Gandhi do?"* when encountering, dealing with, and managing the difficult personalities on our path.

Who Inspires You?—It could be Mohammad, Buddha, Martin Luther King Jr., Dali Lama, Jackie Robinson, Mother Teresa, Jesus, or any spiritual role model who speaks directly to your heart. An old friend of mine always asks herself: "What would Sister Stella do?" Sister Stella is a Catholic nun with 60+ years of service who inspires thousands of children in the greater Los Angeles area. Sister Stella inspires my friend to pursue the "higher path" when dealing with challenging personalities.

Who inspires you? Find your own inner role model (living or dead) who automatically reminds you of your higher calling in life as a maker of peace and sender of love to all. There will always be people who trigger your old wounds, dismiss you and betray you as part of your classroom-of-life experience. The antidote to deescalating any type of violent judgmental attitude, belief or emotional reaction within you is to remember you aren't ego-driven, but rather spiritually motivated. It's imperative to choose love over violence (verbal, emotional and physical) when you're feeling powerless. Anger, fear and aggression are natural ego responses when we feel powerless and at the mercy of old painful circumstances. There is no true or lasting personal power in anger or revenge. ***Your lasting power is always within you, and that is your true essence: Love!*** Saying "What would Gandhi do?" helps to refocus me on my spiritual path and how I want to move beyond feeling powerless, being angry at my old wounded ego patterns. I like to say to myself, *"What would my inner Gandhi do?"* All joking aside, it's humbling and courageous to truly listen to your inner response about a personal "teaching" moment.

What would …...(fill in the blank) do? Then allow your soulful energy to flow through your heart and mind for a loving, divine response. You will be the most surprised at the answers that come to you as a result of asking for the greater good for direction and wisdom.

Never Forgotten or Forsaken: The Power of Being Misunderstood—

"Misunderstanding is the root of all fears and fear is the root of all evil."
—Bill Philipps

This quote is a great way to help explain how evil, sin and hatred operate in this world. I have no idea who created this phrase, but they clearly knew the power of love and it is so easily misunderstood. Choosing love and "turning the other cheek" can feel like you're getting screwed over by your ex-partner, your family, your former business partner or God. Choosing to be non-defensive, peaceful, and soulful can appear as a sign of weakness. The common misunderstanding by people is in trying to understand the divine through the eyes of the ego. The ego/self/Maya perspective on life never comprehends the charity, love and selflessness of the spiritual journey. Failure to keep your ego in control when someone is provoking you to a breaking point can lead to lifelong misunderstanding and hatred. It is at your deepest and darkest moments of feeling separated from your intuitive nature that you stop and wonder where God is.

The answer is that God/Spirit is always within your heart! It's the most perfect timing of untimely events—seemingly unfair circumstances that lead to an inner and outer explosion in your life. The sense of abandonment is real and many times can lead to complete mental, emotional and psychological confusion. The extreme example of this forsaken and spiritually shaken experience is suicide. Becoming so disoriented and spiritually disconnected from your soul/spirit and believing your ego is HELL on earth causes people to end their life.

"Your thoughts and emotions are the drama
(hell) that you create in your mind.
You must be able to end it somewhere-meditating."
—Sadhguru

Hell is Here, Not There—People ask what is hell like? Feeling complete and utter despair is your hell on earth and a very serious crisis to reconcile. It all starts with how your life was and is now becoming, which is overwhelming. So much of the "hell," psychological pain and emotional heartbreak is only within our ego mind. There are the moments when your soul transcends your body ego control and illusion of life by *dethroning your ego*. The only way to gain soul perspective for your life is by experiencing your ego as a follower of your inner wisdom and divine essence of love. This life-changing internal switch (ego-driven to being soul-driven) allows for direct access of the divine to engage your complete conscious and super-conscious awareness. It's at these critical moments that your entire personal life/spiritual perspective is enlarged to include all the limitless possibilities of the universe flowing through you! *Ultimately, you come to realize that you were never truly forsaken, but rather your ego needed to be ejected from the control center of your heart and soul.*

Your Life Never Ends—When Jesus was hanging on a wooden cross waiting for death by extreme physical agony, he knew that his moment to stay connected to his higher power was upon him. The mindset to remain connected is challenged to the point where you give up, but you really don't. *Death isn't the end of your journey, but rather the next step.* Death loses its bite when your soul reconnects you to your homeward journey and takes you to the other side (your awakening). What appears to be a loss is really a gain by losing your old life. Your new life, rebirth and transformation can only be achieved by your own death-birth cycle. Jesus had his, and to this day still enjoys his connection with God. You can also have an eternity of enjoyment by allowing your death-birth cycle to evolve.

When you feel like you're hanging by a thread onto life, ask for your divine nature to remind you of your endless connection to God in spite of the emotional pain in your life. It's all within you to come back from the dead and reinvent your career, marriage, your family, and ultimately, yourself. If there is one last major hurdle to discuss in this book, it is the following three topics: Maya, devil/evil and the illusion of the material world.

Duality of Your Life—It's Natural

Maya-Devil/Evil-Illusion—These words are all the same dynamic for our complete disconnection from our divine nature. Throughout religious literature "Maya" is an Eastern/India cultural term meaning the production of powerful illusions as god-like in experience, but are not real. The deception of Maya is that nothing is permanent or divine in nature, but appears to be. Maya is the infatuation with the outer world of power, position and money. Maya/devil/illusion has no regard, no respect, and no desire to cultivate an inward spiritual connection with you and your world. It's these seemingly real-life illusions that cause all of us to doubt, forget and ignore that still quiet voice within our hearts (God). The intoxicating powerful illusion of Maya is discussed in all cultures as the greatest barrier to reconnecting to the God within you.

As I have come to understand it, illusion, Maya, and evil/devil is anything that isn't permanent, eternal, and unchanging. Anything that changes, shifts and transforms is considered Maya, and this includes practically everything that is perceived through the five senses. That which is unchanging and eternal (your soul) is considered absolute truth and part of your inherent divine nature (see Paramahansa Yogananda and Debra Moffitt in the bibliography for further explanation). The illusion of power, position, and evil are all part of the movie of your life. The idea of evil as a lasting power is also an illusion of this life, movie and play in which you are starring.

The Power Struggle of Your Life—People wonder why God created evil on this planet. Let's get this fact straight, God/Divine didn't create the devil, evil or the illusion of power, *we did!* These forces of this life are here to help us find and discover our deepest and greatest treasures within our heart and soul. The illusion of permanence is deceptive because it causes people to hold onto, grasp and abuse others to have the illusion of Maya/god. It's this epic contrast of illusion versus your soul in this school-of-life which is the *gift of duality*. Our entire life is always in a contrast illustrated by the duality between the sleepwalking state of man and the eternal God-wakefulness soul. This incredible process of developing your inner spiritual eye and overcoming this dream state is our soul's ultimate triumph and purpose. The key is to seek the wisdom and insight to rise above the dualities of your life and awaken to the soulfulness of your God/Divine connection. It's our life journey's opportunity to rediscover our everlasting connection to the bigger universe and not to our little ever-changing dream world state of mind. The short answer to why evil exists is that it's part of the world of illusion that we all live in. It's the choices of people treating others out of fear that creates the tension, hatred and misunderstandings that lead to fatal outcomes.

Why the Emptiness and Feelings of Separation?—The life forces of deception and evil all converge to help you realize that you aren't your body, your mind, or your possessions. The emotional emptiness within you is always the reminder of the gap between your ego and your soul. Maya keeps the barrier wall up between you and your Spirit/Soul until you break through this powerful illusion. It's your own spiritual awakening that allows you to see that the illusion of your deep emotional separation from God, from your world, and from people is false. Your personal experience of the divine connection is the bulldozer to eliminate the illusion of spiritual, emotional, psychological separation within you. Your soulful recognition of your connectedness to *everything* is what begins to permanently fulfill you.

Resisting your divine nature and denying your soulful awakening only deepens the black hole of emptiness and suffering within you. Denying, ignoring and dismissing your divine nature are classic behavior patterns of sleepwalking through your life. It's impossible to avoid, disregard and ignore that "still quiet voice" within when the noise in your life is silent for a few moments. Choosing to live without that "spark of light" triggering your inner consciousness is a very lonely existence. My office is overflowing with people who are in complete despair about the emptiness within them. They feel fooled by life (ego) and feel worse for all the choices, actions and ego decisions of choosing money over people. Remember our discussion about the story of Scrooge? Scrooge did literally and figuratively wake up from his "Maya dream state" to realize the purpose of his own life (giving), and it wasn't to make more money or step over the helpless.

Seeing Beyond and Below the Surface of Your Life—Your body fades over your life cycle like an old jacket covering the soul. Your mind is the conduit to understanding and experiencing your divine nature. Our possessions are for temporary purposes only to help, serve, and allow us to live on the earth. Our soul's awakening develops through this different duality of life experiences, illusions and God realizations. If you allow it, the divine spark that is in everyone begins to burn away all illusions surrounding you. It's the illusions, Maya and evil experiences that cause us, via emotional suffering, to explore and become spiritually aware of our deepest and most powerful inner truths (God within you).

Seeing Your Bigger Picture—Breaking through the intoxicating nature of the world to discover the eternal world within you *always* goes through the process of awakening from Maya. We could discuss these very powerful concepts and philosophical ideas endlessly—to no avail. It's important to remember and be mindful of your own evolving awareness of the distortion of money, wealth and the transitory nature of your worldliness. Your greatest asset isn't your retirement fund or savings account; it's your soul's realization that Maya's promises are empty ones. Maya, illusion and the devil always leave its victims empty, hopeless, fooled and despairing. *The biggest lie in this world is that everything you want can be acquired through the senses and this world!* The truth is that your life is, has been, and will always be within you, not outside of you. Once this awareness becomes your inner guide, the world begins to look and feel like a feature-length movie in which you're an actor or observer.

Fifteen Daily Reminders for Keeping Your Spiritual Balance—There is a classic book, "Pilgrim's Progress," which was written in 1678 while the author, John Bunyan, was jailed for his spiritual beliefs. The book is one of the best metaphors and analog of the deceptive nature of Maya/Devil, the seductive illusive nature of this world, and man's quest for a spiritual awaking. Another brilliant spiritual-minded author is C.S. Lewis and his "Screw Tape Letters," a hypothetical discussion with the devil about the foolishness of man. These two books are incredibly powerful for a commonsense approach to exposing the illumination nature of this world and the deceptive duality of life without God. In order not to live in the

"Valley of Despair" or become kissing-cousins with the enemy of your soul (ignorance), the following 15 ideas are short ideas for those moments when your spiritual truths seem lost under the waves of anxiety, despair, and our fears of life.

1. ***You never die!*** Only your body and ego die, that's why they (ego/body) are so scared of death and abandonment. Remember your life is always a duality between what's real and what's not—choose lasting qualities, actions, and deeds (love). Death of your body has no grip or control of your soul now!

2. ***When in doubt on what to do in any given moment, ask yourself this question: What would love do?*** The answer usually steps around your ego-pride and immediately widens your perspective. Meditate and listen to your inner voice of wisdom. Ask your spiritual guru, role model (Gandhi) what he would do in any particular circumstance. Listen for their answer.

3. ***Miracles are the oxygen of your soul.*** Fear is the lower option of yourself as the controller of everything—don't be a control-freak. Let it go and it all gets done! Whatever that is (only you know).

4. ***It's never too early to apologize, forgive yourself and accept the differences in your friend/partner/family.*** It's never too late to tell someone how much they mean to you! Forgiveness, acceptance and love are the essence of life that everyone craves and needs. Be generous with all these qualities.

5. ***You may be only one person in the world, but you don't know who you mean the world to!*** Remember the movie, "It's A Wonderful Life." You will never know how your life impacts and influences others. Your passion will always lead you to your life purpose. You and your life matter.

6. ***Your life is endless!*** Your spiritual journey will always be a process, not a destination. Don't panic over a bad moment, or a bad year or a bad

10 years. Your life is so much bigger than any moment or moments on your path.

7. ***Death-Rebirth transformation cycle is your secret insight for any day or situation.*** Everything always changes, including you. Allow yourself to change for your highest good. This is a time-limited class project called your "life." Your class is in session as we read this page.

8. ***There are no losses in your life—Never!*** It's through the understanding of losing that you're getting your spiritual insights, awakenings, and learning/mastering your life lessons. Your journey is all about you becoming more and more the soulful person you always desired. You win by losing your ego. Divine love sees the gifts in your emotional hardships—your successful failures!

9. ***Remember to ask yourself, "Where is the duality here (love/anger)?*** Your hardest life lessons are always in a duality context. Dualities are the contrast for finding the "pearl of great price" within you. The biggest barrier to your life journey is the duality of soul vs. ego. Always choose your soul's intentions and watch your life transform.

10. ***Feelings of separation, emptiness, and anxiety are all common side effects of having an ego-driven life.*** Realizing that your soul/intuitive/divine nature is only passing through this life is a perspective that will comfort you in any situation. You're a visitor in this life. Your home is on the other side.

11. ***Heartbreak, divorce, losing a lover, and disappointment are all part of the process of awakening that will create the opening of your inner spiritual eye to your current destiny.*** Listen to your soul, spirit, intuition and guardian angels (we all have several). They are always within hearing distance. They will help you get through this challenge with a wider, deeper and fuller understanding of you and God.

12. ***Whatever has happened or should have happened if you only had known better isn't worth your shame or self-loathing any longer.*** Your deepest essences are pure love—pursue *your* inner awareness/

happiness like a dog chasing a squirrel. Remember that Spirit hides the secret of life/happiness within you. You be the one to look inside and embrace it!! Your lasting happiness is inside of you, not on Wall Street or Disneyland or Beverly Hills.

13. **Your "Hut/Life" might have burned down, and your job, family, or health falls apart.** It's at these moments of utter despair that the endless grace/love of the universe shows up, and it's always a miracle. Don't stop looking! Expect your miracle—your life has sent God major distress signals, and he/she always answers your calls. Keep calling and talking to God.

14. **The illusion Maya of your life isn't your story!** The illusion of wealth, power, prestige, fame, sexual prowess and any material craving are just pieces of your bigger puzzle that starts and finishes with your divine connection. It is never too early to ask God for his/her divine assistance. Your life isn't in this world. It is only living in this world. Your true home and destination is on the other side, the same place you came from—remember that! Take comfort that your worth isn't measured by your ego.

15. **There is nothing that you do that doesn't involve relationships.** Accept the fact that your textbook of life includes every type and kind of emotional relationships. Allow yourself to flow, accept and forgive whatever is needed in any of your various relationships—especially the most important one: you and Spirit! Your divine intuitive connection is the ultimate lifeline you need for any emergency, crisis, loss, death or fear. Dig deep in your heart and find your pearl of great price.

Finally, this whole love story of your life really does turn out well in ways you couldn't have ever imagined. These 15 ideas are just a few of the many spiritual reminders you can consider while sitting at your desk and working on your computer or wherever. Store them on your phone or anywhere you need them. Everything is within you for your greatest and most pleasurable life and fulfilling your passionate purpose. We forget that this whole thing called our "life" is part of something so much bigger than our ego can ever conceive. It's important to remember that we are all part of something much bigger than our own world.

> *"Our universe is much larger than we can conceive. We must keep our minds open and learn to look at things from a spiritual and responsible perspective."*
> —James Van Praagh

Conclusion—First of all, I don't believe in good-byes. This book, story, life, or spiritual ideas will never be done or completed, nor should it. This is just a break in the action. I know more is coming, and I will share it all and pass it all along to you. The "it" is our collective God realization and divine daily experience. I am not an expert on any of these matters—not at all! I just have this burning passion to tell you—keep going deeper into your heart and soul. Demand that the presence of God/Spirit be revealed to you right now—wherever you are! Don't settle for knowledge *about* God, but rather demand from your intuitive nature to *experience* God. The difference is worth the asking. It's the experience of the divine that has caused me to step away from the conservative secular humanistic psychological training/approach and engage in the powerful experience of Love/Spirit/God in my life and in all the people that I encounter.

Experience God—It is the experiences of God that has no regard for your personality, only your openness to the divine. Zip code, gender, country and nationality have nothing to do with your innate ability to find the pearl of great price within you. The pearl, diamond, or treasures are all metaphors for your soulful God awakening and inward-bound journey. Whenever you're feeling hopeless and despairing, be open to the divine coming to you in ways that you could never think of or hope for. The grace of God is like a beagle chasing a squirrel, reckless and determined to catch your inner attention. *The pursuit can take many lifetimes, but now is a good point to surrender to the divine and put your ego in the backseat of your life.* You would not be reading this book or books like this one if you hadn't already started your inner awakening. You're going beyond the duality of illusion of your life to the life within you that is priceless, timeless and unchangeable.

Since the age of four and throughout the subsequent years, I have been alternately open, closed, and avoidant until finally I embraced my spiritual path through the lightning bolt of several death-birth transformation cycles. There is nothing in this book that isn't first-hand experience on my own spiritual/life journey. I am here with you and offer my piece of the divine for your next personal chapter. Your personal experience of God/Divine is the key to open every door you choose. Once you experience the Divine you will never doubt, question or wonder about your purpose and passion and how things work. *Your inner awakening is your soul's only purpose for your life.* How your particular awakening has evolved is the primary theme of this book, leading you inward. The illusion of your particular *life* fades into the dust when you rise above the "Valley of Despair" and see your life from *above.*

I want to thank you from the deepest part of my heart and soul for taking your time to ponder these ideas with me. We are truly friends even if we never see each other in person or via the world at large. It's my soulful passion and purpose to remind you that we all are going back home together. Some sooner than others, but we are all going in the same direction. Sometimes we need to go south before we can find our true northern direction. There is nothing in this book that isn't based on universal spiritual truths that I have experienced to a greater or lesser degree. Yes, unfortunately I have wondered if this spiritual story really does work out. I have wanted to disappear because the pain of the death-birth circumstances pushed me to my utter breaking point. My heart broke into a million pieces, and somehow the divine was able to put me together in a much better fashion. I am telling you as a spiritual eyewitness that everything works out for your highest and greatest good even when you feel like dying or giving up. Don't give up on yourself, don't throw your life away, and always remember you are never alone! We are soulful friends for many eternities to come!

> *"My Soul is not contained within the limits of my body.*
> *My body is contained within the limitlessness of my soul."*
> —*Tim Carrey*

Remember Your Purpose—The powerful duality of illusion and eternity is the premier challenge of all our life/spiritual journeys. This is the big secret of how to continually uncover your inner spirit/intuitive/divine nature while commuting to work, parenting, paying bills, working, and day-to-day living. Your best friend inside of you, your "Soul/God" is always waiting to connect with and talk to you. No illusion of loss can separate you from your greatest version of yourself and the purpose of your destiny. *Lastly, never, and I mean never, forget that everything starts and finishes with you and your soul destiny mission.* What we do between birth and death in this current school-of-life is our full responsibility and privilege. The constant source of our enjoyment, enlightenment, and self-spiritual realization will be determined by our developing patience to explore our inner world. When in doubt about what to do, always consider your ability to be inwardly driven and divinely inspired. Your heart/soul will never disappoint or mislead you in the ways and means of your journey, relationships, and purpose. It doesn't matter how far you feel from your higher-self, you are always within a blink of an eye from connecting to your soul. Never stop looking, blinking, searching and following that small still voice within your heart and soul. It's your intuitive-self/God talking to you. Just like the preschool teacher says to her group of adorable four-year olds before going home: "Look, listen and watch, then cross the street." Let's all keep in touch via our spiritual connection. It's the lasting solution to all the challenges that we all face personally and globally.

Love,

Stephan B. Poulter

> *"When you think everything is someone else's fault, you will suffer a lot.*
> *When you realize that everything springs only from yourself,*
> *you will learn both peace and joy."*
> —*His Holiness the 14th Dalai Lama*

> *"Everything else can wait, but our search for God cannot wait."*
> —*Paramahansa Yogananda*

Epilogue

The 6th Awaking and My Beagle Angel— "Ricardo Poulter"

"The most beautiful people we have known are those who have
known defeat,
known suffering,
known loss,
and have found their way out of the depths of despair.
These persons have appreciation, a sensitivity, and an
understanding of
life that fills them with compassion, gentleness, and
a deep loving concern.
Beautiful people do not just happen."
—Elisabeth Kubler-Ross

The Beagle—This quote and philosophical spiritual summary statement by Elisabeth, about the power of loss, death and grief is perfectly stated. I experienced the complete despair of one of my deepest personal losses on Monday afternoon, November 17th. That day is best described in the above quote. Like all of us walking down the spiritual life path, we know loss, and then there is the ultimate shock—in the wink of an eye, a loss that transcends all our prior experiences. I have suffered terrible upsets, a stroke, grievous romantic breakups, the death of both parents, loss of my kids for a few years, and lived (survived) through all five lightening "awaking" storms to my heart for the purposes of awaking my soul. The rough draft of this book was done, but my death/birth process wasn't; that is how November 17ᵗʰ started and ended. I am not sure where or when the love affair began with Ricardo, the family's pet beagle, but the story is a good one. Sadly, the ending leveled me from behind like a runaway freight train—I never saw it coming! Nothing was unconsciously closer to my heart (I wasn't even aware of it) as that beagle gently changing my entire life from the inside out. Let's go back and paint the backdrop to my "angel/beagle factor."

Everyone has a "Snoopy" Type of Angel—Charles Schultz, the creator of the incredible bigger-than-life cartoon character "Charlie Brown" had a beagle dog named "Snoopy." This pooch had a personality type of the "coolest kid in school" while his owner (Charlie Brown) struggled with all the challenges of life. My beagle, Ricardo, was the present-day version of Snoopy for me. Yes, many times I wonder how we don't all feel like Charlie Brown and have our own Snoopy looking at us with the expression of "really." Ricardo was technically my sons' dog, and like all pets of young/old children, they usually end up being the parents' responsibility. That wasn't a problem for me because I deeply loved Ricardo Poulter. Ricardo and I had that type of intimate "dog and his owner relationship." We lived together through the toughest 12 years of my entire life up to that point. Ricardo would always come and sit on my foot when the waves of despair would hit, and I would be emotionally distraught and heartbroken. He knew the energy of panic and emotional pain in the room.

The back story to Ricardo could be its own book, but let's just say he was a lifesaver for me during the divorce, child custody process, parent's deaths, romantic heartbreaks, financial strains, career challenges and the writing/creation of this book. I have lived through all five awaking events extensively discussed in previous chapters. I had finished this book in late summer and was focusing on editing, selling, and preparing it for publication. Over the years, Ricardo and I had developed a very close emotional spiritual bond. He would go to work with me, sit next to clients on the couch, snore in a chair. He was always the cooler-than-life pooch. If people became emotionally upset in the office, Ricardo would often leave his chair and go sit next to them. He would eat people's food, bark, get irritable, and then sit next to someone who was sobbing. Ricardo was the coolest and most well-balanced soul I had ever met.

Cancer Loss—Ricardo and I had an unspoken agreement that he wouldn't leave this earth until I got remarried, sold/published the book, completely reunited with the kids, and maintained/mastered my inner spiritual intuitive connection. The objectives were high and were very clear. Meanwhile, Ricardo was a "dude," playing cards and smoking a cigar with the other pooches at doggie daycare (so it seemed). It was that simple and felt like a done deal. Well, during the creation of this book, the pooch had a serious cancer bout. He survived it and was given a clean bill of health. Deep down in my heart I never felt relieved or truly resolved about his health. Five months later, I knew something was terribly wrong with him. My psychic 10-year clients all told me within a span of a week that Ricardo seemed off. My daughter (who also knew intuitively something was wrong) was away at college at the time but called me on Saturday afternoon, November 15th, and told me to take Ricardo to the veterinarians immediately. So, I listened to her. We made the trip to the veterinarian that same afternoon.

Time stopped moving when the veterinarian came out of the examining room, saying: *"I am so sorry, but Ricardo has numerous tumors in his stomach, glands and on his head. There isn't much we can do for him other than give him some pain relievers."* My heart literally skipped several beats and the flood of emotional grief hit me like a 100-foot wave of water. Within 48 hours Ricardo was on the other side of life.

I have never sobbed so hard and couldn't remember ever being so heartbroken. I subsequently had many emotional meltdowns on the floor at home and couldn't stop my river of grief during the days, weeks and months that followed his passing. I knew loss, but had never encountered the loss of my soul mate. Ricardo was that piece of me that was so covered up with unresolved pain, suffering and emotional despair that I was suddenly completely and utterly "unzipped." There was no avoidance, denial, anger, or running away from this spiritual awaking. I had to emotionally sit still and meditate to relieve my heavy heart and sad soul. Ricardo was such a big piece of my heart that I couldn't psychologically breathe or pretend my grief didn't exist. I realized that this grieving/sobbing soul process is the transformational power of love via the road of death/loss. This reminded me that the death/birth process is never complete in this school of life—my class was clearly still in session. Book or no book, my spirit was committed to my Self-God realization, and this was beyond words.

> *"Sometimes the bad things that happen in our lives put us*
> *directly on the path to the best things that will ever happen to us."*
> —*Wayne Dyer*

The Last Awaking: Number #6—
Lightning Bolt of Death

Heartbreaking Day of Death—I had asked the Universe/God to help me to present the best possible book about the fine art of our life/spiritual journey leading to ultimate inner divine awaking. I knew the five areas of awaking had been thoroughly discussed and then something happened. My soul mate, Ricardo Poulter, suddenly died within five days of my request. I hadn't considered the actual process of death and dying as its own action for our awaking. Symbolically, the different death/rebirth processes and circumstances are all metaphors in all areas of our life. The actual experience of witnessing someone (any beloved person or pet) going to the other side on this narrow line between the material world and the spiritual world wasn't something I had directly addressed. Clearly, witnessing and feeling the power of the spiritual world transcending this physical life was necessary and highly relevant to our (my) journey.

I had never allowed myself to truly sob from my heart about all of the previous losses, disappointments, deaths, abuses, and heartbreaks that I wrote about. I have cried, but I hadn't cried from the depths of my soul, where your heart literally hurts from the emotional loss. I had been missing and overlooking this major lightning bolt in the Valley of Despair. I didn't directly write about or discuss the sixth awaking event: *Death!*

It seemed obvious, considering the experience of death, but then again it wasn't so simple. The power of death and accepting the truth about how energy only changes forms and is never destroyed was staring me in the face. I lay on the floor the night before Ricardo passed, and sobbed, wondering how I was going to make it without him. He had been my companion for years when the kids were gone, and then during all their comings and goings. Ricardo always reminded me with just a look that the kids would always come back around, my romantic soul mate would show up, and that we are never alone in the world. Ricardo was my angel that reminded me of the greater good, and then he died! I could feel the emotional/spiritual floor fall from underneath me, and fortunately I was already face down on it.

The quote above from Wayne Dyer somehow found its way to me while I was driving to the veterinarians on that fateful Monday afternoon. I couldn't imagine losing a child, a partner, or someone who felt like they were my right arm. Ricardo was my right arm and the channel for my ability to love and be the man, husband, father, psychologist, mentor and friend I had always wanted. Angels come in all shapes and sizes, and I never expected that my son's chronically barking-howling pooch would be a lightning bolt to my heart and soul. I never, and I mean never, saw this relationship ending or changing at this point in my life and my kids' life. Yet I knew that the Divine /God was involved in this act of compassion and self/spiritual awaking.

> *"Remember that our loved ones never die; they shed their physical*
> *bodies to make a transition from one dimension to another.*
> *Death is just the doorway into the next spiritual realm;*
> *Love never dies and neither do we!"*
> —*James Van Praaugh*

Illusion of Maya and Death—there is nothing in life that is more emotional sobering than that moment of conscious recognition of the powerlessness of "Maya" (illusion of the material world) and the deafening power of the silent loving universe (spiritual world) intersecting. Seeing into and feeling the other side in this life is something that is a powerful intuitive experience. You can never go back to sleepwalking after seeing and feeling the Divine Universe and its precise movement. I felt like I was standing on the rim of the Grand Canyon and looking into the vastness of heaven, when Ricardo passed away. *Heaven, paradise, the other side of this world felt very close, and the illusion of distance between this life and the next one was only one breath away.* The deceptive and misleading ego separation between this material world and our spiritual world was never so exposed. The power of this world in West Los Angeles just didn't seem very attractive or interesting that day or any of the days that followed.

Handing Ricardo's leash over to the veterinarian and watching him leave the medical examining room was beyond anything I had felt or knew. Yes, both of my parents had passed, but I was relieved and happy that they were on the other side of this mad world. In my clinical practice, I have had more than 10 different people/clients commit suicide directly, passively and unintentional within a three-year period. As Dr. Steve, That was chilling and heartbreaking to experience. Ricardo was a completely different story. He was my buddy and traveler in this life, and we were partners. Everyone who knew me knew "the beagle" for better or worse. Going home, I drove down Santa Monica Boulevard in rush hour traffic that day after losing my soul mate, and it all seemed like a dream.

No Death—it took me many weeks to ask Spirit/God what was the deeper lesson here? The intuitive answer came back at me within seconds: *"You forgot to mention Death as an awaking, Stephan."* My only response was *"Ugh, you're right my oversight, I will now."* The lifting of the veil of the illusion of this life had previously happened occasionally for me. The soul grieving for Ricardo leveled me like nothing I had allowed myself to ever experience. I had many different experiences of loss but this time I couldn't dismiss it because of my emotional attachment to him. The illusion of death lost its power because we never die! The raw nerve of sorrow that I had never known and unconsciously always avoided was all about this material life—not the bigger view of our spiritual life.

I avoided the deep emotional flood of loss, feeling hopeless, lost and adrift in the sea of life—even though we are always connected spiritually. The illusion of the material/physical world is that we are only our five senses, our bodies and this world of acquiring—which is all terribly misleading. The experience of death changes our inner Maya belief/perspective with divine power and forever transforms our inner connection to our higher-self. This is all part of our spiritual success of realizing our spiritual roots and foundation. Once you have touched and intuitively felt the other side via death, you're never the same person. It's impossible to feel the Divine Universe within and then go back to the sleep/illusion of your daily life.

The Soul's Purpose of Being an Eyewitness of Death—Mediation and intuitive promptings via my grief about Ricardo pushed me to deal with the next layer of my soul. The psychological distorted feelings of shame and feeling disconnected from the Divine were no longer relevant or empowered. The sting of death had lost its teeth and was no longer a player on my spiritual field. Feeling and experiencing Ricardo passing away in the blink of an eye was shocking and liberating simultaneously. Our soul's deepest desire is to reconnect us to our higher-self. The chilling experience of witnessing the powerlessness of death is the fast lane to this experience. The quote below by Jeff Van Praagh summarizes the daily, weekly and lifetime process of walking back home to our true natural habitat. We all have a spiritual home within our hearts that is always awaiting our attention and reconnection. Death serves to remind us of the illusionary myth of this physical life, which is not our primary source or reason for being alive.

> *"God is not limited and neither are you.*
> *Your home is heaven and*
> *your journey on this Earth is your homework.*
> *The key to success on this planet*
> *is a keener awareness of your spiritual heritage."*
> —*Jeff Van Praagh*

As stated throughout this book, we can realize, through our own death/birth experience, that our life is really on the other side of this thin veil of human experience. Not fearing your personally designed death/rebirth process is emotional/spiritual freedom and the key to lasting inner peace. Knowing that there isn't anything to fear (even death) and that we are connected to the greater universe and to God is priceless. Death reminds and awakens within us our latent remembrance of our deepest longing and belonging to everything and everyone. I will always hold a place in my heart and soul for Ricardo Poulter. He was my angel who served his purpose to further wake me up to the ever-expanding greater potential of my (our) spiritual journey. There is no limitation to this journey, including death. That limitation is only the ego's secret for keeping us feeling separated and fearful. Death serves us in moving our souls to the other side with completion (hopefully) of our purpose in this life.

A dear long-time friend of mine said the following to me shortly after Ricardo's passing:

> *"Steve, it seems to me that, as your soul mate, Ricardo elected to be the holder of your "stuff," and once he knew that you could transcend your emotional pain, challenges through and to your soul, his work was done and he passed over to the other side."*
> —*Melissa G.*

Death's Soulful Refocusing Of Your Purpose—We have all had the experience of loss in all of its various forms (money, relationships, family, health, and death). The primary purpose of loss on this earthly material plane is always for our greater good—thus my friend's gentle reminder that Ricardo's passing was as important as his life and all the different contributions that he made to my awaking. It's very emotionally upsetting to know that the important souls in our life have many, many different roles that sometimes cause incredible suffering. Regardless, at the time of the extreme emotional suffering, loss, crisis, tragedy, there is an unfolding divine plan that will prevail and reveal itself to you. The timing, event and circumstances of any death, regardless of its magnitude, are significant for our soul evolution. *You can't have a new beginning without an ending! New births metaphorically are the process of your life, which should always be about your ever-increasing awareness!* Death is a cold, harsh reminder of our limited time, purpose and soulful reasons for everything that will happen in our life. All of you know loss, and we all want to know a new beginning. What new beginnings are in front of you today? What awaits your permission and intention to happen in your life? Death is only one of the many tools that Spirit/Universe uses to shake us out of our sleepwalking state of being. Ricardo's passing pushed me to go inward and find greater peace, clarity and deeper soulful awareness. This last quote pulls together the primary task that death serves for all of us in this school of life:

> *"Often, it's not about becoming a new person, but*
> *becoming the person you were meant to be, and already are,*
> *but don't know how to be—death is always the new*
> *beginning of your inner expression coming out."*
> —Stephan (Author)

Lastly, whatever you're hesitating about, pondering or reluctant to pursue, go toward it, and all the processes of your successful learning via the ego failings will awaken the timeless infinite soul within you. Take care, and let's never lose sight that our greater purpose is to love, serve and reconnect to others and our infinite Spirit within.

Remember the story of the three beagle puppies in the introduction of the book? Your delivery into your next life chapter is here. There is life after this crisis, learning curve and emotional loss. Listen to your Higher Self like the wise puppy told her shelter-mates. We are all in the womb of Spirit waiting to be born over and over again. You want to be the soul that knows her mother's voice and knows that life is on the other side. I trust that we are all moving down the road of our own life/spiritual circumstances via all six power tools of our awaking: money, childhood family, love relationships, parenting, health, and death). Remember, all life paths lead to our spiritual path, just like all rivers lead to the ocean. All paths lead us back to Spirit, Universe, your Higher Power, and/God. You're going in the right direction—just keep asking your soul for guidance, and watch the greatest story ever told unfold within your life: that story is you and your soul awaking.

Bibliography—Resources—References

Allen, Patricia, and Sandra Harmon, *Getting to "I Do": The Secret to Doing Relationships Right*. New York, Quill, 2002.

American Psychiatric Association. *Diagnostic and Statistical Manual of Mental Disorders, 4th edition*. Washington, DC: American Psychiatric Association, 1995.

Angelou, Maya. *Rainbow in the Cloud: The Wisdom and Spirit of Maya Angelou*. New Press Print, 2014.

Beattie, Melody. Codependent No More: How to Stop Controlling Others and Start Caring for Yourself. Hazelden Foundation, U.S.A. 1987

Berne, Rhonda. *The Secret*. New York: Beyond Words, 2006.

Bhaktivedanta, A.C. Swami Prabhupada. *Bhagavad Gita; As It Is, Second Edition Revised and Enlarged*. Los Angeles, Ca. Bhaktivedanta Book Trust, 2011.

Bloch, Douglas and Demetra George. *Astrology for Yourself: How to Understand and Interpret Your Own Birth Chart: A Workbook for Personal Transformation*. Berwick, Me. Ibis Print, 2006.

Bowen, Murray. *The Family Life Cycle*. New York: Gardner, 1988.

_____, *The Use of Family Therapy in Clinical Practice.* Northvale, NJ: Jason Bronson Books, 1988.

Bowl by, John. *A Secure Base: Parent-Child Attachment and Healthy Human Development.* New York: Basic Books, 1988.

Bradshaw, John. Homecoming: Reclaiming and Championing Your Inner Child. New York, Bantam Print, 1990.

Brazen, T. Berry. *Working & Caring.* Reading, MA: Addison-Wesley, 1992.

Brown, Byron. *Soul without Shame: A Guide to Liberating Yourself from the Judge Within.* Boston, Shamble, 1999.

Bryan, Mark. *Codes of Love: How to Rethink Your Family and Remake Your Life.* New York: Pocket Books, 1999.

Chapman, Gary. T*he Five Love Languages: How to Express Heartfelt Commitment to Your Mate.* Chicago, Northfield, 2004.

Chodron, Pema and Emily Hilburn Sell. *Comfortable with Uncertainty: 108 Teachings.* Boston, Shambhala Print, 2002.

Chodron, and Thubten. *Buddhism for Beginners.* Ithaca, NY: Snow Lion Publications, 2001.

Chopra, Deepak and Leonard Mlodinow: *War of the Worldviews: Science vs. Spirituality.* London, Rider Print, 2011.

Chopra, Deepak. *Surgery of the Deep Femoral Artery.* New York, Springer Print 2012.

A Course of Miracles: Combined Volume: Glen Ellen, CA. Foundation for Inner Peace, 1992.

Dass, Ram: *Still Here: Embracing Aging, Changing and Dying.* New York: Riverhead, 2001.

Dass, Ram. *Remember Be Here Now.* San Cristobal Foundation Print, New Mexico, 1975.

Dyer, Wayne W. *Excuses Be Gone! How to Change Lifelong, Self-Defeating Thinking Habits.* Carlsbad, Ca: Hay House Publications, 2009.

Dyer, Wayne W. *Wishes Fulfilled: Mastering the Art of Manifesting.* Carlsbad, Ca: Hay House Publishers, 2012.

Eden, Donna and David Feinstein. *Energy Medicine for Women: Aligning Your Body's Energies to Boost Your Health and Vitality.* New York, New York, Penguin Press, 2008.

Hampel, John. *Wherever You Go, There You Are.* Milwaukee: Bzff Publishers, 1991.

Hay, Louise L. *The Golden Louise L. Hay Collection.* Carlsbad, Ca. Hay House Inc., 2012.

Hay, Louise L. *Modern Day Miracles: Miraculous Moments and Extraordinary Stories from People All Over the World Whose Lives Have Been Touched by Louise L. Hay.* Carlsbad, Ca. Hay House Inc., 2010.

Hay, Louise L. *You Can Heal Your Life.* Santa Monica, Ca. Hay House Inc., 1984.

Hay, Louise L. *Life Loves You; 7 Spiritual Practices to Heal Your Life.* Carlsbad, Ca. Hay House, Inc. 2015.

Isaacson, Walter. *Steve Jobs.* New York, New York. Simon & Schuster, 2011. (hardback)

Kubler-Ross, Elizabeth. *Working It Through: An Elizabeth Kubler-Ross Workshop on Life, Death and Transition.* New York, NY. Simon & Schuster, 1997.

Lamont, Ann. *21 Great Scientists Who Believed the Bible*. Brisbane, Australia: Creation Science Foundation, 1995.

Lewis, C.S.: *The Screw tape Letters: Mere Christianity; Surprised by Joy*. New York: Book of the Month Club Publishers, 1992.

McCullough, Susan. *Beagles for Dummies*. Hoboken, NJ: Wiley Publishers, 2007.

Millman, Dan. *Way of the Peaceful Warrior: A Book That Changes Lives*. Tiburon, Ca. H.J. Kramer Publishers, 2000.

Myss, Caroline M. *Anatomy of the Spirit—The Seven Stages of Power and Healing*. Three Rivers Press, NY, NY. 1996

Myss, Caroline M. *Defy Gravity: Healing beyond the Bounds of Reasons*. Carlsbad, Ca. Hay House Publishers, 2009.

Myss, Caroline M. *Entering the Castle: An Inner Path to God and Your Soul*. New York, NY. Free Publishers, 2007.

Myss, Caroline M. *Invisible Acts of Power: Personal Choices That Create Miracles*. New York, NY. Free Publishers, 2004.

Peck, Scott, M. M.D. *The Road Less Traveled; A New Psychology of Love, Traditional Values and Spiritual Growth: Twenty- Fifth Edition*. New York, NY. Touchstone Press, 2003.

Poulter, Stephan B. (See title page for the complete list of his books and audios).

Praagh, Jeff Van. *Ghosts Among Us: Uncovering the Truth about the Other Side*. New York, Harper One Publishers, 2008.

Praagh, Jeff Van. *Adventures Of The Soul: Journeys Through The Physical and Spiritual Dimensions*. Carlsbad, Ca. Hay House Inc., 2014.

Prabhupada, A.C.. *The Nectar of Devotion: The Complete Science of Bhakti Yoga*. New York, Bhaktivedanta Book Trust, 1970.

Ruiz, Miguel. *The Four Agreements: A Personal Guide to Personal Freedom*. San Rafael, Ca: Amber-Allen Publishers, 1997.

Saxe, John Godfrey. The Six Blind Men and the Elephant. New York, New York. Whittlesey House, 1963.

Schmidt, Gary D., and John Bunyan. *Pilgrim's Progress*. Grand Rapids, MI: W.B. Eerdmans Publishers, 1994.

Sogyal, Rinpoche., *The Tibetan Book of Living and Dying*. San Francisco, Ca. Harper Press, 1992.

Strong, Mary. *Letters of the Scattered Brotherhood*. New York, NY. Harper Press, 1948.

Ullman, Dana. *Homeopathic Medicine for Children and Infants*. New York, NY. Tarcher Perigee Press, 1992.

Walsch, Neale Donald. *Conversations with God for Teens*. New York, NY. Scholastic Press, 2002.

Walsch, Neale Donald. *Conversations with God: Uncommon Dialogue*. New York, NY. Putnam's Sons Publications, 1996.

Walsch, Neale Donald. *Friendship with God: An Uncommon Dialogue*. New York, NY. Putnam Press, 1999.

Walsch, Neale Donald. *What God Said: The 25 Core Messages of Conversations with God That Will Change Your Life and World*. New York, NY. Berkley Books, 2013.

Walsh, Courtney A. *Dear Human: A Manifesto of Love, Invitation and Invocation to Humanity*. New York, New York. Findhorn Press, 2015.

Weil, Andrew. *Spontaneous Healing: How to Discover and Enhance Your Body's Natural Ability to Maintain and Heal itself.* New York, NY. Harper Press, 2006.

Weiss, Brian L, M.D. *Many Lives, Many Masters.* New York, NY. Simon and Schuster, 1988.

Woolfolf, Joanna. The Only Astrology Book You'll Ever Need: Twenty-first Century Edition. National Book Network, 2011.

Yogananda, Paramahansa. *Autobiography of a Yogi.* Los Angeles, Ca. International Publications of Self-Realization Fellowship. Thirteenth Edition, 2009.

Yogananda, Paramahansa. *Man's Eternal Quest: Collected Talks and Essays on Realizing God in Daily Life: Volume I, II, IIII.* International Publications of Self-Realization Fellowship, Edition 2008.

Printed in the United States
By Bookmasters